Frommer's®

PORTABLE

Virgin Islands

5th Edition

by Darwin Porter & Danforth Prince

Here's what critics say about Frommer's:

"Amazingly easy to use. Very portable, very complete."
—**BOOKLIST**

"Detailed, accurate, and easy-to-read information for all price ranges."
—**GLAMOUR MAGAZINE**

WILEY

Wiley Publishing, Inc.

Published by:

WILEY PUBLISHING, INC.

111 River St.
Hoboken, NJ 07030-5774

ISBN 978-0-470-47060-2

Editor: Jennifer Polland
Production Editor: Suzanna R. Thompson
Cartographer: Anton Crane
Photo Editor: Richard Fox
Production by Wiley Indianapolis Composition Services

Front cover photo: Sandy Key, British Virgin Islands: Snorkelers swimming. © Marc Muench / Alamy Images.

For information on our other products and services or to obtain technical support, please contact our Customer Care Department within the U.S. at 877/762-2974, outside the U.S. at 317/572-3993 or fax 317/572-4002.

Wiley also publishes its books in a variety of electronic formats. Some content that appears in print may not be available in electronic formats.

Manufactured in the United States of America

5   4   3   2   1

CONTENTS

5 THE BRITISH VIRGIN ISLANDS 150

6 FAST FACTS 192

INDEX 200

LIST OF MAPS

ABOUT THE AUTHORS

As a well-established team of veteran travel writers, **Darwin Porter** and **Danforth Prince** have produced numerous titles for Frommer's, which have included Italy, France, the C aribbean, Spain, England, Scotland, Austria, and Germany. A film critic, columnist, and broadcaster, Porter is also a noted biographer of Hollywood celebrities. Porter's recent releases include *Merv Griffin: A Life in the Closet*, documenting the career and private life of the richest and most notorious man in television, and *Paul Newman, The Man Behind the Baby Blues*. Prince was formerly employed by the Paris bureau of the *New York Times* and is today the president of Blood Moon Productions and other media-related firms.

HOW TO CONTACT US

In researching this book, we discovered many wonderful places—hotels, restaurants, shops, and more. We're sure you'll find others. Please tell us about them, so we can share the information with your fellow travelers in upcoming editions. If you were disappointed with a recommendation, we'd love to know that, too. Please write to:

Frommer's Portable Virgin Islands, 5th Edition
Wiley Publishing, Inc. • 111 River St. • Hoboken, NJ 07030-5774

AN ADDITIONAL NOTE

Please be advised that travel information is subject to change at any time—and this is especially true of prices. We therefore suggest that you write or call ahead for confirmation when making your travel plans. The authors, editors, and publisher cannot be held responsible for the experiences of readers while traveling. Your safety is important to us, however, so we encourage you to stay alert and be aware of your surroundings. Keep a close eye on cameras, purses, and wallets, all favorite targets of thieves and pickpockets.

FROMMER'S STAR RATINGS, ICONS & ABBREVIATIONS

Every hotel, restaurant, and attraction listing in this guide has been ranked for quality, value, service, amenities, and special features using a **star-rating** system. In country, state, and regional guides, we also rate towns and regions to help you narrow down your choices and budget your time accordingly. Hotels and restaurants are rated on a scale of zero (recommended) to three stars (exceptional). Attractions, shopping, nightlife, towns, and regions are rated according to the following scale: zero stars (recommended), one star (highly recommended), two stars (very highly recommended), and three stars (must-see).

In addition to the star-rating system, we also use **seven feature icons** that point you to the great deals, in-the-know advice, and unique experiences that separate travelers from tourists. Throughout the book, look for:

(**Finds**)	Special finds—those places only insiders know about
(**Fun Facts**)	Fun facts—details that make travelers more informed and their trips more fun
(**Kids**)	Best bets for kids and advice for the whole family
(**Moments**)	Special moments—those experiences that memories are made of
(**Overrated**)	Places or experiences not worth your time or money
(**Tips**)	Insider tips—great ways to save time and money
(**Value**)	Great values—where to get the best deals

The following **abbreviations** are used for credit cards:

AE	American Express	**DISC**	Discover	**V**	Visa
DC	Diners Club	**MC**	MasterCard		

TRAVEL RESOURCES AT FROMMERS.COM

Frommer's travel resources don't end with this guide. Frommer's website, **www.frommers.com** has travel information on more than 4,000 destinations. We update features regularly, giving you access to the most current trip-planning information and the best airfare, lodging, and car-rental bargains. You can also listen to podcasts, connect with other Frommers.com members through our active-reader forums, share your travel photos, read blogs from guidebook editors and fellow travelers, and much more.

Planning Your Trip to the Virgin Islands

If you live on the East Coast of the U.S., getting to the U.S. Virgin Islands is as easy as flying to Florida. If you plan to visit the B.V.I., you'll probably have to make a transfer in lieu of a direct flight. If you live elsewhere, you might have to fly to New York and then transfer to a flight going to the Virgin Islands. Those who reside in Britain often fly first to Miami or San Juan.

If you're an American citizen, visiting the U.S. Virgin Islands is relatively easy and hassle free, since it is part of the U.S. territory. Those from other counties should read "Entry Requirements," later in this chapter.

A little planning can go a long way. In this chapter, we will give you all the information you need to know before you go, including how to get the lowest rates on flights, lodging, and car rentals. We also help you decide which island(s) to visit and when to go.

For additional help in planning your trip and for more on-the-ground resources in the Virgin Islands, turn to "Fast Facts," p. 192.

1 CHOOSING THE PERFECT ISLAND

Peering at the tiny Virgin Islands chain on a world map, you may find it difficult to distinguish the different islands. They vary widely, however, in looks and personality, and so will your vacation, depending on which island or islands you choose. It's important to plan ahead. For example, if you're an avid golfer, you won't want to spend a week on a remote British Virgin Island with only a rinky-dink 9-hole course or no course at all. But that same island might be perfect for a young couple contemplating a romantic honeymoon. By providing detailed information about the character of each inhabited island in both the U.S. Virgin Islands and the British Virgin Islands, we hope to guide you to your own idea of paradise.

The Virgin Islands

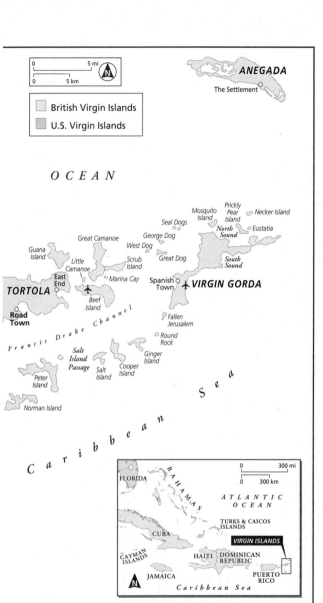

U.S. VS. BRITISH VIRGIN ISLANDS

American and British cultures have left different imprints on the Virgin Islands. The **U.S. Virgin Islands,** except for St. John, offer much of the commercial hustle-and-bustle of the mainland United States, including supermarkets and fast-food chains. In contrast, the British islands are sleepier. Except for a few deluxe hotels (mostly on Virgin Gorda), they recall the way the Caribbean was before the advent of high-rise condos, McDonald's restaurants, and fleets of cruise ships.

If you want shopping, a wide selection of restaurants and hotels, and nightlife, head to the U.S. Virgin Islands, particularly **St. Thomas** and **St. Croix.** With a little research and effort, you can also find peace and quiet on these two islands, most often at outlying resorts. But overall, among the U.S. Virgin Islands, only **St. John** matches the British Virgins for tranquillity. St. John is a rugged mixture of bumpy dirt roads, scattered inhabitants, and a handful of stores and services. It's protected by the U.S. Forest Service, and remains the least developed of the U.S. islands.

The **British Virgin Islands** seem to be lingering in the past, although change is in the air. **Tortola** is the most populated British isle, but its shopping, nightlife, and dining are still limited. It's more of a spot for boaters of all stripes—it's considered the cruising capital of the Caribbean. To the east, **Virgin Gorda** claims most of the B.V.I.'s deluxe hotels. There are also attractive accommodations and restaurants on the smaller islands, such as Jost Van Dyke, Anegada, and Peter Island.

If you'd like to meet and mingle with locals, and get to know the islanders and their lifestyle, it's much easier to do so in the sleepy B.V.I. than in all the comings and goings of St. Thomas or even St. Croix. Again, the only U.S. Virgin Island that has the laid-back quality of the B.V.I. is St. John—except that the "local native" you are likely to meet on St. John is often an expat from the U.S. mainland, not a Virgin Islander born and bred.

There are frequent ferry connections between St. Thomas and St. John, but traveling among the other islands is a bit difficult, requiring private boats in some cases or airplane flights in others (see the "Getting Around" section, later in this chapter). The day will surely come when transportation from island to island will be made more convenient and frequent, but that day hasn't arrived yet.

THE MAJOR ISLANDS IN BRIEF

The islands previewed below are the sites of the most shopping, hotels, restaurants, attractions, and nightlife, and are the most frequently visited. A few words about islands that aren't mentioned below: For those who want to avoid the masses, the British Virgin Islands have a number of escapist-friendly islands such as Peter Island, Mosquito Island, and Guana Island. These are virtually private hideaways, often with expensive resorts (which are the main reason for going there in the first place). Two remote British Virgin Islands with more democratically priced hotels are Anegada and Jost Van Dyke. Even if you're staying at a resort on Virgin Gorda or Tortola, you might want to join a boat excursion to visit some of the lesser-known islands as part of a sightseeing excursion (with time devoted to R & R on a nearly deserted beach, of course).

St. Thomas

The most developed of the U.S. Virgin Islands, St. Thomas resembles a small city at times. There are peaceful retreats here, but you must seek them out. The harbor at **Charlotte Amalie,** the capital, is one of the largest cruise ship magnets in the Caribbean. Many locals try to avoid Charlotte Amalie when the greatest concentration of vessels is in port (usually Dec–Apr). Charlotte Amalie offers the widest selection of duty-free shopping in the Caribbean. However, you must browse carefully through the labyrinth of bazaars to find the real bargains.

St. Thomas, like most of the Virgin Islands, gives you plenty of opportunity to get outside and get active, although many visitors come here simply to sit, sun, and maybe go for a swim. **Magens Bay Beach,** with its tranquil surf and sugar-white sand, is one of the most beautiful beaches in the world, but it is likely to be packed, especially on heavy cruise ship days. More-secluded beaches include **Secret Harbour** and **Sapphire Beach** in East End.

St. Thomas has only one golf course, **Mahogany Run,** but it's a real gem. The three trickiest holes (13, 14, and 15) are known throughout the golfing world as the "Devil's Triangle."

Yachts and boats anchor at **Ramada Yacht Haven Marina** in Charlotte Amalie and at **Red Hook Marina** on the island's somewhat isolated eastern tip, though the serious yachting crowd gathers at Tortola in the British Virgin Islands (see "Tortola," below). Sport fishers angle from the **American Yacht Harbor** at Red Hook. The island also attracts snorkelers and scuba divers—there are many outfitters offering equipment, excursions, and instruction. Kayaking and parasailing also draw beach bums away from the water's edge.

St. Thomas has the most eclectic and sophisticated restaurant scene in the Virgin Islands. Emphasis is on French and Continental fare, but the wide selection of restaurants also includes options from Mexican, West Indian, and Italian to Asian and American. St. Thomas pays more for its imported (usually European) chefs and secures the freshest of ingredients from mainland or Puerto Rican markets.

There's also a wide variety of accommodations on St. Thomas, from the small, historic **Hotel 1829** in Charlotte Amalie, to more modern beachfront complexes in the East End, including the manicured **Elysian Beach Resort.** Apartment and villa rentals abound, and you can also find a handful of old-fashioned B&B-style guesthouses.

St. John
Our favorite of the U.S. Virgin Islands, St. John has only two deluxe hotels, but you'll find several charming inns and plenty of campgrounds. The island's primary attraction is the **U.S. Virgin Islands National Park,** which covers more than half the island. Guided walks and safari bus tours are available to help you navigate the park, which is full of pristine beaches, secret coves, flowering trees, and ghostly remains of sugar cane plantations. An extensive network of trails invites hiking. A third of the park is underwater. **Trunk Bay,** which also boasts the island's finest beach, has an amazing underwater snorkeling trail. As you can imagine, scuba diving is another major attraction on St. John.

St. John has a handful of posh restaurants, as well as a number of colorful, West Indian eateries. Many residents and long-term visitors like to bring ingredients over on the ferry from St. Thomas, where prices are lower and the selection is broader. Nightlife isn't a major attraction here; it usually consists of sipping rum drinks in a bar in **Cruz Bay,** and maybe listening to a local calypso band. After spending a day outdoors, most visitors on St. John are happy to turn in early.

St. Croix
This island is the second-most-visited destination in the U.S. Virgin Islands. Like St. Thomas, St. Croix is highly developed. Cruise ship passengers continue to flood **Frederiksted** and the capital, **Christiansted,** looking for duty-free goods and a handful of white sand to take home in a plastic bag. St. Croix is also the only island that has a casino, which is beginning to attract a new kind of tourist. Although parts of the island resemble American suburbia, some of St. Croix's true West Indian–style buildings have been preserved, along with many of its rich cultural traditions.

One of the best reasons to take a trip to St. Croix, even if only for a day, is to visit **Buck Island National Park,** just 1¹/₂ miles off St. Croix's northeast coast. The park's offshore reef attracts snorkelers and divers from around the world. Signs posted along the ocean floor guide you through a forest of staghorn coral swarming with flamboyant fish.

St. Croix is the premier golfing destination in the Virgin Islands, mainly because it boasts **Carambola,** the archipelago's most challenging several annual tournaments. Other sports for active vacationers include horseback riding, parasailing, sport fishing, and water-skiing.

The restaurants on St. Croix are generally not as good as those on St. Thomas, although they claim to be. You will find plenty of small, local eateries serving up dishes and snacks ranging from West Indian curries to French croissants. Life after dark is mostly confined to a handful of bars in Christiansted.

As for accommodations, St. Croix has only a few real luxury hotels, but there are a lot of small, attractive inns. And it's easy to find villas and condos for rent at reasonable weekly rates.

Tortola

Tortola is the hub of the British Virgin Islands, but not always the best place for visitors, especially if you're planning to spend more than a couple of days here; we think Virgin Gorda (see below) has better hotels and restaurants. **Road Town,** the capital, with its minor shopping, routine restaurants, and uninspired architecture, requires a couple of hours at the most. Once you leave Road Town, however, you'll find Tortola more alluring. The island's best and most unspoiled beaches, including **Smuggler's Cove** (with its collection of snorkeling reefs), lie at the island's western tip. Tortola's premier beach is **Cane Garden Bay,** a 2.4km (1¹/₂-mile) stretch of white sand. Because of the gentle surf, it's one of the safest places for families with small children. For hikers on Tortola, exploring **Sage Mountain National Park,** where trails lead to a 543m (1,781-ft.) peak that offers panoramic views, is a definite highlight. The park is rich in flora and fauna, from mamey trees to mountain doves.

Although many visitors to the Caribbean look forward to fishing, hiking, horseback riding, snorkeling, and surfing, what makes Tortola exceptional is boating. It is *the* boating center of the British Virgin Islands, which are among the most cherished sailing territories on the planet. The island offers some 100 charter yachts and 300 bareboats, and its marina and shore facilities are the most up-to-date and extensive in the Caribbean Basin.

The crystal-clear waters compensate for the island's lackluster bars and restaurants. You can count on simple and straightforward food here; we suggest any locally caught fish grilled with perhaps a little lime butter.

Virgin Gorda

Our favorite British Virgin Island is Virgin Gorda, the third-largest member of the archipelago, with a permanent population of about 1,400 lucky souls. Many visitors come over just for a day to check out the **Baths,** an astounding collection of gigantic rocks, boulders, and tide pools on the southern tip. Crafted by volcanic pressures millions of years ago, the boulders have eroded into shapes reminiscent of a Henry Moore sculpture. With more than 20 uncrowded beaches, the best-known of which are **Spring Beach** and **Trunk Beach,** Virgin Gorda is a sun worshiper's dream come true.

Unlike Tortola, Virgin Gorda has some of the finest hotels in the Virgin Islands, including **Little Dix Bay** and **Biras Creek.** One caveat: You must be willing to pay a high price for the privilege of staying at one of these regal resorts. There are also more reasonably priced places to stay, such as **Virgin Gorda Village.** Outside the upscale hotels, restaurants tend to be simple places serving local West Indian cuisine. No one takes nightlife too seriously on Virgin Gorda, so there isn't very much of it.

2 WHEN TO GO

CLIMATE

Sunshine is practically an everyday affair in the Virgin Islands. Temperatures climb into the 80s (high 20s Celsius) during the day, and drop into the more comfortable 70s (low 20s Celsius) at night. Winter is generally the dry season in the islands, but rainfall can occur at any time of the year. You don't have to worry too much, though—tropical showers usually come and go so quickly you won't even really notice. If you're out exploring for the day, you may want to bring rain gear.

HURRICANES The hurricane season, the dark side of the Caribbean's beautiful weather, officially lasts from June to November. The Virgin Islands chain lies in the main pathway of many a hurricane raging through the Caribbean, and the islands are often hit. If you're planning a vacation in hurricane season, stay abreast of weather conditions. It may pay to get trip-cancellation insurance because of the possibility of hurricanes.

Islanders certainly don't stand around waiting for a hurricane to strike. Satellite forecasts generally give adequate warning to both residents and visitors. And, of course, there's always prayer: Islanders have a legal holiday in the third week of July called Supplication Day, when they ask to be spared from devastating storms. In late October, locals celebrate the end of the season on Hurricane Thanksgiving Day.

THE HIGH SEASON & THE OFF SEASON

High season (or winter season) in the Virgin Islands, when hotel rates are at their peak, runs roughly from mid-December to mid-April. However, package and resort rates are sometimes lower in January, as a tourist slump usually occurs right after the Christmas holidays. February is the busiest month. If you're planning on visiting during the winter months, make reservations as far in advance as possible.

Off season begins when North America starts to warm up, and vacationers, assuming that temperatures in the Virgin Islands are soaring into the 100s (upper 30s Celsius), head for less tropical local beaches. However, it's actually quite balmy year-round in the Virgin Islands—thanks to the fabled trade winds—with temperatures varying little more than 5° between winter and summer.

There are many advantages to off-season travel in the Virgin Islands. First, from mid-April to mid-December, hotel rates are slashed a startling 25% to 50%. Second, you're less likely to encounter crowds at swimming pools, beaches, resorts, restaurants, and shops. Especially in St. Thomas and St. Croix, a slower pace prevails in the off season, and you'll have a better chance to appreciate the local culture and cuisine. Of course, there are disadvantages to off-season travel, too: Many hotels use the slower months for construction and/or restoration, fewer facilities are likely to be open, and some hotels and restaurants may close completely when business is really slow.

Additionally, if you're planning a trip during the off season and traveling alone, ask for the hotel's occupancy rate—you may want crowds. The social scene in both the B.V.I. and the U.S.V.I. is intense from mid-December to mid-April. After that, it slumbers a bit. If you seek escape from the world and its masses, summer is the way to go, especially if you aren't depending on meeting others.

3 ENTRY REQUIREMENTS

PASSPORTS

No passport is required for U.S. Citizens visiting the U.S. Virgin Islands only—but it is highly encouraged to carry one. For non-U.S. citizens, visiting the U.S. Virgin Islands is just like visiting the mainland United States: You need a passport and visa.

A passport is necessary for *all* visitors to the British Virgin Islands (including citizens of the U.K.).

For information on how to get a passport, go to "Passports" in the "Fast Facts" chapter (p. 192)—the websites listed provide downloadable passport applications as well as the current fees for processing passport applications.

VISAS

The U.S. State Department has a **Visa Waiver Program (VWP)** allowing citizens of the following countries to enter the United States without a visa for stays of up to 90 days: Andorra, Australia, Austria, Belgium, Brunei, Denmark, Finland, France, Germany, Iceland, Ireland, Italy, Japan, Liechtenstein, Luxembourg, Monaco, the Netherlands, New Zealand, Norway, Portugal, San Marino, Singapore, Slovenia, Spain, Sweden, Switzerland, and the United Kingdom. Canadian citizens may enter the United States without visas; they will need to show passports and proof of residence, however. *Note:* Any passport issued on or after October 26, 2006, by a VWP country must be an **e-Passport** for VWP travelers to be eligible to enter the U.S. without a visa. Citizens of these nations also need to present a round-trip air or cruise ticket upon arrival. E-Passports contain computer chips capable of storing biometric information, such as the required digital photograph of the holder. (You can identify an e-Passport by the symbol on the bottom center cover of your passport.) If your passport doesn't have this feature, you can still travel without a visa if it is a valid passport issued before October 26, 2005, and includes a machine-readable zone, or between October 26, 2005, and October 25, 2006, and includes a digital photograph. For more information, go to **www.travel.state.gov/visa**.

Citizens of all other countries must have (1) a valid passport that expires at least 6 months later than the scheduled end of their visit to the United States, and (2) a tourist visa, which may be obtained without charge from any U.S. consulate.

As of January 2004, many international visitors traveling on visas to the United States will be photographed and fingerprinted on arrival at Customs in airports and on cruise ships in a program created by the Department of Homeland Security called **US-VISIT.** Exempt from the extra scrutiny are visitors entering by land or those (mostly in Europe) who don't require a visa for short-term visits. For more information, go to the Homeland Security website at **www.dhs.gov/dhspublic**.

U.S. citizens, E.U. citizens, Canadians, Australians, New Zealanders, and South Africans do not require a visa to enter the **British Virgin Islands.** If you are traveling through the U.S. but your final destination is the B.V.I., you may still need to travel with a visa, according to U.S. entry requirements.

Visa requirements are not exactly the same for the B.V.I. as they are for the U.K. A full list of countries that require a visa for entry to the B.V.I. and more information on obtaining a visa can be found on the B.V.I. Immigration website at **www.bviimmigration.gov.vg**.

CUSTOMS
What You Can Bring into the U.S.V.I.

Every visitor more than 21 years of age may bring in, free of duty, the following: (1) 1 liter of wine or hard liquor; (2) 200 cigarettes, 100 cigars (but not from Cuba), or 3 pounds of smoking tobacco; and (3) $100 worth of gifts. These exemptions are offered to travelers who spend at least 72 hours in the United States and who have not claimed them within the preceding 6 months. It is altogether forbidden to bring into the country foodstuffs (particularly fruit, cooked meats, and canned goods) and plants (vegetables, seeds, tropical plants, and the like). Foreign tourists may carry in or out up to $10,000 in U.S. or foreign currency with no formalities; larger sums must be declared to U.S. Customs on entering or leaving, which includes filing form CM 4790. For details regarding U.S. Customs and Border Protection, consult your nearest U.S. embassy or consulate, or **U.S. Customs** (*©* **202/927-1770;** www.cbp.gov).

What You Can Bring into the B.V.I.

Visitors to the B.V.I. can bring in food, with the exception of meat products that are not USDA-approved. Visitors can bring up to $10,000 in currency and 1 liter of alcohol per person.

What You Can Take Home from the Virgin Islands

U.S. Citizens & Residents: Upon return to the mainland U.S. **from the U.S.V.I.,** residents are entitled to $1,600 worth of duty-free exports every 30 days—that's three times the exemption allowed from most foreign destinations. One way to get the most out of your **duty-free allowance** is to send gifts home. You can ship up to $100 worth of unsolicited gifts per day without paying duty, although you do have to declare such gifts on your Customs form when you leave.

Family members traveling together can make joint declarations. For a husband and wife with two children, the exemption in the U.S. Virgin Islands is $4,000.

Unsolicited gifts worth up to $200 per day can be sent from the U.S. Virgin Islands to friends and relatives, and they do not have to be declared as part of your $1,600 duty-free allowance. Gifts mailed from the British Virgin Islands cannot exceed $50 per day.

U.S. citizens can bring back 5 liters of liquor duty-free, plus an extra liter of rum (including Cruzan rum) if one of the bottles is produced in the Virgin Islands. Goods made on the island are also duty-free, including perfume, jewelry, clothing, and original paintings; however, if the price of an item exceeds $25, you must be able to show a certificate of origin.

Be sure to collect receipts for all purchases in the Virgin Islands, and beware of merchants offering to give you a false receipt—he or she might be an informer to U.S. Customs. Also, keep in mind that any gifts received during your stay must be declared.

For the most up-to-date specifics on what you can bring back **from the B.V.I.** and the corresponding fees, download the invaluable free pamphlet *Know Before You Go* online at **www.cbp.gov**. (Click on "Travel," and then click on "Know Before You Go.") Or contact the **U.S. Customs & Border Protection (CBP),** 1300 Pennsylvania Ave. NW, Washington, DC 20229 (𝒞 **877/287-8667**), and request the pamphlet.

Canadian Citizens: For a clear summary of Canadian rules, write for the booklet *I Declare,* issued by the **Canada Border Services Agency** (𝒞 **800/461-9999** in Canada, or 204/983-3500; www.cbsa-asfc.gc.ca).

U.K. Citizens: From the B.V.I., U.K. citizens can bring back (duty-free) 200 cigarettes (250 grams of tobacco), 2 liters wine, 1 liter strong liquor, 60cc perfume, and £145 of goods and souvenirs. Larger amounts are subject to tax.

For further information, contact **HM Revenue & Customs** at 𝒞 **0845/010-9000** (from outside the U.K., 020/8929-0152), or consult their website at www.hmce.gov.uk.

Australian Citizens: A helpful brochure available from Australian consulates or Customs offices is *Know Before You Go.* For more information, call the **Australian Customs Service** at 𝒞 **1300/363-263,** or log on to www.customs.gov.au.

New Zealand Citizens: Most questions are answered in a free pamphlet available at New Zealand consulates and Customs offices: *New Zealand Customs Guide for Travellers, Notice no. 4.* For more information, contact **New Zealand Customs Service,** The Customhouse, 17–21 Whitmore St., Box 2218, Wellington (𝒞 **04/473-6099** or 0800/428-786; www.customs.govt.nz).

MEDICAL REQUIREMENTS

Unless you're arriving from an area known to be suffering from an epidemic (particularly cholera or yellow fever), inoculations or vaccinations are not required for entry into the United States. If you have a medical condition that requires **syringe-administered medications,** carry a valid signed prescription from your physician; syringes in carry-on baggage will be inspected. Insulin in any form should have the proper pharmaceutical documentation. If you have a disease that requires treatment with **narcotics,** you should also carry documented proof with you—smuggling narcotics aboard a plane carries severe penalties in the U.S.

For **HIV-positive visitors,** requirements for entering the United States are somewhat vague and change frequently. For up-to-the-minute information, contact **AIDSinfo** (𝒞 **800/448-0440** or 301/519-0459 outside the U.S.; www.aidsinfo.nih.gov) or the **Gay Men's Health Crisis** (𝒞 **212/367-1000;** www.gmhc.org).

4 GETTING THERE & GETTING AROUND

GETTING TO THE VIRGIN ISLANDS
By Plane

The bigger islands, like St. Thomas, have regularly scheduled air service on North American carriers, and the smaller islands are tied into this network through their own carriers.

If you're coming from the United Kingdom, you'll likely fly first to Miami and then take American Airlines or some other carrier on to your final destination. There are no direct flights from North America or Europe to any of the B.V.I. You will most likely make a connection in St. Thomas, St. Croix, or San Juan in Puerto Rico after first connecting in the mainland U.S.

For more information on how to reach each island, refer to the "Getting There" sections in the individual island chapters. To find out which airlines travel to the Virgin Islands, see "Airline, Hotel & Car-Rental Websites," p. 198.

GETTING AROUND

Here are some general comments about getting around the islands. For more information, read the "Getting Around" sections in the individual island chapters.

By Plane

Travelers can fly between St. Thomas and St. Croix, and between St. Thomas and Virgin Gorda. St. John doesn't have an airport; passengers usually land at St. Thomas, then travel to St. John by boat.

By Boat

Ferry service is a vital link between St. Thomas and St. John; private water taxis also operate on this route. Launch services link Red Hook, on the East End of St. Thomas, with both Charlotte Amalie in St. Thomas and Cruz Bay in St. John. **Seaborne Airlines (© 888/359-8687;** www.seaborneairlines.com) makes the trips between St. Thomas and St. Croix.

In the B.V.I., ferries and private boats link Road Town, Tortola, with the island's West End; there's also service to and from Virgin Gorda and some of the smaller islands, such as Anegada and Jost Van Dyke. However, on some of the really remote islands, boat service may be only once a week. Many of the private islands, such as Peter Island, provide launches from Tortola.

You can travel by ferry from Charlotte Amalie, on St. Thomas, to West End and Road Town on Tortola, a 45-minute voyage. Boats making this run include **Native Son** (✆ 284/495-4617; www.nativesonferry.com) and **Smith's Ferry Service** (✆ 284/495-4495; www.smithsferry.com). **Inter-Island Boat Services** (✆ 284/495-4166) brings passengers from St. John to the West End on Tortola.

For details on specific ferry connections, including sample fares, see the "Getting Around" sections of the individual island chapters.

By Car

A rented car is often the best way to get around each of the Virgin Islands. Just remember the most important rule: In both the U.S. and the British Virgin Islands, *you must drive on the left.*

All the major car-rental companies are represented in the U.S. Virgin Islands, including **Avis** (✆ 800/331-1212; www.avis.com), **Budget** (✆ 800/472-3325; www.budget.com), and **Hertz** (✆ 800/654-3131; www.hertz.com); many local agencies also compete in the car-rental market (for detailed information, refer to the "Getting Around" sections in individual island chapters). On St. Thomas and St. Croix, you can pick up most rental cars at the airport. On St. John there are car-rental stands at the ferry dock. Cars are sometimes in short supply during the high season, so reserve as far in advance as possible.

Parking lots in the U.S. Virgin Islands can be found in Charlotte Amalie, on St. Thomas, and in Christiansted, on St. Croix (in Frederiksted, you can generally park on the street). Most hotels, except those in the congested center of Charlotte Amalie, have free parking lots.

In the British Virgin Islands, many visitors don't even bother renting a car, mainly because taxi service is adequate, but also because they'll have to drive on the left along roads that can be hairy when they exist at all—some of the roads are like roller coaster rides. To rent a car on the B.V.I., you must purchase a local driver's license for $10 from police headquarters or a car-rental desk in town, and you must be at least 25 years old. Major U.S. companies are represented in these islands, and there are many local companies as well. Note that there are no car-rental agencies at the airports on Tortola or Virgin Gorda. Vehicles come in a wide range of styles and prices, including Jeeps, Land Rovers, mini mokes, and even six- to eight-passenger Suzukis. Weekly rates are usually slightly cheaper.

By Taxi

Taxis are the main mode of transport on all the Virgin Islands. On **St. Thomas,** taxi vans carry up to a dozen passengers to multiple destinations, and smaller private taxis are also available. Rates are posted at the airport, where you'll find plenty of taxis on arrival. On **St. John,** both private taxis and vans for three or more passengers are available.

On **St. Croix,** taxis congregate at the airport, in Christiansted, and in Frederiksted, where the cruise ships arrive. Many hotels often have a "fleet" of taxis available for guests. Taxis here are unmetered, and you should always negotiate the rate before taking off.

On the **British Virgin Islands,** taxis are sometimes the only way to get around. Service is available on Tortola, Virgin Gorda, and Anegada, and rates are fixed by the local government.

By Bus

The only islands with recommendable bus service are **St. Thomas** and **St. Croix.** On St. Thomas, buses leave from Charlotte Amalie and circle the island; on St. Croix, air-conditioned buses run from Christiansted to Frederiksted. Bus service elsewhere is highly erratic; it's mostly used by locals going to and from work.

---

5 MONEY & COSTS

Both the U.S. Virgin Islands and the British Virgin Islands use the **U.S. dollar** as the form of currency.

British and Canadian travelers will have to convert their currency into U.S. dollars. Banks on the islands are your only option if you need to exchange currency. These rates can be expensive, and additional charges are often tacked on; it is recommended to change money before arriving. Conversions between the U.S. dollar and other currencies fluctuate, and the differences could affect the relative costs of your trip.

There seems to be no shortage of ATM machines in the Virgin Islands, all of which dispense U.S. dollars. They are everywhere—on the downtown streets of Charlotte Amalie, within the large resorts, and in shopping arcades—making it easy to get quick cash. ATMs are most prevalent in Charlotte Amalie on St. Thomas, and in Christiansted on St. Croix. They are also available in Cruz Bay on St. John and in the British Virgin Islands on Tortola and Virgin Gorda. The other islands do not have ATMs, so if you're planning a visit, be sure to visit an ATM to get some cash first.

Each machine charges around $2 to $3 for a transaction fee. Nearly all of the machines are operated by three banks: **Scotiabank** (www.scotiabank.com), **FirstBank** (www.firstbankvi.com), and **Banco Popular** (www.bancopopular.com/vi).

Many establishments in the Virgin Islands, including most of those recommended in this guide, accept credit cards. However, visitors should be aware that a lot of establishments accept only cash. In recent years, though, local hotels, restaurants, and stores have begun accepting credit cards in order to survive. Some shop owners have said that they fear a great loss of business if they don't take plastic.

MasterCard and **Visa** are widely accepted on all the islands that cater to visitors, especially Virgin Gorda, Tortola, St. John, St. Croix, and, of course, St. Thomas. In the past few years, there has been a tendency to drop **American Express** because of the high percentage it takes from transactions with shopkeepers.

However, visitors should not rely solely on credit cards, since many establishments in the Virgin Islands accept only cash. Often, villas and condos or small inns will accept only cash or personal checks in advance. You will also want to arm yourself with cash while browsing the small boutiques and curio shops throughout the islands, as most do not take credit cards.

1

6 HEALTH

GENERAL AVAILABILITY OF HEALTHCARE

Finding a good doctor in the Virgin Islands is not a problem. We list **hospitals** and **emergency numbers** under "Fast Facts," in individual island chapters. If you do get sick, you may want to ask the concierge at your hotel to recommend a local doctor—even his or her own physician. This will probably yield a better recommendation than any toll-free number would.

COMMON AILMENTS

DIETARY RED FLAGS   If you experience **diarrhea,** moderate your eating habits, and drink only bottled water until you recover. If symptoms persist, consult a doctor. Much of the fresh water on the Virgin Islands is stored in cisterns and filtered before it's served. Delicate stomachs might opt for bottled water.

SEASICKNESS   The best way to prevent **seasickness** is with the scopolamine patch by Transderm Scop, a prescription medication. Bonine and Dramamine are good over-the-counter medications, although each causes drowsiness. Smooth Sailing is a ginger drink that works quite well to settle your stomach. You might also opt for an acupressure wristband available at drugstores (www.sea-band. com). We find that a ginger pill taken with a meal and followed by Dramamine an hour before boating also does the job.

SUN EXPOSURE   The Virgin Islands' sun can be brutal. To protect yourself, consider wearing sunglasses and a hat, and use **sunscreen** (SPF 15 and higher) liberally. Limit your time on the beach for the first few days. If you overexpose yourself, stay out of the sun until you recover. If your sunburn is followed by fever, chills, a headache, nausea, or dizziness, see a doctor.

BUGS & BITES **Mosquitoes** do exist in the Virgin Islands, but they aren't the malaria-carrying mosquitoes that you might find elsewhere in the Caribbean. They're still a nuisance, though. **Sand flies,** which appear mainly in the evening, are a bigger annoyance. Screens can't keep these critters out, so carry your bug repellent.

WHAT TO DO IF YOU GET SICK AWAY FROM HOME

The largest hospital in St. Thomas—and the only emergency room on the island—is the **Roy Lester Schneider Hospital** (p. 38). Islanders from St. John also use this hospital, which is about a 5-minute drive from Charlotte Amalie.

The other major hospital is the **Governor Juan F. Luis Hospital & Medical Center** on St. Croix (p. 115). The payment of Medicare and Medicaid operates as it does in the United States. If you walk into a hospital without any coverage or insurance, you are expected to pay.

On Tortola in the British Virgin Islands, the main hospital in the little country is **Peebles Hospital** (p. 157). If you are on one of the out islands, you are generally taken to Tortola for treatment. In addition to these hospitals, there are a number of private doctors' offices throughout the islands, charging higher rates than the hospitals. It is not difficult to get a prescription filled or find a doctor on St. Thomas, St. Croix, and Tortola. You should get your prescriptions filled before heading to the other islands.

It's sometimes tricky and complicated to get prescriptions from the mainland refilled. Often it requires a phone call from the U.S.V.I. to a stateside pharmacy or to the doctor who prescribed the medicine in the first place. CVS and Wal-Mart are the best for contacting a Stateside branch of CVS or Wal-Mart if your prescription is on a computer file. To avoid possible hassles and delays, it is best to arrive in both the B.V.I. and the U.S.V.I. with the adequate medication you'll need for your vacation.

---

7 SAFETY

The Virgin Islands are a relatively safe destination. The small permanent populations are generally friendly and welcoming. That being said, **St. Thomas** is no longer as safe as it once was. Crime against tourists has been on the rise, and muggings are frequent. Wandering the island at night, especially on the back streets of Charlotte Amalie (particularly on Back St.), is not recommended. For a town of this small size, there is an unusually high crime rate. Guard your valuables or store them in hotel safes if possible.

The same holds true for **St. Croix** and the back streets of Christiansted and Frederiksted. Although these areas are safer than St. Thomas, random acts of violence against tourists in the past, even murder, have been known to happen. Know that most crime on the island is petty theft aimed at unguarded possessions on the beach, unlocked parked cars, or muggings (rarely violent) of visitors at night. Exercise the same amount of caution you would if you were traveling to an unfamiliar town on the mainland. Whether on St. Thomas or St. Croix, always take a taxi home after a night out.

St. John is a bit different, since there is no major town and most of the island is uninhabited. Muggings and petty theft do happen, but such occurrences are rarely violent. You are most likely to find your camera stolen if you leave it unattended on the beach.

The **British Virgin Islands** are a different story. Crime is practically nonexistent on these islands. Minor robberies do occur on Tortola, with less trouble reported on Virgin Gorda.

In general, the Virgin Islands' steep, curvy roads are often poorly lit at night. St. Croix's road network is particularly poor and is composed of rocky, steep dirt roads through the interior. As a result, car-rental insurance is higher on this island than the others. For those travelers who are unaccustomed to driving on the left, we suggest leaving the night driving up to a taxi driver. Do not attempt the most rural roads at night, since cellphone service is spotty at best and breakdowns or robberies are an all-too-perfect way to ruin your Virgin Islands vacation; see "Getting Around," earlier in this chapter.

8 SPECIALIZED TRAVEL RESOURCES

In addition to the destination-specific resources listed below, visit Frommers.com for additional specialized travel resources.

GAY & LESBIAN TRAVELERS

The Virgin Islands, along with Puerto Rico, are some of the most gay-friendly destinations in the Caribbean. However, discretion is still advised in some parts. Islanders tend to be very religious and conservative, and displays of same-sex affection, such as hand holding, are frowned upon.

St. Thomas is the most cosmopolitan of the Virgin Islands, but it is no longer the "gay paradise" it was in the 1960s and 1970s. Most gay vacationers now head for Frederiksted in St. Croix, which has more hotels and other establishments catering primarily to the gay market, none better than the **Sand Castle on the Beach** (p. 123) or the **Palms at Pelican Cove** (p. 118).

In Charlotte Amalie on St. Thomas, the most boisterous gay nightlife takes place in the Frenchtown section of the city. On Thursday, Friday, and Saturday nights beginning at around 11pm, gay men and women flock to **Stereo,** Frenchtown Mall, 24-A Honduras, in Frenchtown (© **340/774-5348**), which is upstairs over the Epernay Bistro.

The B.V.I., however, still remain uptight and closeted toward gay visitors, almost evoking the 1950s. Sometimes when a gay man wants to let loose, he takes the boat to Charlotte Amalie.

TRAVELERS WITH DISABILITIES

Some resorts on St. Thomas and St. Croix have made inroads in catering to persons with disabilities; St. John and all of the British Islands lag far behind in this regard. As of this writing, about a third of the major resorts (and none of the cheaper guesthouses or villas) in St. Thomas or St. Croix have the facilities to accommodate vacationers who have disabilities. If you're planning a vacation in the Virgin Islands, you should contact a travel agent or call the hotel of your choice (an even better option) to discuss your requirements, see if a particular resort is prepared to cater to your needs, and obtain specific information.

For the most part the accessibility of hotels and restaurants in the U.S.V.I. remains far behind the progress made on the mainland, and you must take this into account if you're planning a vacation here. Of the three U.S. Virgins, St. Thomas and St. John, because of their hilly terrain, remain the most unfriendly islands to those who are wheelchair bound. Because it is flat, St. Croix is an easier place to get around.

Of all the hotels in the U.S.V.I., the **Ritz-Carlton** (p. 46) on St. Thomas is the most hospitable to persons with disabilities. It maintains what it calls "accessible rooms," meaning that a selection of accommodations in every price category can be reached without navigating stairs. The staff even offers beach wheelchairs (resting on balloon tires), allowing a person with disabilities to be wheeled into the surf by a member of the watersports staff. Most hotels, however, have a long way to go before they become a friend of a person with disabilities. The big factor hindering such a program is money, of course. Making buildings wheelchair accessible is very costly, and in these days money is in short supply.

There is no organization in the islands that is specifically charged with the care and comfort of vacationers arriving with disabilities.

General Resources for Green Travel

In addition to the resources for the Virgin Islands listed above, the following websites provide valuable wide-ranging information on sustainable travel. For a list of even more sustainable resources, as well as tips and explanations on how to travel greener, visit www.frommers.com/planning.

- **Responsible Travel** (www.responsibletravel.com) is a great source of sustainable travel ideas; the site is run by a spokesperson for ethical tourism in the travel industry. **Sustainable Travel International** (www.sustainabletravel international.org) promotes ethical tourism practices, and manages an extensive directory of sustainable properties and tour operators around the world.
- In the U.K., **Tourism Concern** (www.tourismconcern.org. uk) works to reduce social and environmental problems connected to tourism. The **Association of Independent Tour Operators (AITO)** (www.aito.co.uk) is a group of specialist operators leading the field in making holidays sustainable.
- In Canada, **www.greenlivingonline.com** offers extensive content on how to travel sustainably, including a travel and transport section and profiles of the best green shops and services in Toronto, Vancouver, and Calgary.
- In Australia, the national body which sets guidelines and standards for ecotourism is **Ecotourism Australia** (www. ecotourism.org.au). **The Green Directory** (www.thegreen directory.com.au), **Green Pages** (www.thegreenpages. com.au), and **Eco Directory** (www.ecodirectory.com.au) offer sustainable travel tips and directories of green businesses.

9 SUSTAINABLE TOURISM

Eco-tourism is a relatively new concept to the Virgin Islands. Many of the islands were clear-cut in the 1700s to make way for sugar plantations, destroying much of the natural landscape. All through the 1900s, while real estate developments on St. Thomas continued to grow, little concern was given to preserving and sustaining the natural resources of the U.S.V.I. Today, there is a very different attitude

- **Carbonfund** (www.carbonfund.org), **TerraPass** (www.terrapass.org), and **Carbon Neutral** (www.carbonneutral.org) provide info on "carbon offsetting," or offsetting the greenhouse gas emitted during flights.
- **Greenhotels** (www.greenhotels.com) recommends green-rated member hotels around the world that fulfill the company's stringent environmental requirements. **Environmentally Friendly Hotels** (www.environmentally friendlyhotels.com) offers more green accommodation ratings. The **Hotel Association of Canada** (www.hacgreen hotels.com) has a Green Key Eco-Rating Program, which audits the environmental performance of Canadian hotels, motels, and resorts.
- **Sustain Lane** (www.sustainlane.com) lists sustainable eating and drinking choices around the U.S.; also visit **www.eatwellguide.org** for tips on eating sustainably in the U.S. and Canada.
- For information on animal-friendly issues throughout the world, visit **Tread Lightly** (www.treadlightly.org). For information about the ethics of swimming with dolphins, visit the **Whale and Dolphin Conservation Society** (www.wdcs.org).
- **Volunteer International** (www.volunteerinternational.org) has a list of questions to help you determine the intentions and the nature of a volunteer program. For general info on volunteer travel, visit **www.volunteer abroad.org** and **www.idealist.org**.

toward the ecosystem of the Virgin Islands among permanent residents and visitors alike.

While the eco-tourism infrastructure is still underdeveloped, and the terms "eco-friendly" and "sustainable" can be misused, it is still possible to find truly eco-friendly lodgings on the islands. Camping is always an option. St. John, which is almost entirely a national park, has numerous campsites. Aside from those run by the National Park Service, there is the **Maho Bay Campground** (p. 94), which is an umbrella name for two campsites with several types of eco-friendly lodgings ranging from bare cottages to comfortable studios. On St. Croix, there is **Mount Victory Camp,** which relies on renewable energy to power its cottages. The British Virgin Islands are less developed than their American cousins, so lodgings tend to be more eco-friendly by nature. You don't have to camp out to stay in eco-sensitive lodging.

Low-impact activities like hiking, snorkeling, and kayaking abound in the Virgin Islands. While on St. Croix, contact the **St. Croix Environmental Association** (p. 136), which hosts hikes, tours of research facilities, and events based around the hatching of baby sea turtles. Aside from the many companies that offer tours, the St. Thomas–based **Virgin Islands Ecotours/Mangrove Adventures** (p. 64) offers tours with professional naturalists of the mangrove lagoon and nature reserve at Cas Cay.

St. Thomas, with all its development and modern conveniences, faces the biggest challenges in regard to sustainable development.

10 THE ACTIVE VACATION PLANNER

There's no rule that says you have to confine yourself to a beach chair within arm's length of the bar while visiting the Virgin Islands (though there's no rule against it, either). You will have endless opportunities to sit by the surf sipping rum drinks, but remember that these islands offer more than just a coastline. Coral reefs and stunning beaches provide breathtaking backdrops for a variety of watersports, from snorkeling to sea kayaking and sailing, and there's also plenty of golf, tennis, hiking, and even horseback riding. This section presents an overview of the outdoor activities on the Virgin Islands. See individual chapters for more specific information on locations and outfitters.

ACTIVITIES A TO Z

CAMPING   The best campsites in the Virgin Islands are on St. John, at **Maho Bay** and **Cinnamon Bay** (the Cinnamon Bay campground is considered one of the finest campgrounds in the Caribbean). Both facilities are open year-round and are so popular that reservations need to be made far in advance during the winter months. In the British Virgin Islands, the best campsite is Tortola's **Brewers Bay Campground,** which rents tents and basic equipment and is open year-round.

FISHING   In the past 25 years or so, more than 20 sport-fishing world records have been set in the Virgin Islands, mostly for the mega blue marlin. Other abundant fish in these waters are bonito, tuna, wahoo, sailfish, and skipjack. Sport-fishing charters, led by experienced local captains, abound in the islands; both half-day and full-day trips are available. But you needn't go out to sea to fish. On St. Thomas, St. John, and St. Croix, the U.S. government publishes lists of legal shoreline fishing spots (contact local tourist offices for more information). Closer inshore, you'll find kingfish, mackerel, bonefish, tarpon, amberjack, grouper, and snapper.

On St. Thomas, many people line-fish from the rocky shore along Mandahl Beach, which is also a popular spot for family picnics. The shore here is not the best place for swimming, because the sea floor drops off dramatically and the surf tends to be rough. On St. John, the waters in Virgin Islands National Park are open to fishermen with hand-held rods. No fishing license is required for shoreline fishing, and government pamphlets available at tourist offices list some 100 good spots. Call ✆ **340/774-8784** for more information.

GOLF   The golfing hub of the Virgin Islands is the challenging **Carambola Golf & Country Club** (✆ **340/778-5638;** www.golf carambola.com) in St. Croix. Also on St. Croix is the excellent course at the **Buccaneer** (✆ **340/773-2100**), just outside Christiansted. The highlight on St. Thomas is the **Mahogany Run** (✆ **800/253-7103** or 340/777-6006; www.mahoganyrungolf.com). There aren't any courses on St. John or the British Virgin Islands.

HIKING   The best islands for hiking are **Tortola** and **St. John.** In Tortola, the best hiking is through Sage Mountain National Park, spread across 37 hectares (91 acres) of luxuriant flora and fauna. On St. John, the most intriguing hike is the Annaberg Historic Trail, which takes you by former plantation sites. Most of St. John is itself a National Park, so there are dozens of opportunities for hiking. **St. Croix** also has good hiking in its "Rain Forest" area. **Buck Island,** off the coast of St. Croix, is beloved by snorkelers and scuba divers but also fascinating to hike. You can easily explore the island in a day, as it is only half a mile wide and a mile long. While hiking in the Virgin Islands, you'll encounter many birds and flowers—but no poisonous snakes. Be sure to look for the trumpet-shaped "ginger thomas," the U.S. Virgin Island's official flower.

HORSEBACK RIDING   Equestrians should head for St. Croix. **Paul and Jill's Equestrian Stables** (✆ **340/772-2880;** www.paulandjills. com), at Sprat Hall Plantation, are the best stables not only in the Virgin Islands but also in all the Caribbean. The outfit is known for the quality of both its horses and its riding trails. Neophytes and experts are welcome.

SAILING & YACHTING   The Virgin Islands are a sailor's paradise, offering crystal-clear turquoise waters, secluded coves and inlets, and protected harbors for anchoring.

Most visitors, however, are content with **day sails,** which are easy to organize, especially at the harbors in St. Thomas, Tortola, and Virgin Gorda. Regardless of where you decide to cruise, you really shouldn't leave the islands without spending at least 1 day on the water, even if you have to load up on Dramamine or snap on your acupressure wristbands before you go.

The most popular cruising area around the Virgin Islands is the deep and incredibly scenic **Sir Francis Drake Channel,** which runs from St. John to Virgin Gorda's North Sound. The channel is surrounded by mountainous islands, and boasts crisp breezes year-round. In heavy weather, the network of tiny islands shelters yachties from the brute force of the open sea. The waters surrounding St. Croix to the south are also appealing, especially near Buck Island.

Outside the channel, the Virgin Islands archipelago contains reefy areas that separate many of the islands from their neighbors. To navigate these areas, you need to use a depth chart (available from charter companies or any marine supply outlet) and have some local knowledge. *Tip:* Locals and temporarily shore-bound sailors willingly offer free advice, often enough to last a couple of drinks, at almost any dockside watering hole.

For more than a quarter of a century, *The Yachtsman's Guide to the Virgin Islands* has been the classic cruising guide to this area (it's updated periodically). The detailed, 240-page text is supplemented by 22 sketch charts, more than 100 photographs and illustrations, and numerous landfall sketches showing harbors, channels, landmarks, and such. Subjects covered include piloting, anchoring, communication, weather, fishing, and more. The guide also covers the eastern end of Puerto Rico, Vieques, and Culebra. Copies are available at major marine outlets, bookstores, and direct from **Yachtman's Guide** (© 877/923-9653; www.yachtsmansguide.com).

Except for **Anegada,** which is a low-lying atoll of coral limestone and sandstone, all the Virgin Islands are high and easily spotted. The water here is very clear. The shortest distance between St. Thomas and St. Croix is 35 nautical miles; from St. John to St. Croix, 35 nautical miles; from St. Thomas to St. John, 2 nautical miles; from Tortola to St. Thomas, 10 nautical miles; from Virgin Gorda to Anegada, 13 nautical miles; and from St. John to Anegada, 30 nautical miles. Virgin Gorda to St. Croix is about the longest run, at 45 nautical miles. (Specific distances between the islands can be misleading, though, because often you may need to take roundabout routes from one point to another.)

If you don't know how to sail but would like to learn, contact one of the sailing schools on St. Croix. **Jones Maritime Sailing School,** 1215 King Cross St., Christiansted, St. Croix, U.S.V.I.

00820 (© **340/773-4709;** www.jonesmaritime.com), has three 24-foot day-sailors and charges $295 per person for a 2-day course, on Saturdays and Sundays.

Womanship, 137 Conduit St., Annapolis, MD 21401 (© **800/342-9295** in the U.S.; www.womanship.com), offers a sailing program for women of all ages and levels of nautical expertise in the British Virgin Islands. Groups consist of a maximum of six students with two female instructors. Participants sleep aboard the boat, meals included. Courses normally last a week. The cost is $2,065 to $2,795 from January to May; October to December, $1,995 to $2,695.

The British Virgin Islands are also the headquarters of the **Off-shore Sailing School,** Prospect Reef Resort, Road Town (© **284/494-5119**). This school offers sailing instruction year-round. For information before you go, write or call Offshore Sailing School, 16731 McGregor Blvd., Ft. Myers, FL 33908 (© **800/221-4326** or 239/454-1700; www.offshore-sailing.com).

SEA KAYAKING **Arawak Expeditions,** Cruz Bay, St. John (© **800/238-8687** or 340/693-8312 in the U.S.; www.arawakexp.com), is the only outfitter in the Virgin Islands offering multiple-day sea-kayaking/island-camping excursions, although numerous outfitters and hotels throughout the chain provide kayaks for day trips. The vessels with Arawak Expeditions are in two-person fiberglass kayaks, complete with foot-controlled rudders. The outfit provides all the kayaking gear, healthy meals, camping equipment, and experienced guides. The cost of a full-day trip is $110, half-day, $65; you can also book longer expeditions, such as a 5-day excursion costing $1,195 per person or a 7-day trip going for $2,495 per person.

SNORKELING & SCUBA DIVING On St. Croix, the best site for both is **Buck Island,** easily accessible by day sails from the harbor in Christiansted. St. Croix is also known for its dramatic "drop-offs," including the famous Puerto Rico Trench.

On St. Thomas, all major hotels rent fins and masks for snorkelers, and most day-sail charters have equipment onboard. Many outfitters, like the **St. Thomas Diving Club** (© **340/776-2381;** www.stthomas divingclub.com), also feature scuba programs.

As for the British Virgin Islands, the best snorkeling is around the **Baths,** Virgin Gorda's major attraction. **Anegada Reef,** which lies off Anegada Island, has been a "burial ground" for ships for centuries; an estimated 300 wrecks, including many pirate ships, have perished here. The wreckage of the **HMS *Rhone,*** near the westerly tip of Salt Island, is the most celebrated dive spot in the B.V.I. This ship went under in 1867 in one of the most disastrous hurricanes ever to hit the Virgin Islands.

Diving cruises are packaged by **Oceanic Society Expeditions,** Fort Mason Center, San Francisco, CA 94123 (© **800/326-7491** or 415/441-1106 in San Francisco; www.oceanicsociety.org), which also offers whale-watching and some research-oriented trips. **Caradonna Dive Adventures** (© **800/328-2288;** www.caradonna.com) offers all sorts of diving packages. See individual destination chapters for information on snorkeling and scuba outfitters and lessons.

11 STAYING CONNECTED

In the Virgin Islands, hotel surcharges on long-distance and local calls are usually astronomical, so you're better off using your **cellphone** or a **public pay telephone.** Many convenience stores, groceries, and packaging services sell **prepaid calling cards** in denominations up to $50; for international visitors these can be the least expensive way to call home. Many public pay phones at airports now accept American Express, MasterCard, and Visa credit cards. **Local calls** made from pay phones in most locales cost either 25¢ or 35¢ (no pennies, please). Many of the most rural or expressly private resorts and hotels in the Virgin Islands do not provide phones in the rooms, but have phones in their lobbies or common areas.

Most long-distance and international calls can be dialed directly from any phone. **For calls within the United States, including the U.S. Virgins, and to Canada,** dial 1 followed by the area code and the seven-digit number. **For other international calls,** dial 011 followed by the country code, the city code, and the number you are calling.

You can **call the British Virgins** from the United States by just dialing **1,** the area code **284,** and the number; from the U.K. dial **011-44,** then the number. **To call the U.S. from the B.V.I.,** just dial 1 + area code and the number; **to call the U.K. from the B.V.I.,** dial 011-44-, then the number.

For calls from **within the British Virgin Islands,** the same calling procedure as in the U.S.V.I. applies.

Calls to area codes **800, 888, 877,** and **866** are toll-free. However, calls to area codes **700** and **900** (chat lines, bulletin boards, "dating" services, and so on) can be very expensive—usually a charge of 95¢ to $3 or more per minute, and they sometimes have minimum charges that can run as high as $15 or more.

For **reversed-charge or collect calls,** and for person-to-person calls, dial the number 0, then the area code and number; an operator will come on the line, and you should specify whether you are calling collect, person-to-person, or both. If your operator-assisted call is international, ask for the overseas operator.

distance information, dial 1, then the appropriate area code and 555-
1212.

CELLPHONES

While traveling through the less-developed regions of the Virgin
Islands, you might find your cellphone to be completely useless. To
some vacationers this is a major perk, while to others this is a frighten-
ing prospect.

It's acknowledged by cellphone users that the best reception in the
U.S.V.I. or B.V.I. is provided by Sprint and AT&T. If you're using an
American cellphone in the Virgin Islands, the same rates and price
plans that you would have in the U.S. should apply. However, cellphone reception is spotty and sometimes calls are dropped in mountainous regions, deep valleys, or rural areas in both the U.S.V.I. and the
B.V.I. The use of cellphones in both the U.S.V.I. and the B.V.I. has
become a way of life for most residents, just like it is on the mainland.

INTERNET & E-MAIL

Your hotel remains the best bet for Internet access. The day of the
grand Internet cafe has not arrived in the Virgin Islands. The best
chances for Internet access are found in St. Thomas, less so in St.
Croix, and even less so in St. John, except for two deluxe hotels.

In Charlotte Amalie, you will find a few small cafes that will let you
use an Internet-ready computer for the price of a coffee.

Throughout the British Virgin Islands, it is difficult to find places
where you can use the Internet. Increasingly, Tortola and Virgin
Gorda have Internet access, but it is very rare in the out islands of the
B.V.I., although modern technology is slowly creeping in.

If your hotel is small and doesn't have Internet access, refer to the
"Fast Facts" section of each island chapter for specific recommenda-
tions of where to go.

---

12 TIPS ON ACCOMMODATIONS

Resorts and hotels in the Virgin Islands offer package deals galore,
and though they have many disadvantages, the deals are always
cheaper than rack rates. It's always best to consult a reliable travel
agent to find out what's available in the way of land-and-air packages
before booking accommodations.

There is no rigid classification of hotel properties on the islands. The
word "deluxe" is often used, or misused, when "first-class" might be
more appropriate. "First-class" itself isn't always what it's touted to be.

For that and other reasons, we've presented fairly detailed descriptions of the properties so that you'll get an idea of what to expect. However, even in the deluxe and first-class properties, don't expect top-rate service and efficiency. Life here moves pretty slowly, and that can have its disadvantages.

The facilities available at hotels in the Virgin Islands vary widely. All the big, first-class hotels have swimming pools and are usually located on or near a beach. If you book at less expensive accommodations, you can often pay a small fee to use the facilities of a larger, more expensive resort.

The good news: During the **off season** (mid-Apr to mid-Dec) hotels slash prices 25% to 50%.

Renting Your Own Villa or Vacation Home

Looking for something a little different? You might decide to rent a villa, condo, apartment, or cottage for your Virgin Islands vacation.

Private apartments and cottages are more no-frills options than villas and condos. Most can be rented with or without maid service. Cottages usually contain a simple bedroom with a small kitchen and bathroom. Many open onto a beach, while others are clustered around a communal swimming pool. If you're planning your trip for the high season, reservations should be made at least 5 to 6 months in advance.

Sometimes local tourist offices will advise you on vacation home rentals if you write or call them directly. In addition, dozens of agencies throughout the United States and Canada offer rentals in the Virgin Islands. Here are some of the best:

At Home Abroad, 405 E. 56th St., Suite 6H, New York, NY 10022 (© **212/421-9165;** www.athomeabroadinc.com), has a roster of private homes, villas, and condos for rent in St. Thomas, St. John, Tortola, and Virgin Gorda; maid service is included in the price.

Hideaways International, 767 Islington St., Portsmouth, NH 03801 (© **800/843-4433** or 603/430-4433; www.hideaways.com), has rentals ranging from cottages to villas to entire islands. In most cases, you deal directly with the owners. The company also arranges specialty cruises, yacht charters, airline tickets, rental cars, and hotel reservations. Annual membership is $195.

In the U.K., browse the options offered through **Holiday Rentals** (© **020/8846-3444;** www.holiday-rentals.co.uk).

Island Villas, 340 Strand St., Frederiksted, St. Croix, U.S.V.I. 00840 (© **800/626-4512** or 340/773-8821; www.stcroixislandvillas.com), offers some of the best properties on St. Croix, specializing in villas, condos, and private homes, many of which are on the beach.

One- to seven-bedroom units are available, with prices from $1,000 to $15,000 per week.

Villas of Distinction, P.O. Box 55, Armonk, NY 10504 (© **800/ 289-0900;** www.villasofdistinction.com), offers "complete vacations," including car rental and domestic help. Its private villas have one to six bedrooms, and almost every villa has a pool.

St. Thomas

St. Thomas, the busiest cruise ship harbor in the West Indies, is not the largest of the U.S. Virgins—St. Croix, 40 miles south, holds that distinction. But bustling Charlotte Amalie, at the heart of St. Thomas, is the capital of the U.S.V.I., and it remains *the* shopping hub of the Caribbean. The beaches on this island are renowned for their white sand and calm, turquoise waters, including the very best of them all, Magens Bay. *National Geographic* has rated the island as one of the top destinations in the world for sailing, scuba diving, and fishing.

Charlotte Amalie, with its white houses and bright red roofs glistening in the sun, is one of the most beautiful towns in the Caribbean. It's most famous for shopping, but the town is also filled with historic sights, like Fort Christian, an intriguing 17th-century building constructed by the Danes. The town's architecture reflects the island's culturally diverse past: You'll pass Dutch doors, Danish red-tile roofs, French iron grillwork, and Spanish-style patios.

However, thanks to St. Thomas's thriving commercial activity—as well as its lingering drug and crime problems—the island is often referred to as the most "unvirgin" of the Virgin Islands. Charlotte Amalie is heavily developed and Main Street is virtually a 3- to 4-block-long shopping center. Although this area tends to be overcrowded, the island's beaches, major hotels, most restaurants, and entertainment facilities are, to an extent, removed from the cruise ship chaos. And you can always find seclusion at a hotel in more remote sections of the island.

St. Thomas has much to recommend it—not only perfect sandy beaches but also the best dining in the islands and a string of the most upmarket resorts. But no one ever said St. Thomas was the friendliest of the Virgin Islands. It is, in fact, the unfriendliest—a rather impersonal place overrun with cruise ship passengers and locals who cast a rather cynical eye toward tourists. It can even be dangerous at night, especially on the back streets of Charlotte Amalie.

If you want to escape the masses, don't come here, as the rush-hour traffic in and out of Charlotte Amalie will reveal. If you're seeking something laid-back, with friendlier people, all you have to do is take the ferry over to St. John (see chapter 3), and you'll enter a world that's more evocative of the sleepier 1950s. In short, St. Thomas is for those who want action.

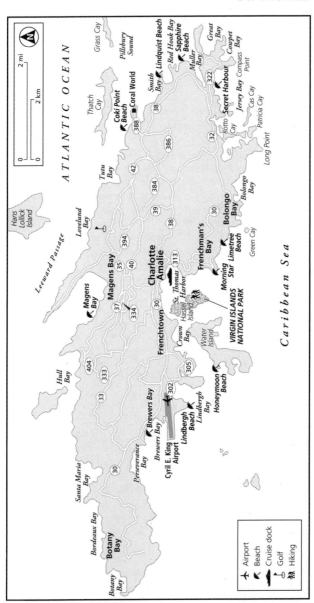

1 ORIENTATION

GETTING THERE
By Plane

If you're flying to St. Thomas, you will land at the **Cyril E. King Airport** (✆ **340/774-5100**), to the west of Charlotte Amalie on Route 30. From here, you can easily grab a taxi to your hotel or villa. Chances are you will be staying east of Charlotte Amalie, so keep in mind that getting through town often involves long delays and traffic jams.

Nonstop flights to the U.S. Virgin Islands from New York City take $3^3/_4$ hours. Flight time from Miami is about $2^1/_2$ hours. Flight time between St. Thomas and St. Croix is only 20 minutes. Flying to San Juan, Puerto Rico, from mainland cities and connecting to St. Thomas may cost less than regular nonstop fares.

American Airlines (✆ **800/433-7300** in the U.S.; www.aa.com) offers frequent service to St. Thomas and St. Croix from the U.S. mainland, with two daily flights from New York to St. Thomas in high season. Passengers flying from other parts of the world are usually routed to St. Thomas through American's hubs in Miami or San Juan, both of which offer nonstop service (often several times a day) to St. Thomas. (American Eagle alone has 12 nonstop flights daily from San Juan to St. Thomas.)

Delta (✆ **800/241-4141** in the U.S.; www.delta.com) offers two daily nonstop flights between Atlanta and St. Thomas in winter. **US Airways** (✆ **800/428-4322** in the U.S.; www.usairways.com) has one nonstop daily flight from Philadelphia to St. Thomas, and an additional flight on Saturday.

Cape Air (✆ **800/352-0714** in the U.S.; www.flycapeair.com) has service between St. Thomas and Puerto Rico. This Massachusetts-based airline offers 5 to 12 flights daily. Cape Air has expanded its service to include flights from San Juan to St. Croix and Tortola, and flights between St. Croix and St. Thomas.

United Airlines (✆ **800/538-2929** in the U.S.; www.united.com) has nonstop service on Saturday to St. Thomas from Chicago and Washington, D.C.

Continental Airlines (✆ **800/231-0856** in the U.S.; www.continental.com) has daily flights from Newark International Airport, in New Jersey, to St. Thomas.

A final hint: Bargain seekers should ask their airline representative to connect them with the tour desk, which can often arrange discounted hotel rates if a hotel reservation is booked simultaneously with airline tickets.

If you're in the British Virgin Islands, you can take a boat to Charlotte Amalie from Tortola. Trip time is only 45 minutes between these two capitals, and a one-way ticket is $30 ($50 round-trip). The major carriers to and from Tortola are **Smith's Ferry** (© **340/775-7292;** www.smithsferry.com) and **Native Son** (© **340/774-8685;** www. nativesonferry.com), which are both based in Charlotte Amalie. Boats arrive in and depart from Tortola's West End.

St. Thomas is also linked by boat to St. John, about 3 to 5 miles away. Ferries depart Red Hook Marina on the East End of St. Thomas and arrive at Cruz Bay on St. John. Trip time is about 15 to 20 minutes; the cost is $6.10 one-way for adults ($1 for kids 2–10). For complete ferry schedules, call **Transportation Services** at © **340/776-6282.**

It's also possible to take a ferry service from Puerto Rico to St. Thomas, with a stop in St. John. The service, however, is available only during Carnival. Trip time between Fajardo and Charlotte Amalie (St. Thomas) is about $1^3/4$ hours, with the departure Saturday morning and the return Sunday afternoon. The cost is $100 one-way, $125 round-trip. For more information, call **Transportation Services** at © **340/776-6282.**

VISITOR INFORMATION

At 78 1-2-3 Estate Constant, across from the Nisky Shopping Center, on the waterfront in downtown Charlotte Amalie, the **visitor center** (© **340/774-8784;** www.visitusvi.com) is open Monday to Friday from 9am to 5pm and Saturday 8am to 2pm. You can get maps and a list of legal shoreline fishing sites throughout the islands here. There's also an information desk at the cruise ship terminal.

ISLAND LAYOUT
Charlotte Amalie

Charlotte Amalie, the capital of St. Thomas, is the only town on the island. Its seaside promenade is called **Waterfront Highway,** or simply, **the Waterfront.** From here, you can take any of the streets or alleyways into town to **Main Street** (also called Dronningens Gade). Principal links between Main Street and the Waterfront include **Raadets Gade, Tolbod Gade, Store Tvaer Gade,** and **Strand Gade.**

Main Street is home to all of the major shops. The western end (near the intersection with Strand Gade) is known as **Market Square.** Once the site of the biggest slave market auctions in the Caribbean Basin, today it's an open-air cluster of stalls where native farmers and gardeners gather daily (except Sun) to sell their produce. Go early in the morning to see the market at its best.

Running parallel to and north of Main Street is **Back Street** (also known as Vimmelskaft Gade), which is also lined with stores, including some of the less expensive choices. ***Beware:*** It can be dangerous to walk along Back Street at night, but it's reasonably safe for daytime shopping.

In the eastern part of town, between Tolbod Gade and Fort Pladsen (northwest of Fort Christian), lies **Emancipation Park,** commemorating the liberation of the slaves in 1848. Most of the major historical buildings, including the Legislature, Fort Christian, and Government House, lie within a short walk of this park.

Southeast of the park looms **Fort Christian.** Crowned by a clock tower and painted rusty red, it was constructed by the Danes in 1671. The **Legislative Building,** seat of the elected government of the U.S. Virgin Islands, lies on the harbor side of the fort.

Kongens Gade (or King's St.) leads to **Government Hill,** which overlooks the town and St. Thomas Harbor. **Government House,** a white brick building dating from 1867, stands atop the hill.

Between **Hotel 1829** (a mansion built that year by a French sea captain) and Government House is a staircase known as the **Street of 99 Steps.** Actually, someone miscounted: It should be called the Street of 103 Steps. Regardless, the steps lead to the summit of Government Hill.

West of Charlotte Amalie

The most important of the outlying neighborhoods to the west of Charlotte Amalie is **Frenchtown.** Some of the older islanders still speak a distinctive Norman-French dialect here. Because the heart of Charlotte Amalie is dangerous at night, Frenchtown, with its finer restaurants and interesting bars, has become the place to go after dark. To reach Frenchtown, take Veterans Drive west of town along the Waterfront, turning left (shortly after passing the Windward Passage Hotel on your right) at the sign pointing to the Villa Olga.

The middle-grade hotels which lie to the immediate west of Charlotte Amalie attract visitors who are seeking more moderate hotel rates than those charged at the mega-resorts that lie along the gold-plated South Coast. The disadvantage is that you may have to depend on public transportation to reach the sands. The biggest attraction is that you're on the very doorstep of Charlotte Amalie, with all its amusements.

East of Charlotte Amalie

Traveling east from Charlotte Amalie, along a traffic-clogged highway, you'll see St. Thomas Harbor on your right. If you stay in this area, you'll be in a tranquil setting just a short car or taxi ride from the bustle of Charlotte Amalie. The major disadvantage is that you must reach the sands by some form of transportation; if you want to run out of your hotel-room door onto the beach, look elsewhere.

The South Coast

This fabled strip, with its good sandy beaches, has put St. Thomas on the tourist maps of the Caribbean. If you don't mind paying the big bucks, you can stay here in grand style. Many visitors prefer the resorts on the South Coast because they want to be far removed from the hustle and bustle of Charlotte Amalie, especially during the day, when it's overrun by cruise ship passengers and others. But if you feel the need for a shopping binge, cars, buses, hotel shuttles, and taxis can quickly deliver you to Charlotte Amalie if you wish.

The East End

The East End is reached by traversing a long, difficult, traffic-clogged road. Once you're here, you can enjoy sea, sand, and sun with little to disturb you (the East End offers even more isolation than the South Coast). This is the site of great beaches such as Sapphire Beach and Lindquist Beach. This section of bays and golden sands offers some ritzy, expensive properties that compete with the mega-resorts of the South Coast, but smaller, less-expensive gems also exist. The little settlement at **Red Hook** is a bustling community with raffish charm and lots of loud bars and affordable eateries. It is also the departure point for ferries to St. John.

The North Coast

The renowned beach at **Magens Bay,** celebrated as one of the finest strips of sands in the Caribbean, lies on the lush North Coast. Be aware, though, that the beach is often overrun with visitors, especially when cruise ship arrivals are heavy. The North Coast has few buildings and not much traffic, making it a destination for those who'd like to dine in a less heavily visited area of the island. The vistas here are among the most panoramic on the island, though traveling the roads is like a ride on a roller coaster—the roads have no shoulders and are especially scary for those not familiar with driving on the left. A lot of the northwest coast, especially at Botany Bay, Bordeaux Bay, and Santa Maria Bay, isn't linked to any roads.

---

2 GETTING AROUND

BY CAR

St. Thomas has many leading North American **car-rental firms** at the airport, and competition is stiff. Before you go, compare the rates of the "big three": **Avis** (© **800/331-1212** or 340/774-1468; www.avis. com), **Budget** (© **800/626-4516** or 340/776-5774; www.budget stt.com), and **Hertz** (© **800/654-3131** or 340/774-1879; www.hertz. com). You can often save money by renting from a local agency, although vehicles sometimes aren't as well-maintained. Try **Dependable Car Rental,** 3901 B Altona, Welgunst, behind the Bank of Nova Scotia and the Medical Arts Complex (© **800/522-3076** or 340/774-2253; www.dependablecar.com), which will pick up renters at the airport or their hotel; or the aptly named **Discount Car Rental,** 14 Harwood Hwy., outside the airport on the main highway (© **877/478-2833** or 340/776-4858; www.discountcar.vi), which grants drivers a 12% discount on rivals' rates. There is no tax on car rentals in the Virgin Islands.

DRIVING RULES   *Always drive on the left.* The speed limit is 20 mph in town, 35 mph outside town. Remember, there is often a lot of traffic on the roads going east out of Charlotte Amalie. Take extra caution when driving in St. Thomas, especially at night. Many roads are narrow, curvy, and poorly lit.

PARKING   Because Charlotte Amalie is a labyrinth of congested one-way streets, don't try to drive within town looking for a parking spot. If you can't find a place to park along the Waterfront (free), go to the sprawling lot to the east of Fort Christian, across from the Legislature Building. Parking fees are nominal here, and you can park your car and walk northwest toward Emancipation Park, or along the Waterfront, until you reach the shops and attractions.

BY TAXI

Taxis are unmetered, but fares are controlled and widely posted; however, we still recommend that you negotiate a fare (usually per person) with the driver before you get into the car. A typical fare from Charlotte Amalie to Sapphire Beach is $13 per person to the East End, about $25 per person. Surcharges, one-third of the price of the excursion, are added after midnight. You'll pay $2 to $4 per bag for luggage. You can easily hail a taxi in Charlotte Amalie, although it's not so easy throughout the island. Reason? The taxis are all waiting for cruise passengers at the dock in Charlotte Amalie. You will more than likely have to call a taxi to pick you up while out on the island. Of course, your hotel can always call one for you. For 24-hour radio-dispatch taxi service, call © **340/774-7457.** If you want to hire a taxi and a driver (who just may be a great tour guide) for a day, expect to pay about $40 per person for 2 hours of sightseeing in a shared car, or $55 to $80 per hour for two to four people.

Taxi vans transport 8 to 12 passengers to multiple destinations on the island. It's cheaper to take a van instead of a taxi if you're going

$1 to $2 per bag. Call 🕿 **340/774-7457** to order a taxi van.

BY BUS

Buses, called **Vitrans,** leave from streetside stops in the center of Charlotte Amalie, fanning out east and west along all of the most important highways. They run between 5:30am and 9pm daily, but waits can be very long and this is a difficult way to get about. A ride within Charlotte Amalie is 75¢; a ride to anywhere else is $1. The Fortuna buses are run by Vitrans and have no set schedule. A ride from Charlotte Amalie to Brewers Bay or Lindbergh Beach is $6 to $8 per person. For schedule and bus-stop information, call 🕿 **340/774-5678** or www.vinow.com.

ON FOOT

Trust us: This is the *only* way to explore the heart of Charlotte Amalie. All the major attractions and main stores are within easy walking distance. However, other island attractions, like Coral World and Magens Bay, require you to take a bus or taxi.

⦅Fast Facts⦆ St. Thomas

Banks Several major U.S. banks are represented on St. Thomas, including **First Bank,** 11A Curaçao Gade, Charlotte Amalie (🕿 **340/775-7777**). Most island banks are open Monday to Thursday 8:30am to 3pm, and Friday 8:30am to 4pm. The banks are your only option if you need to exchange currency. More than 50 ATMs are available on the island.

Bookstores **Dockside Bookshop,** Havensight Mall, Charlotte Amalie (🕿 **340/774-4937**), where the cruise ships dock, sells books, cards, maps, and board games.

Business Hours Typical business and store hours are Monday to Friday 9am to 5pm and Saturday 9am to 1pm. Some shops open Sunday for cruise ship arrivals. Bars are usually open daily 11am to midnight or 1am, although some hot spots stay open later.

Cameras & Film Try **Blazing Photos,** Havensight Mall, Charlotte Amalie (🕿 **340/776-5547**), near the cruise ship dock. There's a branch at **Nisky Shopping Center,** Frenchtown (🕿 **340/774-1005**).

Dentists The **Smile Center** (🕿 **340/775-9110**) is a member of the American Dental Association and is also linked with various specialists. Call for information or an appointment.

Doctors **Roy Lester Schneider Hospital,** 9048 Sugar Estate, Charlotte Amalie (✆ **340/776-8311;** www.rlshospital.org), provides services for locals and visitors.

Drugstores Go to **Drug Farm,** 2–4 Ninth St., Charlotte Amalie (✆ **340/776-7098**), or **Havensight Pharmacy,** Havensight Mall, Building 4, Charlotte Amalie (✆ **340/776-1235**).

Emergencies For the police, call ✆ **911;** ambulance, **911;** fire, **921.**

Hospitals The **Roy Lester Schneider Hospital** is at 9048 Sugar Estate, Charlotte Amalie (✆ **340/776-8311**).

Hot Lines Call the **police** at ✆ **911** in case of emergency. If you have or witness a boating mishap, call the **U.S. Coast Guard Rescue** (✆ **787/729-6800**), which operates out of San Juan, Puerto Rico. Scuba divers should note the number of a **decompression chamber** (✆ **340/776-8311**) at the Roy Schneider Community Hospital on St. Thomas.

Internet Access The best cybercafe is **Beans, Bytes, and Websites** at the Royal Dane Mall (✆ **340/777-7089;** www.beansbytesandwebsites.com), in the center of Charlotte Amalie. It is open daily 7am to 10pm, charging 10¢ a minute with a $1 minimum. Not only do you face a myriad of options for your computer needs, but you can enjoy rich coffee, tropical juices, fruit smoothies, and pastries as well.

Laundry & Dry Cleaning The major hotels provide laundry service, but it's more expensive than a laundromat. For dry cleaning, go to **One-Hour Martinizing,** Barbel Plaza, Charlotte Amalie (✆ **340/774-5452**). A good full-service laundromat is **4-Star Laundromat,** 68 Kronprindsens Gade (✆ **340/774-8689**), also in Charlotte Amalie.

Mail Postage rates are the same as on the U.S. mainland: 28¢ for a postcard and 44¢ for a letter to U.S. addresses. For international mail, a first-class letter of up to 1 ounce costs 98¢ (75¢ to Canada and 79¢ to Mexico); a first-class postcard costs the same as a letter.

Maps See "Visitor Information," earlier in this chapter.

Newspapers & Magazines Copies of U.S. mainland newspapers, such as the *New York Times, USA Today,* and *The Miami Herald,* arrive daily in St. Thomas and are sold at hotels and newsstands. The latest copies of *Time* and *Newsweek* are also for sale. *St. Thomas Daily News* covers local, national, and international events. *Virgin Islands Playground* and *St. Thomas This Week,* both of which are packed with visitor information, are distributed free on the island.

Police The main police headquarters is at the **Alexander A. Farrelly Justice Center,** 8172 Sub Base, Charlotte Amalie (*(C)* **340/774-2211**).

Post Office The main post office is at 9846 Estate Thomas, Charlotte Amalie (*(C)* **340/774-1950**), and is open Monday to Friday 7:30am to 5pm and Saturday 7:30am to noon.

Safety St. Thomas has an unusually high crime rate, particularly in Charlotte Amalie. Don't wander around town at night, particularly on Back Street. Single women should avoid frequenting Charlotte Amalie's bars alone at night. Guard your valuables. Store them in hotel safes if possible, and make sure you keep your doors and windows shut at night.

Taxes The only local tax is an 8% surcharge added to all hotel rates.

Telephone & Fax All island phone numbers have seven digits. It is not necessary to use the 340 area code when dialing within St. Thomas. Numbers for all three islands, including St. John and St. Croix, are found in the U.S. Virgin Islands phone book. Hotels will send faxes and telexes for you, usually for a small service charge. Make long-distance, international, and collect calls as you would on the U.S. mainland by dialing 0 or your long-distance provider.

Tipping Tip as you would on the U.S. mainland—15% or so on a restaurant check, and a few dollars a day for housekeeping services in a hotel.

Toilets You'll find public toilets at beaches and at the airport, but they are limited in town. Most visitors use the facilities of a bar or restaurant.

Transit Information Call *(C)* **340/774-7457** to order a taxi 24 hours a day. Call *(C)* **340/774-5100** for airport information and *(C)* **340/776-6282** for information about ferry departures for St. John.

Weather For emergency (hurricane and disaster) weather reports, call **Vietema** at *(C)* **340/774-2244.**

3 WHERE TO STAY

Nearly every beach on St. Thomas has its own hotel, and the island also has more quaint inns than any other place in the Caribbean. The choice of hotels on St. Thomas divides almost evenly between places to stay in Charlotte Amalie, and grand resorts along the East End that front the fabulous beaches. There are advantages and disadvantages to both, and your choice becomes a matter of personal taste.

Say you're in St. Thomas for shopping and you want to be near the best stores, the widest choice of restaurants and bars, and nearly all the historic attractions. Chances are you'll elect to stay in Charlotte Amalie. And if you're looking for budget accommodations, or a choice of moderately priced inns, you'll need to be in or near Charlotte Amalie. The downside to staying here is that you'll have to take a shuttle over to a good beach, a ride of no more than 10 to 15 minutes from most Charlotte Amalie properties. If you want the isolation of a resort along with proximity to Charlotte Amalie, with all the attractions and shops, you can book into the Marriott property directly to the east of Charlotte Amalie at Flamboyant Point.

If your dream is to arrive in St. Thomas and anchor yourself directly on a beach, then the East End is your best bet. All the properties here are grand, luxurious resorts with many attractions, including watersports and nightlife. The downside is that if you don't want to take expensive transportation, or drive along narrow, dark, and unfamiliar roads at night, you'll be resort-bound for the evening, as commutes to some of the island's best restaurants are difficult after sunset. You'll also have to spend time and money if you want to get into Charlotte Amalie for shopping. Almost without exception, the East End beachfront resorts are very expensive. In spite of the high costs, these hotels attract customers who want the decadent resort life that is impossible to find at the smaller inns of Charlotte Amalie.

Hotels in the Virgin Islands slash their prices in summer by 20% to 60%. Unless otherwise noted, the rates listed below *do not* include the 8% government tax.

IN CHARLOTTE AMALIE
Expensive

Villa Santana ★ This unique country villa is an all-suite property. It was originally built by General Antonio Lopez de Santa Anna of Mexico in the 1850s. Offering a panoramic view of Charlotte Amalie and the St. Thomas harbor, this place is more luxurious than its closest competitor, Villa Blanca (which is also good; p. 45). The shopping district in Charlotte Amalie is just a 5-minute walk away; Magens Bay Beach is a 15-minute drive north. Each guest room is

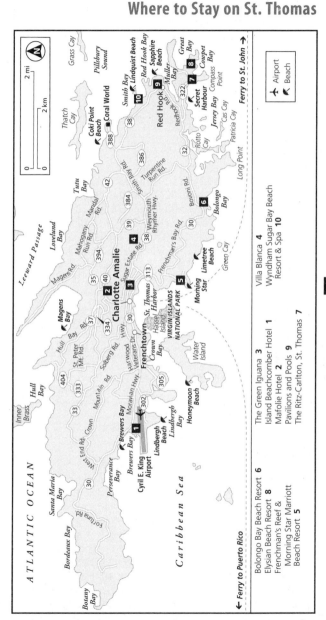

ST. THOMAS

2

WHERE TO STAY

Bolongo Bay Beach Resort **6**
Elysian Beach Resort **8**
Frenchman's Reef & Morning Star Marriott Beach Resort **5**

The Green Iguana **3**
Island Beachcomber Hotel **1**
Mafolie Hotel **2**
Pavilions and Pools **9**
The Ritz-Carlton, St. Thomas **7**

Villa Blanca **4**
Wyndham Sugar Bay Beach Resort & Spa **10**

located in a different part of the villa. You might go for La Mansion, the former library; La Casa de Piedra, a former bedroom; or La Torre, the old pump house, which has been converted into a modern lookout tower. The Mexican-style decor features clay tiles, rattan furniture, and stonework. There is also a sun deck and small garden with hibiscus and bougainvillea.

2602 Bjere Gade #2D, Denmark Hill, Charlotte Amalie, St. Thomas, U.S.V.I. 00802. ©/fax **340/776-1311.** www.villasantana.com. 6 units. Winter $150–$234 suite for 2; off season $114–$124 suite for 2. AE, MC, V. **Amenities:** Outdoor pool. *In room:* Ceiling fan, TV, kitchen, Wi-Fi (free).

Moderate

Hotel 1829 ★   This national historic site is one of the leading small hotels in the Caribbean. It was designed in a Spanish motif, with French grillwork, Danish bricks, and sturdy Dutch doors. Danish and African labor completed the structure in 1829 (hence the name), and since then it has entertained the likes of Edna St. Vincent Millay and Mikhail Baryshnikov. The place stands right in the heart of town, on a hillside 3 minutes from Government House. Magens Bay Beach is about a 10-minute drive. It's a bit of a climb to the top of this multitiered structure—there are many steps, but no elevator. Amid a cascade of flowering bougainvillea are the upper rooms, which overlook a central courtyard with a miniature pool. The rooms in the main house are well designed and attractive, and most face the water. All have wood beams and stone walls. The smallest units, in the former slave quarters, are the least comfortable. Children 11 and under aren't really encouraged here.

Kongens Gade (P.O. Box 1567), Charlotte Amalie, St. Thomas, U.S.V.I. 00804. © **800/ 524-2002** or 340/776-1829. Fax 340/776-4313. www.hotel1829.com. 15 units. Winter $105–$155 double, from $190 suite; off season $90–$125 double, from $190 suite. Rates include continental breakfast. DISC, MC, V. **Amenities:** Bar; small outdoor pool. *In room:* A/C, TV, fridge, hair dryer, no phone.

Inexpensive

The Crystal Palace   This is one of the few B&Bs on St. Thomas. It occupies a building that was rebuilt in 1932 on early-19th-century foundations after a series of fires and hurricanes that left other parts of the island homeless. Today, its owner is the kindly but crusty Ronnie Lockhart, president of the St. Thomas & St. John Friends of Denmark Society, Inc., who showcases the home he was raised in as a genuinely historical but somewhat battered mansion. There's a stateliness to this elegant antique building. Views from the covered balconies sweep out over the city and the harbor. Furnishings include a mixture of the modern, prosaic, and serviceable and the genuinely antique, scattered rather formally amid souvenirs from the Lockhart

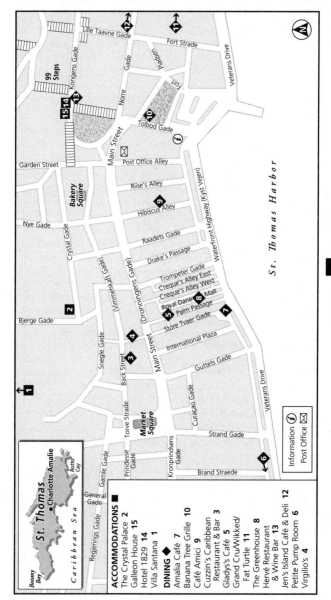

family of long ago. Only two of the building's five accommodations contain a private bathroom—the others are shared facilities in the corridors.

12 Crystalgade, Synagogue Hill, St. Thomas, U.S.V.I. 00802. ✆ **866/502-2277** or 340/777-2277. www.crystalpalaceusvi.com. 5 units, 2 with bath. Winter $119 double without bathroom, $149 double with bathroom; off season $99 double without bathroom, $119 double with bathroom. Rates include breakfast. AE, DISC, MC, V. *In room:* A/C, TV, no phone, Wi-Fi (free).

Galleon House   At the east end of Main Street, about a block from the main shopping area, Galleon House is accessible via a difficult climb, especially in sweltering heat. Nevertheless, its rates are among the most competitive in town, if you don't mind a place operated without state-of-art maintenance and a staff attitude that many readers have complained about. The small rooms, located in scattered hillside buildings, each have a ceiling fan and so-so air-conditioning, plus a cramped bathroom. If you want character, check into the older rooms in the main building. More spacious units with better views lie up the hill in a pair of dull apartment buildings. Breakfast is served on a veranda overlooking the harbor, and Magens Bay Beach is 15 minutes by car or taxi from the hotel. If you check in, say hi to the iguanas for us.

Government Hill (P.O. Box 6577), Charlotte Amalie, St. Thomas, U.S.V.I. 00804. ✆ **800/524-2052** or 340/774-6952. Fax 340/774-6952. www.galleonhouse.com. 12 units, 11 with bathroom. Winter $85 double without bathroom, $109–$159 double with bathroom; off season $75 double without bathroom, $89–$125 double with bathroom. Rates include full breakfast. AE, MC, V. **Amenities:** Pool (outdoor); snorkeling equipment. *In room:* A/C, ceiling fan, TV, Wi-Fi ($10–$15 per day).

WEST OF CHARLOTTE AMALIE
Moderate

Island Beachcomber Hotel (Value)   This rather standard inn near the airport is known for its affordable rates and its beautiful location near one of the island's best sandy beaches, on Lindbergh Bay. Many guests are 1-nighters staying over between yacht charters. A beach-party atmosphere prevails here, and there's a Tahitian aura to the place, created by tropical foliage, bird cages, bridges, and thatched umbrellas. The well-maintained rooms are medium in size, with louvered doors and jalousies, excellent lighting, and ceiling fans, plus a patio or porch. Accommodations face either the garden or the beach; those opening onto the water are grabbed up first, so if you're interested, call well ahead.

Lindberg Beach Rd., Lindbergh Bay, St. Thomas, U.S.V.I. 00802. ✆ **340/774-5250.** Fax 340/774-5615. www.islandbeachcomber.net. 48 units. Winter $189–$219 double; off season $119–$169 double. Extra person $15. AE, DC, DISC, MC, V. **Amenities:** Restaurant; bar. *In room:* A/C, ceiling fan, TV, fridge, hair dyer, Wi-Fi (free).

Moderate

The Green Iguana ★ (Value) Sitting on Blackbeard's Hill, in the center of Charlotte Amalie, this is one of the best run and most economical inns on the island. There's a remnant within the construction from a much older building, but much of what you'll see today is an unpretentious concrete structure from the 1970s and 1980s. Bedrooms have panoramic views of the harbor, the constantly arriving cruise ships, and the other Virgin Islands. The little inn lies only a 5-minute walk from the town's shops, restaurants, and bars, and Magens Beach is a 10-minute drive over the hill. Bedrooms are mid-size and done in a tropical motif with wicker. You have a choice of a king-size, queen-size, or twin-size bed.

37B Blackbeard's Hill, Charlotte Amalie, St. Thomas, U.S.V.I. 00802. (C) **800/484-8634** or 340/776-7654. Fax 340/777-4312. www.thegreeniguana.com. 9 units. Winter $135–$165 double; off season $95–$125 double. AE, MC, V. *In room:* A/C, ceiling fan, hair dryer, kitchenette, Wi-Fi (free).

Mafolie Hotel ★ (Finds) A unique gem among many bland cookie-cutter hotels, this stunning guesthouse is perched 800 feet above Charlotte Amalie's harbor. Its proprietor, Michael Sigler, and his wife, Helga, provide very friendly service at the hotel, while their daughter Natasha and son-in-law AJ take care of the superb restaurant, which draws customers from the upscale Ritz and Marriott nearby. Mike said to us, "We insist on giving good service; that's just how a family works." Each room is different from the next, all decorated by Helga with a personal touch that you can't get at a chain. There is a free shuttle to the beach.

7091 Estate Mafolie, Mafolie Hill, Charlotte Amalie, St. Thomas, U.S.V.I. 00802. (C) **800/225-7035** or 340/774-2790. Fax 340/774-4091. www.mafolie.com. 22 units. Winter $134–$154 double, $164 junior suite; off season $108–$124 double, $144 junior suite. Rates include continental breakfast. Up to 2 children 12 and under stay free in parent's room. Extra person $15. AE, MC, V. **Amenities:** Restaurant; bar; concierge. *In room:* A/C, TV, fridge.

Villa Blanca ★ (Value) Small, intimate, and charming, this hotel lies 1¹/₂ miles east of Charlotte Amalie on 3 secluded acres of hilltop land. Views are among the most panoramic on the island, looking out over the harbor and the green rolling hills. Once the home of owner Blanca Terrasa Smith, today, a homey and caring ambience prevails. Each room has air-conditioning, a well-equipped kitchenette, a good bed with a firm mattress, and a private balcony or terrace with sweeping views either eastward to St. John or westward to the harbor of Charlotte Amalie and Puerto Rico. While there's no restaurant, the rates include a light continental breakfast and each room has a kitchenette, so you can easily prepare modest meals. On the premises are a freshwater pool and a large covered patio where you can enjoy the sunset. The closest beach is Morningstar Bay, about 4 miles away.

4 Raphune Hill, Rte. 38, Charlotte Amalie, St. Thomas, U.S.V.I. 00801. ℭ **800/231-0034** or 340/776-0749. Fax 340/779-2661. www.villablancahotel.com. 14 units. Winter $135–$155 double; off season $95–$125 double. Rates include continental breakfast. Children 9 and under stay free in parent's room. AE, DISC, MC, V. **Amenities:** Pool (outdoor); Wi-Fi (free in lobby). *In room:* A/C, ceiling fan, TV, kitchenette.

THE SOUTH COAST
Very Expensive

Frenchman's Reef & Morning Star Marriott Beach Resort ★★★ Lying 3 miles east of Charlotte Amalie on the south shore, this is the largest hotel in the U.S. Virgin Islands, but since the opening of the Ritz-Carlton, it is no longer the most plush or most glamorous. In 2005, the two separate parts of this resort, Frenchman's Reef and Morning Star, were officially conglomerated into one mega-resort with an excellent location on a bluff overlooking both the harbor and the Caribbean.

This is a full-service, American-style mega-resort. Facilities devoted to the good life are everywhere: To reach the secluded beach, for example, you take a glass-enclosed elevator. The accommodations here have all you'll need for comfort, including generally spacious bathrooms. The bedrooms at Frenchman's Reef are traditionally furnished and quite comfortable, while those at the Morning Star are more luxurious. All units have private balconies with sea views.

There is enough variety in dining to keep you on the premises at night, and the cuisine has become better and better. In general, we prefer the seafood to the frozen meat imported from the U.S. mainland. The complex boasts the hip **Havana Blue** (p. 59), a cocktail/cigar lounge with a truly inspired menu.

No. 5 Estate Bakkeroe, Flamboyant Point (P.O. Box 7100), St. Thomas, U.S.V.I. 00801. ℭ **800/524-2000** or 340/776-8500. Fax 340/715-6193. www.marriott.com. 506 units. Winter $349–$700 double; from $1,009 suite. Off season $208–$435 double; from $750 suite. Children 12 and under stay free in parent's room. AE, DC, DISC, MC, V. **Amenities:** 6 restaurants; 3 bars; babysitting; health club & spa; room service; 2 tennis courts (lit); watersports equipment/rentals. *In room:* A/C, TV, fridge, hair dryer, Wi-Fi ($16).

The Ritz-Carlton, St. Thomas ★ (Kids) Fronted by white-sand beaches, the Ritz-Carlton stands on 30 acres of oceanfront at the island's southeastern tip, 4 miles from Charlotte Amalie. The hotel's architecture evokes a *palazzo* in Venice, as befitting of a Ritz property, and is set amid landscaped gardens, with bubbling fountains and hidden courtyards evoking the feel of a truly sprawling villa.

Also befitting of the Ritz is the special, key-activated Club Lounge featuring 75 well-appointed units, each with views of the Caribbean and a private balcony. Some of the rooms also contain separate tubs and "rainshower stalls." The resort features an extensive spa with 11 luxurious treatment rooms and more open-air cabanas. The recent renovation has seen improvements all around, and a most notable change has been in the quality of the dining and an improvement in the service. Of the restaurants, **Bleuwater** (p. 57) is highly recommended and has the best chef on the island; the **Great Bay Lounge** is a chic place for cocktails, tapas, and sushi. The Ritz Kids program is one of the best on the island, with such features as snorkeling and scuba diving. Finally, the property has its own scuba diving school and private yacht, readily available for guests.

6900 Great Bay, St. Thomas, U.S.V.I. 00802. ✆ **800/241-3333** or 340/775-3333. Fax 340/775-4444. www.ritzcarlton.com. 204 units. Winter $619–$869 double, from $1,129 suite; off season $609–$759 double, from $1,099 suite. AE, DC, DISC, MC, V. **Amenities:** 4 restaurants; 3 bars; babysitting; children's programs; concierge; health club & spa; 2 pools (outdoor); room service; 2 tennis courts (lit); watersports equipment/rentals. *In room:* A/C, TV, Internet (free), minibar.

Expensive

Bolongo Bay Beach Resort ★ (Kids)   This is an unpretentious, bare-feet-welcome kind of place. You'll find a half-moon-shaped white-sand beach, and a cluster of pink two- and three-story buildings, plus some motel-like units closer to the sands. There's also a social center consisting of a smallish pool and a beachfront bar, replete with palm fronds. It's a relatively small property, but it offers all the facilities of a big resort. Many guests check in on the European Plan, which includes watersports activities and even a scuba diving lesson; others opt for all-inclusive plans that include all meals, drinks, a sailboat excursion to St. John, and use of scuba equipment. Rooms are simple, summery, and filled with unremarkable but comfortable furniture. Each unit has its own balcony or patio, a refrigerator, and one king-size or two double beds. Some of the units on the beach come with kitchenettes, and the apartment-style condos, in a three-story building, have full kitchens.

7150 Bolongo, St. Thomas, U.S.V.I. 00802. ✆ **800/524-4746** or 340/775-1800. Fax 340/775-3208. www.bolongobay.com. 65 units. Winter $195–$360 double; off season $170–$295 double. Ask about other packages and various meal plans. AE, MC, V. **Amenities:** 2 restaurants; 2 bars; babysitting; children's programs (ages 4–12); exercise room; 2 pools (outdoor); 2 tennis courts (lit); watersports equipment/rentals; Wi-Fi by pool (free). *In room:* A/C, ceiling fan, TV, fridge, hair dryer, kitchenette (in some).

THE EAST END
Very Expensive

Wyndham Sugar Bay Resort & Spa ★★ (Kids)   At the eastern end of the island, on a desirable 32-acre plot of steeply sloping terrain, within a 5-minute ride from Red Hook, this well-maintained, much-improved hotel caters very clearly to a conservative, mainstream clientele who often opt to bring their families and young children along with them on holiday. Since about 60% of the guests who stay here opt for a full-board plan, it is the largest all-inclusive hotel on St. Thomas. It has panoramic views that sweep out over the sea from its position atop a rocky headland, although its secluded beach is really too small for a resort of this size. Many of the attractive rooms are decorated with rattan pieces and pastels. This is not the most cutting-edge or stylish hotel on the island, but guest rooms have modern carpeting, Balinese furnishings, electronics, wall treatments, and state-of-the-art plumbing. The hotel has one of only two casinos (slot machines only) on the island, and the hotel's spa, Journeys, is the largest full-service spa in the U.S. Virgins.

6500 Estate Smith Bay, St. Thomas, U.S.V.I. 00802. (C) **877/999-3223** or 340/777-7100. Fax 340/777-7200. www.wyndham.com. 294 units. Winter $338–$519 double, from $750 suite; off season $183–$332 double, from $650 suite. Ask about packages and various meal plans. AE, DC, DISC, MC, V. **Amenities:** 3 restaurants; 2 bars; babysitting; casino (slot machines only); children's programs; exercise room; 4 tennis courts (lit). *In room:* A/C, ceiling fan, TV, fridge, hair dryer, Internet ($15).

Expensive

Elysian Beach Resort ★   This timeshare resort on Cowpet Bay, a 30-minute drive from Charlotte Amalie, is imbued with a certain European resort chic. If you seek tranquillity and seclusion without all the razzle-dazzle of other East End competitors, stay here. The beautiful white-sand beach is another compelling reason to choose this place. There are free shuttles to Charlotte Amalie and Magens Bay Beach, should you decide to leave.

The thoughtfully planned bedrooms contain balconies, and 14 offer sleeping lofts that are reached by a spiral staircase. The decor is tropical, with rattan and bamboo furnishings, ceiling fans, and natural-wood ceilings. Try to avoid rooms in buildings V to Z, as they are some distance from the beach.

The hotel also boasts **Robert's American Grille** (p. 58), a peaceful spot to enjoy creative American and West Indian cuisine.

6800 Estate Nazareth, Cowpet Bay, St. Thomas, U.S.V.I. 00802. (C) **800/347-8182** or 340/775-1000. Fax 340/776-0910. www.elysianbeachresort.net. 180 units. Winter $234–$259 double, $459 suite; off season $195–$239 double, $399 suite. AE, DC, DISC, MC, V. **Amenities:** 2 restaurants; 2 bars; exercise room; pool (outdoor); small spa; tennis court (lit); watersports equipment/rentals. *In room:* A/C, TV, hair dryer, kitchenette, Wi-Fi ($9.95).

Pavilions and Pools ★ Ideal for a honeymoon, this resort lets you have your own villa, with floor-to-ceiling glass doors opening onto your own private swimming pool. It's perfect for those who want to run around nude as Adam and Eve, Eve and Eve, or Adam and Adam. The resort, 7 miles east of Charlotte Amalie, is actually just a string of condominium units, tastefully furnished according to the tastes of each individual owner. After checking in and following a landscaped pathway to your villa, you don't have to see another soul until you leave if you so wish—the fence and gate around your space are that high. Your swimming pool is encircled by a deck and plenty of tropical greenery. Inside, a room divider screens a well-equipped kitchen. The place is not posh, and an average good motel in the States will have better-quality furniture. The resort is a steep uphill walk from Sapphire Bay, which boasts one of the island's best beaches and many watersports concessions. Honeymooning couples should inquire about packages.

6400 Estate Smith Bay, St. Thomas, U.S.V.I. 00802. ⓒ **800/524-2001** or 340/775-6110. Fax 340/775-6110. www.pavilionsandpools.com. 25 units. Winter $275–$360 double; off season $200–$275 double. Rates include continental breakfast. AE, MC, V. **Amenities:** Restaurant; watersports equipment/rentals; Wi-Fi (free in lobby), private pools. *In room:* A/C, ceiling fan, TV, hair dryer, kitchen.

4 WHERE TO DINE

The dining scene in St. Thomas these days is among the best in the West Indies, but it has its drawbacks: Fine dining (and even not-so-fine dining) tends to be expensive, and the best spots (with a few exceptions) are actually not right in Charlotte Amalie and can be reached only by taxi or car.

You'll find an eclectic mix of cuisines on St. Thomas, including American, Italian, Mexican, Asian, and other options. We recommend exploring some of the local Caribbean dishes at least once or twice, especially the seafood specialties like "ole wife" and yellowtail, which are usually prepared with a spicy Creole mixture of peppers, onions, and tomatoes. The winner among native side dishes is *fungi* (pronounced *foon*-gee), made with okra and cornmeal. Most local restaurants serve johnnycake, a popular fried, unleavened bread.

IN CHARLOTTE AMALIE
Expensive
Amalia Café ★ SPANISH Even though the owners, Randolph and Helga Maynard, are not from Spain (he's from Antigua and she's from Germany), they offer the most savory Spanish cuisine in town, including a varied selection of tasty tapas. Their location is romantically

located in a Spanish meson in the cobblestone Palm Passage in the center of Charlotte Amalie. The razor-sharp Spanish cooking techniques are generated by a team of chefs from the Dominican Republic, who have been extensively trained in the preparation of Spanish culinary traditions.

We like to make a full meal just out of the tapas, especially garlic shrimp, clams in green sauce, and delightful mussels in a brandy sauce. That Castilian classic, garlic soup, is also offered as a starter. These DR chefs make the best *paella Valenciana* in town (the secret is in the fish stock). Their *zarzuela de mariscos,* or seafood casserole, is as good as you might get along Spain's Costa Brava. A pasta of the day is offered but one of their best specialties is oven-roasted lamb shank in pan juices and sherry flavoring. Not only do they serve the best pitchers of sangria on the island, but the cooks also make the best caramel flan for dessert.

24 Palm Passage. ⓒ **340/714-7373.** www.amaliacafe.com. Reservations recommended. Main courses lunch $13–$20, dinner $21–$28. AE, MC, V. Mon–Fri 11am–3pm and 6–10pm; Sun 11am–3pm (winter only).

Banana Tree Grille INTERNATIONAL   This place offers candlelit dinners, sweeping views over the busy harbor, and a decor that includes genuine banana plants artfully scattered through the two dining rooms. The cuisine is creative and changes frequently; the patrons are often hip and laid-back. Start off with grilled bacon-wrapped horseradish shrimp over a mango glaze. Main dishes are filled with flavors influenced by Asian, Caribbean, and Italian cuisines. Especially noted are the house specialties of sugar-cane-and-cocoa-lacquered tuna, lobster tail tempura with an orange-pepper sauce, and the divine mango-and-mustard-glazed salmon. Try the aïoli shank, a house specialty, if it's offered: A shank of lamb is slowly braised in Chianti and served with an aïoli sauce over white beans and garlic mashed potatoes. The desserts are truly decadent. The hotel itself, once the most famous in the U.S. Virgin Islands, is now devoted to timeshares.

In Bluebeard's Castle, Bluebeard's Hill. ⓒ **340/776-4050.** www.bananatreegrille. com. Reservations recommended. Main courses $20–$49. AE, MC, V. Tues–Sun 6–9:30pm.

Grande Cru/Wikked/Fat Turtle ★ INTERNATIONAL   This trio of the genuinely intriguing restaurants of Charlotte Amalie lie side by side beside the WICO docks, immediately adjacent to where some of the world's biggest cruise ships moor. Each of the three is part of a fast-evolving marina/hotel/condo development, Yacht Haven Grande. The most expensive, formal, and elegant of the three restaurants is Grande Cru, whose meticulously crafted dining room manages

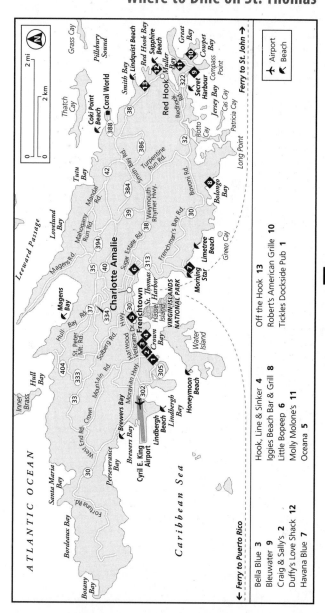

← Ferry to Puerto Rico

↑ Ferry to St. John →

✈ Airport
⚓ Beach

Bella Blue **3**
Bleuwater **9**
Craig & Sally's **2**
Duffy's Love Shack **12**
Havana Blue **7**

Hook, Line & Sinker **4**
Iggies Beach Bar & Grill **8**
Little Bopeep **6**
Molly Molone's **11**
Oceana **5**

Off the Hook **13**
Robert's American Grille **10**
Tickles Dockside Pub **1**

to be both romantic and jazzy at the same time. Tables spill outdoors onto a covered veranda that's open to a view of privately owned yachts. Look for stylish menu items which include braised short ribs on horseradish and lemon risotto, pistachio and basil-crusted goat cheese on greens with a truffle-flavored vinaigrette, and a succulent version of roasted chicken with preserved lemon and sun-dried tomatoes.

The charming middle-bracket contender within the group is Wikked, a breezy, amiable, and likable restaurant that some of the local boat and condo owners have transformed into their favorite. And the most raucous and animated is Fat Turtle, a booze-and-burger joint that's a favorite with the college crowd looking for flavorful grub, very stiff drinks, and large-screen TVs broadcasting sporting events.

In the Yacht Haven Marina. Grande Cru ✆ **340/775-8CRU** (775-8278); Wikked ✆ **340/775-8WKD** (775-8953); Fat Turtle **340/775-8FAT** (775-8328). Reservations recommended at Grande Cru, not necessary at Wikked or Fat Turtle. Main courses at Grande Cru $24–$38; platters and main courses at Wikked and Fat Turtle $12–$28. AE, MC, V. Grande Cru Mon–Fri noon–3pm; daily 5–10pm. Wikked Mon–Sat 11am–10pm; Sun 8am–10pm. Fat Turtle daily 11am–10pm.

Hervé Restaurant & Wine Bar ★ AMERICAN/CARIBBEAN/ FRENCH A panoramic view of Charlotte Amalie and a historic setting are side benefits—it's the cuisine that matters. Hervé Paul Chassin is a restaurateur with a vast classical background. In an unpretentious setting, he offers high-quality food at reasonable prices. There are two dining areas: a large open-air terrace and a more intimate wine room. Start with the pistachio-encrusted brie, shrimp in a stuffed crab shell, or conch fritters with mango chutney. For a main course, try the house special bouillabaisse, or a delectable blacksesame-crusted tuna with a ginger/raspberry sauce. There are also nightly specials of game, fish, and pasta. Desserts are divine—you'll rarely taste a creamier crème caramel or a lighter, fluffier mango or raspberry cheesecake.

Next to Hotel 1829, Government Hill. ✆ **340/777-9703.** www.herverestaurant. com. Reservations required. Main courses lunch $9–$48, dinner $21–$49. AE, MC, V. Mon–Fri 11am–3pm; daily 6–10pm.

Petite Pump Room ★ WEST INDIAN/INTERNATIONAL This restaurant is housed on the second floor of the industrial-looking ferryboat terminal at the edge of the harborfront in Charlotte Amalie, departure point for boats headed off to the British Virgin Islands and St. Croix. Established in 1963 by the then-owner of the famous Pump Room restaurant in Chicago, it does a thriving breakfast and lunch business among local boat owners and downtown office workers. The draw is some of the best West Indian cooking on the island, a cuisine that takes the preparation of callaloo greens very seriously (they're fabulous), and the nuances of pounded conch steak and grouper

with fries with devotion. If you want something "international" (that
is, American), the menu lists club sandwiches, steaks, chicken dishes,
and burgers, but virtually everyone who comes here orders the West
Indian food. Examples? Stewed oxtail or chicken, or fried potfish with
Creole sauce, always served with your choice of pigeon peas and rice,
mashed potatoes, dumplings, macaroni and cheese, *fungi* with vegetables, fried plantains, or two kinds of potatoes.

In the Edward Wilmoth Blyden Building, Veterans Dr. *C* **340/776-2976.** www.
petitepumproom.com. Breakfasts $7–$13; sandwiches and salads $8–$13; platters
$11–$20. Daily 7am–4:30pm.

Virgilio's ★ NORTHERN ITALIAN   Virgilio's is the best northern Italian restaurant in the Virgin Islands. Its neobaroque interior is
sheltered under heavy ceiling beams and brick vaulting. A well-
trained staff serves meals against a backdrop of stained-glass windows,
crystal chandeliers, and soft Italian music. The *cinco peche* (clams,
mussels, scallops, oysters, and crayfish simmered in a saffron broth) is
delicious, and the fettuccine Alfredo is one of the best we've tasted.
Classic dishes are served with a distinctive flair—the lamb shank, for
example, is filled with a porcini-mushroom stuffing and glazed with
a roasted garlic aïoli. The marinated grilled duck is served chilled. You
can also order individual pizzas. The place does a thriving take-away
business as well.

18 Dronningens Gade (entrance on a narrow alley running btwn Main and Back
sts.). *C* **340/776-4920.** Reservations recommended. Main courses lunch $11–
$26, dinner $19–$46. AE, MC, V. Mon–Sat 11:30am–10:30pm; Sun 5–10:30pm.

Moderate

Cuzzin's Caribbean Restaurant & Bar ★ (Finds) CARIBBEAN
For some real, old-fashioned Virgin Islands cooking, head to this
offbeat place installed in an 18th-century stable on Back Street. The
dining room is comfortable, with stone-and-brick walls. The restaurant boasts island dishes, with a focus on seafood, especially conch,
lobster, and freshly caught fish that arrives the day it's served. Native
dishes include stews and curries, such as island-style mutton, curried
chicken, and conch stewed in a rich onion-butter sauce. The signature
dish is Cuzzin' Nemo, a mélange of lobster, conch, scallops, and shrimp
served over pasta. Fried green bananas or fried plantains accompany
most dishes, and desserts are rich and luscious. The drinks of choice
include local beverages such as ginger beer, mauby, and sea moss.

7 Wimmelskafts Gade (Back St.). *C* **340/777-4711.** Reservations recommended.
Main courses $11–$40. AE, DISC, MC, V. Tues–Sat 11am–9:30pm; Mon 11am–4pm.

The Greenhouse AMERICAN/CARIBBEAN   Fronted by big
windows, this sunny waterfront restaurant attracts cruise ship passengers who need a place to drop. The food here is not the island's

best, but it's satisfying if you're not too demanding. The house specializes in chicken, often with exotic fruit flavors, such as mango-banana chicken or coconut chicken. The excellent appetizers range from conch fritters to stuffed jalapeño peppers. A kettle of soup is always on the stove, and you can make a meal of the freshly made salads. The most popular item on the menu is the big, juicy burger, the island's finest, made with certified Angus beef. There's a wide selection of seafood, like the baked stuffed swordfish with garlic cream sauce, plus chef's specialties such as baby back ribs.

The Greenhouse is also a prime nightlife spot. A daily happy hour from 4:30 to 7pm seduces party animals early. On Tuesday nights after 9:30pm, The Greenhouse turns into a hip nightclub attracting a 21-and-over crowd with two-for-one drinks. This is the biggest event on Tuesday night in St. Thomas. On Friday nights there's live reggae music; on other nights the sounds are selected by a DJ.

Veterans Dr. ✆ **340/774-7998.** www.thegreenhouserestaurant.com. Main courses $8.95–$28. AE, DISC, MC, V. Daily 11am–10pm; bar daily 11am until the last customer leaves.

Inexpensive

Café Amici ITALIAN/CARIBBEAN Many times when shopping in Charlotte Amalie, we stop for lunch in this alley with its buildings of old stone and its cascading tropical plants. Select a seat at this open-air cafe and dig into the day's offerings. There's always a delightful variety of antipasti, salads, and a soup du jour. Pastas are also menu standards, including the famous "rasta pasta," with grilled vegetables, olive oil, garlic, and the chef's "secret" spices. The pizzas and sandwiches are the best in the center of town. We always gravitate to the clams casino pizza, which has added flavorings of bacon, mozzarella, and garlic. A rarer pizza is called tropical, and it's served with a hot, spicy tamarind sauce, grilled cheese, and both feta and mozzarella cheese. Vegetarians will be glad to see the grilled portobello mushroom served with roasted red pepper and smothered in melted provolone cheese and offered on homemade bread with pesto mayonnaise.

Riise's Alley. ✆ **340/776-5670.** Lunch specials $9.95–$13; pizza $9.95–$14. MC, V. Mon–Sat 11am–4pm.

Gladys's Café ★ ⓕⓘⓝⓓⓢ CARIBBEAN/AMERICAN Antigua-born Gladys Isles is a warm, gracious woman who makes a visit here all the more special. Gladys's Café is housed in a 1700 pump house with a stonework courtyard that has a well (one of only three on the island) in the middle. The good, standard breakfast here is the best value in town. Lunch offerings feature various sandwiches, salads, and fresh seafood, including an excellent swordfish and dumplings. Along with local lobster, shrimp, and fish dishes, the house specialty is the hot chicken salad, made with pieces of sautéed breast with red-wine vinegar, pine nuts, and dill, all nestled on a bed of lettuce.

Royal Dane Mall. ℂ **340/774-6604.** Reservations required for groups of 6 or more. Breakfast $5.50–$12; lunch main courses $9–$18. AE, MC, V. Mon–Sat 7am–5pm; Sun 8am–3pm.

Jen's Island Café & Deli AMERICAN/DELI   Homesick New Yorkers especially head for this small eatery for breakfast or lunch while touring or shopping in Charlotte Amalie. You can go healthy at breakfast, ordering yogurt with granola, or a three-cheese omelet with sausage, bacon, or ham. Want more? Order the buttermilk pancakes and to hell with the waistline. The smoked salmon platter is a morning favorite with lovers of deli food. At lunch you can enjoy fresh salad platters, including a grilled chicken salad or a chef's salad—or opt for one of the well-stuffed sandwiches, including slow-roasted beef, pastrami, or albacore tuna. Desserts are homemade daily.

Grand Hotel, 43–46 Norre Gade. ℂ **340/777-4611** or 340/514-5345. www.jens deli.com. Breakfast $4–$7.75; main courses $6.75–$9. MC, V. Mon–Sat 7am–4:30pm.

EAST OF CHARLOTTE AMALIE
Inexpensive
Little Bopeep ⓥ**alue** CARIBBEAN   This plain little brick tavern serves up some of the best West Indian food on the island. No one puts on any airs at this place, and breakfast here is the least expensive in town. You can order (to go) meat patties and sandwiches, such as egg, bacon, and cheese. Lunch gets more interesting and a lot spicier, with curried chicken and curried conch. Fried plantains accompany most dishes.

Barber Plaza. ℂ **340/774-1959.** Breakfast $3–$6; main courses $7–$11. No credit cards. Mon–Fri 7am–5pm; Sat 7am–3pm.

WEST OF CHARLOTTE AMALIE
Moderate
Bella Blu ★ MEDITERRANEAN   West of Charlotte Amalie, this restaurant's 14 tables overlook the harbor. The fare here is light and focuses on the sunny flavors of the Mediterranean. You might start with the tuna tartare, and move on to a Moroccan-inspired chicken or lamb dish. Schnitzels are still on the menu, if you're so inclined. The menu changes with the season and what's fresh at the marketplace.

French Town Mall. ℂ **340/774-4349.** Reservations recommended. Main courses $7–$28 lunch, $16–$28 dinner. AE, MC, V. Mon–Sat 11:30am–10pm.

Craig & Sally's ★ SEAFOOD   This Caribbean cafe is set in an airy, open-sided pavilion in Frenchtown. Its eclectic cuisine is, according to the owner, "not for the faint of heart, but for the adventurous soul." Views of the sky and sea are complemented by a cuisine that ranges from pasta to seafood, with influences from Europe and Asia. Roast pork with clams, filet mignon with macadamia nut sauce, and grilled swordfish with a sauce of fresh herbs and tomatoes are examples from a menu that changes every day. The lobster-stuffed, twice-baked potatoes are inspired. The wine list is the most extensive and sophisticated on St. Thomas.

3525 Honduras, Frenchtown. ℂ 340/777-9949. www.craigandsallys.com. Reservations recommended. Main courses $18–$40. MC, V. Wed–Fri 11:30am–3pm; Wed–Sun 5:30–10pm.

Hook, Line & Sinker AMERICAN   Locals and visitors alike flock to this rendezvous, where they get friendly service, good food at reasonable prices, and a panoramic view of the harbor. The setting evokes a New England seaport village; the building has a pitched roof and skylights, along with wraparound French doors and windows. A *Cheers*-like crowd frequents the bar. Breakfast, except for Sunday brunch, is standard. Lunch choices range from a Caesar salad to various grilled chicken dishes. The dinner menu is usually a delight, featuring delicious dishes such as mango-rum tuna, jerk swordfish, and snapper stuffed with mushrooms and red peppers and covered in a garlic sauce. Locals call the hearty soups "outrageous."

62 Honduras, Frenchtown. ℂ **340/776-9708.** www.hooklineandsinkervi.com. Main courses $9–$15 lunch, $10–$28 dinner; Sun brunch $8.50–$15. AE, MC, V. Mon–Sat 11:30am–4pm and 6–10pm; Sun 10am–2:30pm.

Oceana SEAFOOD   Upscale, hip, and stylish, this local favorite occupies what functioned as the Russian consulate during the Danish occupation of the island. Outfitted with slabs of carefully oiled paneling, and painted in bright blues and greens inspired by the colors of the ocean, the restaurant offers two distinctly different venues. The street level has a wine bar–cum–singles bar, where small platters of food (blini, crostinis, and cheese platters) are specifically designed to go with the changing array of wine. This area buzzes with convivial after-work chitchat. Upstairs, within a relaxed but relatively formal dining room, candles and oil lamps flicker amid bouquets of flowers. Menu items focus mainly on fish, with a healthy roster of beef and lamb as well. Expect a menu that includes spicy shrimp served with a cup of Andalusian-style gazpacho; house-marinated salmon; mussels in white-wine sauce; pan-fried freshwater trout from Idaho; oven-roasted sea bass with a white-wine, thyme, and olive oil sauce; grilled sirloin of lamb; several different preparations of Caribbean lobster; and New York strip, porterhouse, and filet mignon steaks. If the ambience and conviviality of the wine bar appeal to you more than the relative formality of the upstairs dining room, the staff will set up a dining table for you downstairs.

In the Villa Olga, 8 Honduras. (© **340/774-4262.** www.oceana.vi. Reservations required. Tapas $12–$18; main courses $25–$48. AE, DC, MC, V. Restaurant Mon– Sat 5:30–10pm; bar Mon–Sat 5pm–midnight, daily Jan–Apr.

Inexpensive

Tickles Dockside Pub AMERICAN   This joint is dedicated to the concept of fun, comfort, and reasonably priced food in a friendly atmosphere. Diners at this open-air restaurant can sit back and relax while watching the sailboats and cruise ships on the water. The menu features a simple American-pub fare of burgers, including a veggie burger; sandwiches; fish; and pasta. Start off with a plate of "gator eggs" (lightly breaded jalapeño peppers stuffed with cheese) or "sweet lips" (strips of sweet, fried chicken served with a honey-mustard sauce), or a local version of conch chowder. Choose from ham, turkey, or corned beef for your Reuben, grilled with Tickles' own special Russian dressing, Swiss cheese, and sauerkraut. The cooks also turn out an array of classic dishes: chicken Alfredo, prime rib, baby back ribs, fried catfish, and a fisherman's platter served over pasta.

Crown Bay Marina. (© **340/776-1595.** www.ticklesdocksidepub.com. Main courses lunch $8–$11, dinner $11–$25. AE, MC, V. Daily 7am–10:30pm (bar until midnight).

THE SOUTH COAST

Iggies Beach Bar & Grill AMERICAN/CONTINENTAL   Sports fans and others patronize this action-packed seaside spot. It's the island's best sports bar and grill, with giant TVs broadcasting the latest games. To make things even livelier, there's karaoke. The place has "indestructible" furniture, and an aggressively informal crowd. Bring the kids along; no one will mind if they make a ruckus, and they can order from the basic kids' menu. The regular menu changes nightly, and every night there's a theme, such as lobster night or Italian night. Most popular is carnival night, when a West Indian all-you-can-eat buffet is presented along with a limbo show. Adults can order such tropical drinks as "Iggie's Queen" (coconut cream, crème de Noyaux, and rum) or the "Ultimate Kamikazi," the ingredients of which are a secret. There's a fine-dining restaurant in the back that has good fare at shockingly low prices.

At the Bolongo Bay Beach Resort (p. 47), 7150 Bolongo (Rte. 30). (© **340/693-2600.** www.iggiesbeachbar.com. Burgers and sandwiches $6.50–$15; lunch and dinner main courses $14–$30. AE, MC, V. Mon–Fri 3–10pm; Sat–Sun 11:30am–11pm.

THE EAST END
Very Expensive

Bleuwater ★★ SEAFOOD/INTERNATIONAL   One of the grandest dining spots on the island lies in the Ritz-Carlton hotel. It is decorated in a West Indian style, taking its decor from its name—candles, plates, cushions, and wall accents are all in blue. The executive chef, Jasper Schneider, is one of the finest on the island, carefully shopping for only the finest in top-quality ingredients to construct his divine meals. Guests dine in air-conditioned comfort or select an umbrella-shaded table on the patio.

Breakfast dishes are about the best on the island, including both a hot and a cold buffet. The bananas foster French toast with whipped butter and aged rum is almost irresistible, as are the buttermilk pancakes with blueberries, strawberries, bananas, toasted coconut whipped butter, and maple syrup. Of course, if you order the Bleuwater Bloody Mary mimosa, the day is yours.

At dinner, such exotica as duck wontons with pickled cucumber salad or scallop carpaccio are served as starters. You can follow with main dish selections "from the sea" or "from the farm." Our oven-roasted grouper came with leeks and a chorizo-clam broth. Another specialty is a duo of beef—pan-seared *côte de boeuf* and red-wine-braised Kobe short ribs. A "tasting plate" is the way to go in desserts, though you may opt for the warm chocolate tart with a white-chocolate-and-ginger ice cream.

In the Ritz-Carlton (p. 46), 6900 Great Bay. *C* 340/775-3333. www.ritzcarlton.com/en/Properties/StThomas/Dining/Bleuwater. Reservations required. Breakfast main courses $10–$30; dinner main courses $40–$65. Wed–Mon 7–10am and 6–10pm.

Expensive

Robert's American Grille ★ Finds AMERICAN When the shopping bazaars and the glut of cruise ship passengers flooding Charlotte Amalie have got you down, head to this peaceful retreat in the Elysian Beach Resort. The restaurant opens onto the beach at Cowpet Bay, providing a great open-air setting for chef/owner Kevin Kuepper's cuisine. He takes regional American dishes and applies his own creative and imaginative interpretations. You might start with his salad of mesclun, walnuts, and Gruyère all topped with a house-made poppy seed dressing. His "cherry chicken" is a delight, with dried cherries and tarragon, on top of buttermilk mashed potatoes. His pan-fried pork loin medallions are also excellent; the boneless center cut is sautéed and then deglazed with their honey-lime wasabi glaze. Another treat for the palate is the tandoori-marinated mahimahi with purple sticky rice.

In the Elysian Beach Resort (p. 48), 6800 Estate Nazareth, Cowpet Bay. *C* 340/714-3663. www.robertsamericangrille.com. Reservations recommended. Main courses $16–$34; lunch $6–$22. AE, MC, V. Tues–Sat 11:30am–2:30pm and 5:30–10:30pm; Sun 5:30–9pm.

Moderate

Havana Blue ★★ CUBAN FUSION   This chic venue at the Marriott enjoys a beachfront ambience and a sophisticated menu that is the island's most inspired. An inventive crew is in the kitchen, running wild in their culinary imagination. Cool cigars, hip drinks (mango mojitos), and an ultrachic decor draw serious foodies to this cutting-edge restaurant, where chef Jose Rodriguez intoxicates with his tantalizing aromas and flavors. Even the side dishes are called "sexy sides." After launching yourself into the black-bean hummus or the tuna tartare with soy-lime vinaigrette, it's on to such delights as star anise duck confit or a miso-crusted sea bass. What about ancho chile-rubbed beef filet with espresso sauce? Desserts are worth crossing the island for if it means Cuban chocolate cake with coconut ice cream or a warm banana and macadamia spring rolls with a strawberry balsamic purée.

In Frenchman's Reef & Morning Star Marriott Beach Resort (p. 46), 5 Estate Bakkeroe. ✆ **340/776-8500.** www.havanabluerestaurant.com. Reservations required. Main courses $28–$46. AE, DC, MC, V. Daily 5:30–10pm.

Molly Malone's IRISH/CARIBBEAN   At the Red Hook American Yacht Harbor, join the good ol' boys and dig into some baby back ribs. You can dine outdoors under a canopy, right on the dock at the eastern end of Red Hook, where the ferry from St. John pulls in. If you're finding yourself nostalgic for the Emerald Isle, go for the shepherd's pie. The conch fritters are the best in the East End, or opt for the savory conch chowder. In one of the wildest culinary offerings we've seen lately, an "Irish/Caribbean stew" is a nightly feature. If the day's catch netted a big wahoo, game-fish steaks will be on the menu. No one can drink more brew than the boisterous crowd that assembles here every night to let the good times roll.

6100 Red Hook Quarters. ✆ **340/775-1270.** Main courses $12–$30. AE, MC, V. Daily 7am–midnight.

Off the Hook ★ ASIAN/CARIBBEAN   Diners here enjoy an eclectic medley of specialties inspired by Asia, which the chefs concoct from the freshest and finest ingredients in the West Indies. In an open-air dining room also near the American Yacht Harbor, close to the departure point for the ferry to St. John, the fresh catch of the day—hauled off the little fishing boats that pull in—is delivered to the kitchen, where it's grilled to perfection. The yellowfin tuna keeps us coming back. The chef is adept at preparing a tuna and salmon sushi platter, and the Black Angus steak is always a pure delight. The decor is rustic, with outdoor dining and wooden tables.

6300 Estate Smith Bay. ✆ **340/775-6350.** Reservations required. Main courses $17–$28. AE, MC, V. Daily 6–10pm. Closed Sept 15–Oct 15.

Duffy's Love Shack ★ (Finds) CARIBBEAN This is a fun and happening place where you can mingle with the locals. As the evening wears on, the customers become the entertainment, often dancing on tables or forming conga lines. Yes, Duffy's also serves food. The restaurant is open-air, with lots of bamboo and a thatched roof over the bar. Even the menu appears on a bamboo stick, like an old-fashioned fan. A standard American cuisine is spiced up with Caribbean flair. Start with the honey-barbecued ribs and conch fritters, then move on to jerk chicken or macadamia-nut mahimahi. After midnight, a late-night menu appears, mostly featuring sandwiches. The bar business is huge, and the bartender is known for his lethal rum drinks.

650 Red Hook Plaza, Rte. 38. (C) **340/779-2080.** www.duffysloveshack.com. Main courses $10–$23. No credit cards. Daily 11am–2am.

5 BEACHES

Chances are that your hotel will be right on the beach, or very close to one. All the beaches in the Virgin Islands are public, and most St. Thomas beaches lie anywhere from 2 to 5 miles from Charlotte Amalie.

THE NORTH COAST

The gorgeous white sands of **Magens Bay** ★★—the family favorite of St. Thomas—lie between two mountains 3 miles north of the capital. The turquoise waters here are calm and ideal for swimming, though the snorkeling isn't as good. The beach is no secret, and it's usually terribly overcrowded, though it gets better in the midafternoon. Changing facilities, snorkeling gear, lounge chairs, paddle boats, and kayaks are available. There is no public transportation to get here (though some hotels provide shuttle buses). A taxi from Charlotte Amalie will cost about $8.50 per person. If you've rented a car, from Charlotte Amalie take Route 35 north all the way. The gates to the beach are open daily from 6am to 6pm. After 4pm, you'll need insect repellent. Admission is $1 per person and $1 per car. Don't bring valuables, and certainly don't leave anything of value in your parked car. Break-ins of cars and a few muggings are reported monthly.

A marked trail leads to **Little Magens Bay,** a separate, clothing-optional beach that's especially popular with gay and lesbian visitors. This is former President Clinton's preferred beach on St. Thomas (no, he doesn't go nude).

Coki Point Beach, in the northeast near Coral World, is good but often very crowded with both singles and families. It's noted for its warm, crystal-clear water, ideal for swimming and snorkeling; you'll see thousands of rainbow-hued fish swimming among the beautiful corals. Vendors even sell small bags of fish food, so you can feed the sea creatures while you're snorkeling. From the beach, there's a panoramic view of offshore Thatch Cay. Concessions can arrange everything from water-skiing to parasailing. A Vitrans East End bus runs to Smith Bay and lets you off at the gate to Coral World and Coki. Watch out for pickpockets.

Also on the north side of the island is luscious **Grand Beach,** one of St. Thomas's most beautiful, attracting families and couples. It opens onto Smith Bay and is near Coral World. Many watersports are available here. The beach is right off Route 38.

THE EAST END

Small and special, **Secret Harbour** is near a collection of condos and has long been favored by singles of either sex and by those of all sexual persuasions. With its white sand and coconut palms, it's the epitome of Caribbean charm. The snorkeling near the rocks is some of the best on the island. No public transportation stops here, but it's an easy taxi ride east of Charlotte Amalie heading toward Red Hook.

Sapphire Beach ★ is set against the backdrop of the Sapphire Beach Resort & Marina, where you can have lunch or order drinks. Like Magens Bay Beach, this good, wide, safe beach is one of the most frequented by families. There are good views of offshore cays and St. John, and a large reef is close to the shore. Windsurfers like this beach a lot. Snorkeling gear and lounge chairs can be rented. Take the Vitrans East End bus from Charlotte Amalie, via Red Hook. Ask to be let off at the entrance to Sapphire Bay; it's not too far a walk from here to the water.

White-sand **Lindquist Beach** isn't a long strip, but it's one of the island's prettiest beaches. It's between Wyndham Sugar Bay Resort & Spa and the Sapphire Beach Resort. Many films and TV commercials have used this photogenic beach as a backdrop. It's not likely to be crowded, as it's not very well known. Couples in the know retreat here for sun and romance.

THE SOUTH COAST

Morning Star ★—also known as Frenchman's Bay Beach—is near the Frenchman's Reef & Morning Star Marriott Beach Resort, about 2 miles east of Charlotte Amalie. Here, among the hip, savvy, often young crowds (many of whom are gay singles and couples), you can don your skimpiest bikini. Sailboats, snorkeling equipment, and lounge chairs are available for rent. The beach is easily reached by a cliff-front elevator at Frenchman's Reef. **Limetree Beach,** set against

Taking to the Seas

On St. Thomas, most of the boat business centers around the marina in Red Hook and Yacht Haven Marina in Charlotte Amalie.

The 50-foot *Yacht Nightwind,* Sapphire Marina (© 340/775-7017; www.stjohndaysail.com), offers full-day sails to St. John and the outer islands. The $120 price includes continental breakfast, a champagne buffet lunch, and an open bar aboard. You're also given free snorkeling equipment and instruction.

New Horizons, 6501 Red Hook Plaza, Suite 16, Red Hook (© 800/808-7604 or 340/775-1171; http://newhorizonsvi. com), offers wind-borne excursions amid the cays and reefs of the Virgin Islands. The two-masted, 65-foot sloop has circumnavigated the globe, and has even been used as a design prototype for other boats. Owned and operated by Canadian Tim Krygsveld, it contains a hot-water shower, serves a specialty drink called a "New Horizons Nooner," and carries a complete line of snorkeling equipment for adults and children. A full-day excursion with a continental breakfast, an Italian buffet lunch, and an open bar costs $120 per person ($60 for children ages 2–12). Excursions depart daily, weather permitting, from the Sapphire Beach Resort and Marina. Call ahead for reservations.

New Horizons also offers *New Horizons II* (http://new horizonscharters.com), a 44-foot custom-made speedboat that takes you on a full-day trip, from 7:30am to 4:30pm and also leaving from the Sapphire Beach Resort, to some of the most scenic highlights of the British Virgin Islands. Trips cost $145 for adults or $95 for children ages 2 to 12. You will need your passport and will have to pay an additional $30-per-person customs fee.

a backdrop of sea-grape trees and shady palms, also lures the hip folk. On this serene spread, you can bask in the sun and even feed hibiscus blossoms to the friendly iguanas. Snorkeling gear, lounge and beach chairs, towels, and drinks are available. There's no public transportation, but the beach can easily be reached by taxi from Charlotte Amalie.

You can avoid the crowds by sailing aboard the **Fantasy,** 6100 Leeward Way, no. 28 (✆ **340/775-5652;** fax 340/775-6256; http://daysailfantasy.com), which departs daily from the American Yacht Harbor at Red Hook at 9:30am and returns at 3pm. The boat takes a maximum of six passengers to St. John and nearby islands for swimming, snorkeling, and beachcombing. Snorkel gear and expert instruction are provided, as is a champagne lunch. The full-day trip costs $130 per person for adults and children. A half-day sail, usually offered only during the low season, lasts 3 hours and costs $90 for adults and children.

American Yacht Harbor Marina, Red Hook (✆ **340/775-6454;** www.igy-americanyachtharbor.com), offers both bareboat and fully crewed charters. Boats leave from a colorful yacht-filled harbor set against the backdrop of Heritage Gade, a reproduction of a Caribbean village. The harbor is home to numerous boat companies, including day-trippers, fishing boats, and sailing charters like **Nauti Nymph Powerboat Rentals** (✆ **340/775-5066**). There are also five restaurants on the property, serving everything from Continental to Caribbean cuisine. Another reliable charter-boat outfitter is **Charteryacht League,** at Flagship (✆ **800/524-2061** or 340/774-3944; www.vicl.org).

Sailors may want to check out the *Yachtsman's Guide to the Virgin Islands,* available at major marine outlets, at bookstores, through catalog merchandisers, or direct from **Tropic Isle Publishers,** P.O. Box 12, Adelphia, NJ 07710 (✆ **877/923-9653;** http://yachtsmansguide.com). This annual guide, which costs $16, is supplemented by photographs; landfall sketches and charts showing harbors and harbor entrances, anchorages, channels, and landmarks; and information on preparations necessary for cruising the islands.

WEST OF CHARLOTTE AMALIE

Near the University of the Virgin Islands, in the southwest, **Brewers Bay** is one of the island's most popular beaches for families. The strip of white coral sand is almost as long as the beach at Magens Bay. Unfortunately, this isn't a good place for snorkeling. Vendors here sell light meals and drinks. From Charlotte Amalie, take the Fortuna bus heading west; get off at the edge of Brewers Bay, across from the Reichhold Center.

Lindbergh Beach, with a lifeguard, restrooms, and a bathhouse, is at the Island Beachcomber Hotel (p. 44) and is used extensively by locals, who stage events from political rallies to Carnival parties here. Beach-loving couples are also attracted to this beach. It's not good for snorkeling. Drinks are served on the beach. Take the Fortuna bus route west from Charlotte Amalie.

6 FUN IN THE SURF & SUN

WATERSPORTS

FISHING The U.S. Virgins have excellent deep-sea fishing—some 19 world records (8 for blue marlin) have been set in these waters. Outfitters abound at the major marinas like Red Hook. We recommend angling off the *Fish Hawk* (© 340/775-9058), which Captain Al Petrosky sails out of Fish Hawk Marina Lagoon on the east end. His 48-foot diesel-powered craft is fully equipped with rods and reels. For the trip, all equipment, and drinks (but not meals) you'll pay $600 per half-day for up to six passengers. Full-day excursions start at $1,100. **Peanut Gallery Fishing Charters,** 8168 Crown Bay Marina, Suite 310 (© 340/642-7423; www.fishingstthomas.com), offers both light-tackle inshore sports fishing and deep-sea sports fishing. Your captain will be Captain Steve Malpere, who has been fishing in Caribbean waters for more than 30 years, or Captain David Pearsall. The vessels provide inshore fishing year-round for the likes of barracuda, bonefish, kingfish, mackerel, and tarpon. The cost for 4 hours is $500; 6 hours, $550 to $650; 8 hours, $800 to $880.

You can also line-fish from the rocky shore along Mandahl Beach on the north coast. The tourist office in Charlotte Amalie should have a listing of legal spots for line fishing around the island.

GOLF **Mahogany Run,** on the north shore at Mahogany Run Road (© 800/253-7103; www.mahoganyrungolf.com), is an 18-hole, par-70 course. This beautiful course rises and drops like a roller coaster on its journey to the sea; cliffs and crashing sea waves are the ultimate hazards at the 13th and 14th holes. Former President Clinton pronounced this course very challenging. Greens fees are $140 to $160 for 18 holes, reduced to $100 to $120 in the late afternoon. Carts are included. Club rental costs $40.

KAYAK TOURS **Virgin Islands Ecotours/Mangrove Adventures** (© 340/779-2155; www.viecotours.com) offers half-day kayak trips through the mangrove lagoon on the southern coastline. The cost is

$69 per person. The tour is led by professional naturalists who allow for 30 to 40 minutes of snorkeling.

SAILING ★   **Yacht Haven Grande St. Thomas,** 9100 Port of Sale, Charlotte Amalie (© 340/774-9500), is the premier marine facilities for megayachts in the Caribbean. Located alongside Charlotte Amalie harbor, it encompasses a 48-slip facility, with dining, entertainment, and recreational options. **American Yacht Harbor** ★★, Red Hook (© 340/775-6454; www.igy-americanyachtharbor.com), can refer both bareboat and fully crewed charters. It leaves from the east end of St. Thomas in Vessup Bay. The harbor is home to numerous boat companies, including day-trippers, fishing boats, and sailing charters. There are also five restaurants on the property, serving everything from Continental to Caribbean cuisine. Another reliable outfitter is **Charteryacht League** ★★, at Gregory East (© 800/524-2061 in the U.S., or 340/774-3944; www.vicl.org).

Sailors may want to check out the *Yachtsman's Guide to the Virgin Islands,* available at major marine outlets, at bookstores, through catalog merchandisers, or directly from **Tropical Publishers,** P.O. Box 12, Adelphia, NJ 07710 (© 877/923-9653; www.yachtsmansguide.com). This annual guide, which costs $16, is supplemented by sketch charts, photographs, and landfall sketches and charts showing harbors and harbor entrances, anchorages, channels, and landmarks, plus information on preparations necessary for cruising the islands.

SCUBA DIVING & SNORKELING   The best scuba diving site off St. Thomas, especially for novices, has to be **Cow and Calf Rocks,** off the southeast end (45 min. from Charlotte Amalie by boat); here, you'll discover a network of coral tunnels filled with caves, reefs, and ancient boulders encrusted with coral. The *Cartanser Sr.,* a sunken World War II cargo ship that lies in about 35 feet of water, is beautifully encrusted with coral and is home to myriad colorful resident fish. Another popular wreck dive is the *Maj. General Rogers,* the stripped-down hull of a former Coast Guard cutter.

Experienced divers may want to dive at exposed sheer rock pinnacles like **Sail Rock** and **French Cap Pinnacle,** which are encrusted with hard and soft corals, and are frequented by lobsters and green and hawksbill turtles. Both spots are exposed to open-ocean currents, making these very challenging dives.

Coki Beach Dive Club, Coki Beach (© 800/474-COKI [474-2654] or 340/775-4220; www.cokidive.com), a PADI center, offers scuba diving courses and guided dive tours for both beginners and certified divers. You can also rent diving and snorkeling gear here. A one-tank dive costs $55, a two-tank dive $85, if you use the club's equipment.

(Moments) Under the Sea (Without Getting Wet)

The air-conditioned **Atlantis** submarine will take you on a 50-minute voyage (the whole experience is really 2 hr., when you include transportation to and from the sub) to depths of 90 feet, where an amazing world of exotic marine life unfolds. You'll have close-up views of coral reefs and sponge gardens through the sub's 2-foot windows. On some voyages, Atlantis divers swim with the fish and bring them close to the windows for photos.

Passengers take a surface boat from the West Indies Dock, right outside Charlotte Amalie, to the submarine, which is near Buck Island (the St. Thomas version, not the more famous Buck Island near St. Croix). The fare is $99 for adults, $49 for children 12 and under; children under 36 inches are not allowed. The Atlantis dives daily and reservations are suggested, as the sub carries only 48 passengers. For tickets, go to the Havensight shopping mall, building 6, or call (C) **866/ 546-7820** or 340/776-5650. You can also reserve tickets online at www.atlantisadventures.com.

St. Thomas Diving Club, 7147 Bolongo Bay (© **877/538-8734** in the U.S., or 340/776-2381; www.stthomasdivingclub.com), is a full-service, PADI five-star IDC center, and the best on the island. An open-water certification course, including four scuba dives, costs $429. An advanced open-water certification course, including five dives that can be accomplished in 2 days, goes for $425. You can also enjoy local snorkeling for $55.

DIVE IN!, in the Sapphire Beach Resort & Marina, Smith Bay Road, Route 36 (© **866/434-8346,** ext. 2144, in the U.S., or 340/777-5255; www.diveinusvi.com), is a well-recommended, complete diving center that offers some of the finest services in the U.S. Virgin Islands, including professional instruction (beginner to advanced), daily beach and boat dives, custom dive packages, snorkeling trips, and a full-service PADI dive center. An introductory resort course costs $105, with a one-tank dive going for $80 and two-tank dives costing $110. A six-dive pass costs $300.

Media such as *The Miami Herald* and the *Detroit Free Press* has written up the night snorkeling adventures offered by **Homer's Scuba and Snorkel Tours** (© **866/719-1856** or 340/774-7606; www.night snorkel.com). You're provided with a submersible flashlight, glow stick, and wet suit, and taken on an eerie underwater experience at night to meet the denizens of the deep. Various sea creatures such as an octopus will glide before you. The cost is $45 per person, and tours are conducted Tuesday to Saturday with reservations required.

TENNIS   The best tennis on the island is at the **Wyndham Sugar Bay Beach Club,** 6500 Estate Smith Bay (© **340/777-7100**), which has three Laykold courts lit at night and a pro shop. Nonguests pay $8 per hour.

Another good resort for tennis is the **Bolongo Bay Beach Resort,** Bolongo Bay (© **340/775-1800**), which has two courts that are lit until 6pm. They're free to members and hotel guests, but cost $10 per hour for nonguests.

Marriott Frenchman's Reef Tennis Courts, Flamboyant Point (© **340/776-8500**), has two courts. Again, nonguests are charged $10 per hour per court. Lights stay on until 10pm.

---

7 SEEING THE SIGHTS

ATTRACTIONS IN CHARLOTTE AMALIE

Even with the crowds and shops, it is easy to see how the natural colors and charm of the Caribbean come to life in the waterfront town of **Charlotte Amalie.** The capital of St. Thomas once attracted seafarers from all over the globe, and pirates and sailors of the Confederacy used the port during the American Civil War. At one time, St. Thomas was the biggest slave market in the world.

Today, the old warehouses, once used for storing stolen pirate goods, have been converted to shops. In fact, the main streets, called "gade" (a reflection of their Danish heritage), now coalesce into a virtual shopping mall, and are often packed. Sandwiched among these shops are a few historic buildings, most of which can be seen on foot in about 2 hours.

We recommend you set out to see the sites before 10am to avoid the rush of cruise ship passengers and steer clear of 4pm when traffic and pedestrians are at their most plentiful.

Along the eastern harborfront is **King's Wharf,** the site of the Virgin Islands Legislature, which is housed in apple-green military barracks dating from 1874. From here, you will see **Fort Christian** (© **340/776-8605**), which dates from 1672 and is named after the Danish king Christian V. This structure was a governor's residence, police station, court, and jail until it became a national historic landmark in 1977. A museum here illuminates the island's history and culture. Inside you'll see cultural workshops and an exhibit of late-Victorian furnishings. A museum shop features local crafts, maps, and prints. Fort Christian is open Monday through Friday from 9am to 4pm; admission is $4.

Emancipation Park is near the fort. This is where a proclamation freeing African slaves and indentured European servants was read on July 3, 1848. The park is now mostly a picnic area for local workers and visitors. Northwest of the park, at Main Street and Tolbod Gade, stands the **Central Post Office.** On display here are murals by Stephen Dohanos, who became famous as an artist for *The Saturday Evening Post.*

Frederik Lutheran Church, on Norre Gade, was built between 1780 and 1793. The original Georgian-style building, financed by a free black parishioner, Jean Reeneaus, was reconstructed in 1825 and again in 1870, after it was damaged in a hurricane.

Just up Lille Taarne Gade is **Government House,** the administrative headquarters for the U.S. Virgin Islands. It's been the center of political life in the islands since it was built around the time of the American Civil War. Visitors can take a tour on the first two floors for free Monday through Saturday from 8am to noon and from 1 to 5pm.

The **Seven Arches Museum** (© **340/774-9295**) is just to the left of Government House. Browsers and gapers love checking out this museum, which is actually the private home of longtime residents Philibert Fluck and Barbara Demaras. This 2-century-old Danish house has been completely restored and furnished with antiques. Walk through the yellow ballast arches into the Great Room, which has a wonderful view of the Caribbean's busiest harbor. The $5 admission fee includes a cold tropical drink served in a beautiful, walled flower garden. Open daily from 10am to 4pm, or by appointment. Next door is the **Frederik Church Parsonage,** dating from 1725. It's one of the oldest houses on the island, and the only structure in the Government Hill district to retain its simple 18th-century lines.

If you're up for it, climb the **99 Steps** (actually 103 in total), just off Kongens Gade. The steps were erected in the early 1700s, and take you to the summit of Government Hill, from where you'll see the 18th-century **Crown House.** This stately private house was the home of von Scholten, the Danish ruler who issued the famous proclamation of emancipation in 1848 (see Emancipation Park, above). At the foot of the steps is the **Hotel 1829** (© **340/776-1829**), a landmark building and a charming hotel that has attracted many of the island's most famous visitors. Formerly known as the Lavalette House, this place was designed in 1829 by one of the leading merchants of Charlotte Amalie. Next door to the Hotel 1829 is the **Yellow-Brick Building,** a structure that was built in 1854 in what local architects called "the style of Copenhagen." You can go inside and browse the many shops within.

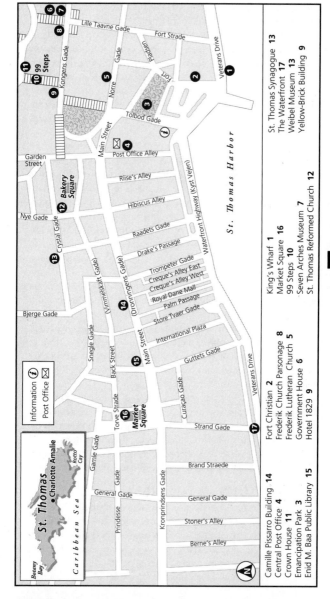

St. Thomas Synagogue **13**
The Waterfront **17**
Weibel Museum **13**
Yellow-Brick Building **9**

King's Wharf **1**
Market Square **16**
99 Steps **10**
Seven Arches Museum **7**
St. Thomas Reformed Church **12**

Fort Christian **2**
Frederik Church Parsonage **8**
Frederik Lutheran Church **5**
Government House **6**
Hotel 1829 **9**

Camille Pissarro Building **14**
Central Post Office **4**
Crown House **11**
Emancipation Park **3**
Enid M. Baa Public Library **15**

ST. THOMAS

2

SEEING THE SIGHTS

The St. Thomas Reformed Church, on Crystal Gade and Nye Gade, was built in 1844. Much of its original structure, designed like a Greek temple, has been preserved intact. Just a block away is the **St. Thomas Synagogue,** the oldest synagogue in continuous use under the American flag, and the second oldest in the Western Hemisphere. It was erected in 1833 by Sephardic Jews, and it still maintains the tradition of having sand on the floor, commemorating the exodus from Egypt. The structure was built of local stone, ballast brick from Denmark, and mortar made of molasses and sand. It's open to visitors Monday to Friday 9am to 4pm. Next door, the **Weibel Museum** (© 340/774-4312) showcases 300 years of Jewish history. It keeps the same hours.

Be sure to visit **Main Street,** Charlotte Amalie's major artery and most famous shopping street. This is where you'll find the **Camille Pissarro Building,** at the Amsterdam Sauer Jewelry Store. Pissarro, a Spanish Jew who became one of the founders of French Impressionism, was born in this building as Jacob Pizarro in 1830. Before moving to Paris, he worked for his father in a store on Main Street. Also housed in the building is **Gallery Camille Pissarro,** with a few Pissarro paintings on display and prints by local artists for sale. Also on Main Street is The **Enid M. Baa Public Library;** formerly the von Bretton House, this building dates from 1818.

At the end of Main Street is **Market Square.** This was the center of a large slave-trading market before the 1848 emancipation and is officially called Rothschild Francis Square. Today it's an open-air fruit and vegetable market, selling, among other items, *genips* (grape-type fruit; to eat one, break open the skin and suck the pulp off the pit). The wrought-iron roof covered a railway station at the turn of the 20th century. The market is open Monday to Saturday, its busiest day; hours vary, but it's busiest from 9am to 3pm.

If the *genip* doesn't satisfy you, take Strand Gade down (south) to **The Waterfront,** also known as Kyst Vejen. This is where you can purchase a fresh coconut. One of the vendors here will whack off the top with a machete so that you can drink the sweet milk from its hull. You'll have an up-close view of one of the most scenic harbors in the West Indies, though it's usually filled with cruise ships.

ATTRACTIONS IN THE WEST

Route 30 (Veterans Dr.) will take you west of Charlotte Amalie to **Frenchtown** (turn left at the sign to the Admiral's Inn). Early French-speaking settlers arrived on St. Thomas from St. Bart's after they were uprooted by the Swedes. Many of today's island residents are the direct descendants of those long-ago immigrants, who were known for speaking a distinctive French patois. This colorful village contains a bevy of restaurants and taverns. Because Charlotte Amalie has become somewhat dangerous at night, Frenchtown has picked up its after-dark business and is the best spot for dancing, drinking, and other local entertainment.

Farther west, Harwood Highway (Rte. 308) will lead you to **Crown Mountain Road,** a scenic drive opening onto the best views of the hills, beaches, and crystal-clear waters around St. Thomas.

ATTRACTIONS AROUND THE ISLAND

A driving tour is the best way to see the island. **Tropic Tours,** 14AB The Guardian Building (✆ 800/524-4334 or 340/774-1855; www. tropictoursusvi.com), offers a tour of St. Thomas, including Drake's Seat, the Estate St. Peter Greathouse, and Charlotte Amalie shopping. The cost is $45 per person.

Coral World Ocean Park ★ (Kids) This marine complex, which is St. Thomas's number-one tourist attraction, features a three-story underwater observation tower 100 feet offshore. Inside, you'll spy sea sponges, fish, coral, and other aquatic creatures in their natural state. An 80,000-gallon reef tank features exotic marine life of the Caribbean; another tank is devoted to sea predators, with circling sharks and giant moray eels. Activities include daily fish and shark feedings. The latest addition to the park is a semisubmarine that lets you enjoy the panoramic view and the "down under" feeling of a submarine without truly submerging.

Nondivers can get some of the thrill long known to scuba aficionados by participating in **Sea Trek.** For $68, or $59 for children, you can get a full immersion undersea with no experience necessary. Participants are given a helmet and a tube to breathe through. The tube is attached to an air source at the observatory tower. You then enjoy a 20-minute stroll in water that's 18 feet deep, observing rainbow-hued tropical fish and the coral reefs as you move along the sea floor. It's a marvelous way to experience the world through the eyes of a fish. *Note:* Reservations are required, so call ahead or log on to the park's website.

Coral World's guests can take advantage of adjacent **Coki Beach** for snorkel rentals, scuba lessons, or simply swimming and relaxing. Lockers and showers are available. Also included in the marine park are the Tropical Terrace Restaurant, duty-free shops, and a nature trail.

6450 Estates Smith Bay, a 20-min. drive from Charlotte Amalie off Rte. 38. ✆ 340/775-1555. www.coralworldvi.com. Admission $21 adults, $12 children ages 3–12. Daily 9am–5pm.

Estate St. Peter Greathouse & Botanical Gardens This estate consists of 11 acres set at the foot of volcanic peaks on the northern rim of the island. The grounds are laced with self-guided nature walks that will acquaint you with some 200 varieties of West

ST. THOMAS

2

SEEING THE SIGHTS

Indian plants and trees, including an umbrella plant from Madagascar. From a panoramic deck in the gardens, you can see some 20 of the Virgin Islands, including Hans Lollick, an uninhabited island between Thatched Cay and Madahl Point. The house itself, filled with local art, is worth a visit.

At the corner of Rte. 40 (6A St. Peter Mountain Rd.) and Barrett Hill Rd. (C) **340/ 774-4999.** www.greathouse-mountaintop.com. Admission $10 adults, $5 children 11 and under. Daily 8am–4pm.

EXCURSIONS FROM ST. THOMAS
Water Island

Water Island, ³/₄ mile off the coast from the harbor at Charlotte Amalie, is the fourth-largest island in the U.S. Virgins, with nearly 500 acres of land. Irregular in shape, 2¹/₂-mile-long Water Island is filled with many bays and peninsulas, studded with several good, sandy beaches along with secluded coves and rocky headlands. Established as the fourth U.S. Virgin Island in 1996, Water Island was once a part of a peninsula jutting out from St. Thomas, but a channel was cut through, allowing U.S. submarines to reach their base in a bay to the west.

At palm-shaded **Honeymoon Beach,** you can swim, snorkel, sail, water-ski, or sunbathe. The beach has been significantly improved in the past few years, as loads of rocks and gravel were hauled off and trees and brush removed. The sand was sifted to get rid of debris, and a dredge removed the seaweed and deposited white sand on the shore. Today it looks quite beautiful.

There is no commerce on the island—no taxis, gas stations, hotels, shops, or even a main town. Residents are totally dependent on Charlotte Amalie, lying half a mile away. If you're planning on a visit, bring water and your own food supplies and other needs. Don't count on it, but there is often a food cart on Honeymoon Beach, serving surprisingly good meals, including an all-steak lunch.

A ferry runs between Crown Bay Marina and Water Island several times a day for $5 one way, $9 round-trip (Crown Bay Marina, (C) **340/774-2255,** is part of the St. Thomas submarine base). If you prefer a guided tour, check in with **Water Island Adventures** ((C) **340/714-2186;** www.waterislandadventures.biz). For $60 per person, including transportation and equipment, a trip to Water Island includes a cycling tour. In the 3¹/₂ hours of the tour, beach time is allowed. Departures are from the dock at Havensight Mall or Crown Bay Marina.

Hassel Island

In the same bay, and even closer to shore, is **Hassel Island** (www. hasselisland.org). This island is almost completely deserted, and is protected as part of a U.S. National Park, which prohibits most forms of development. There are no hotels or services of any kind here, and swimming is limited to narrow, rocky beaches. Even so, many visitors hire a boat to drop them off for an hour or two.

A hike along the shoreline is a welcome relief from the cruise ship congestion of Charlotte Amalie. The island is riddled with some trails which can be traversed, taking you across gentle hills with dry woods, lots of plants, and plenty of cacti—you'll think you're in the Arizona desert. Beach lovers head for the western shore where they find white sands shaded by seagrapes. You can also explore the ruins of early-19th-century English fortifications and mid-19th-century shopping and coal stations. Bring water and food if you plan to spend more than 3 hours. The rather barren island has little shade, so dress accordingly and make sure you carry plenty of drinking water.

A small ferry runs from the Crown Bay Marina on St. Thomas to Hassel, costing $5 to $10 round-trip.

8 SHOPPING

The discounted, duty-free shopping in the Virgin Islands makes St. Thomas a shopping mecca. It's possible to find well-known brand names here at savings of up to 60% off mainland prices. But be warned—savings are not always good, so make sure you know the price of the item back home to determine if you are truly getting a good deal. Having sounded that warning, we'll mention some St. Thomas shops where we have indeed found really good buys. For more help, the local publications *This Week in St. Thomas* and *Best Buys* have updates on sales and shop openings.

Most shops are open Monday to Saturday 9am to 5pm. Some stores are open Sunday and holidays if a cruise ship is in port.

THE BEST BUYS & WHERE TO FIND THEM

The best buys on St. Thomas include china, crystal, perfumes, jewelry (especially emeralds), Haitian art, clothing, watches, and items made of wood. St. Thomas is also the best place in the Caribbean for discounts in porcelain, but remember that U.S. brands may often be purchased for 25% off the retail price on the mainland. Look for imported patterns for the biggest savings. Cameras and electronic items, based on our experience, are not the good buys they're reputed to be.

Nearly all the major shopping in St. Thomas is along the harbor of Charlotte Amalie. Cruise ship passengers mainly shop at the **Havensight Mall,** at the eastern edge of Charlotte Amalie, where they disembark. The principal shopping street is **Main Street** or Dronningens

Gade (the old Danish name). Some of the shops occupy former pirate warehouses. To the north is another merchandise-loaded street called **Back Street** or Vimmelskaft. Many shops are also spread along the **Waterfront Highway** (also called Kyst Vejen). Between these major streets is a series of side streets, walkways, and alleys—each one filled with shops. Other shopping streets are Tolbod Gade, Raadets Gade, Royal Dane Mall, Palm Passage, Storetvaer Gade, and Strand Gade.

It is illegal for most street vendors (food vendors are about the only exception) to ply their trades outside of the designated area called **Vendors Plaza,** at the corner of Veterans Drive and Tolbod Gade. Hundreds of vendors converge here Monday through Saturday at 7:30am; they usually pack up around 5:30pm. (Very few hawk their wares on Sun, unless a cruise ship is scheduled to arrive.)

When you tire of French perfumes and Swiss watches, head for **Market Square,** as it's called locally, or more formally, Rothschild Francis Square. Here, on the site of a former slave market and under a Victorian tin roof, locals with machetes slice open fresh coconuts so you can drink the milk, and women sell ackee, cassava, and breadfruit.

Other noteworthy shopping districts include **Tillett Gardens,** a virtual oasis of arts and crafts—pottery, silk-screened fabrics, candles, watercolors, jewelry, and more—located on the highway across from Four Winds Shopping Center. The Jim Tillett Gallery here is a major island attraction in itself.

All the major stores in St. Thomas are located by number on an excellent map in the center of the publication *St. Thomas This Week,* distributed free to all arriving plane and boat passengers, and available at the visitor center. A lot of the stores on the island don't have street numbers or don't display them, so look for their signs instead.

SHOPPING A TO Z
Art

Bernard K. Passman ★★ Bernard K. Passman is the world's leading sculptor of black coral art and jewelry. He's famous for his *Can Can Girl* and his four statues of Charlie Chaplin. On Grand Cayman, he learned to fashion exquisite treasures from black coral found 200 feet under the sea. After being polished and embellished with gold and diamonds, some of Passman's work has been treasured by royalty. For us laymen with an eye for good sculpture, there are simpler and more affordable pieces for sale. There is also a sister location in the Havensight Mall. 5195 Dronningens Gade, Suite #2. ℭ **340/777-4580.** www. passman.com.

The Color of Joy This is a showcase for the vivid watercolors of Corinne Van Rensselaer, who also does custom framing (the best on the island). This little gallery also sells original prints by local artists, crafts, and gifts, including batiks, etchings, cards, and prints, along with glass and larimar (a type of volcanic stone) jewelry. There is also a selection of ceramics, coral sculptures (much of it done locally), and Haitian artwork. The shop lies a mile out of Red Hook on Route 322, about 110 yards west of the Ritz-Carlton. © **340/775-4020.** www.the colorofjoy.com.

Gallery Camille Pissarro   This art gallery, accessible by stairs, is located in the house where Pissarro, a paragon of Impressionism, was born in 1830. In three high-ceilinged and airy rooms, you can see Pissarro paintings relating to the islands. Many prints by local artists are available, and the gallery also sells original batiks, alive with vibrant colors. Caribbean Cultural Centre, 14 Main St. © **340/774-4621.**

Gallery St. Thomas ★   This is a showcase for the works of Virgin Islands painters, notably Lucinda Schutt, who is best known for her Caribbean land- and seascapes. At this second-floor gallery, to the west of Hotel 1829, Schutt not only sells artwork beginning at $18, but also teaches watercolor painting. First building on Garden St., Government Hill. © **877/797-6363** or 340/777-6363. www.gallerystthomas.com.

Mango Tango Art Gallery   This is one of the largest art galleries in St. Thomas, closely connected with half a dozen internationally recognized artists. Original artwork begins at $500; prints and posters are cheaper. Represented are internationally known artists who spend at least part of their year in the Virgin Islands, many of them sailing during breaks from their studio time. Examples include Don Dahlke, Max Johnson, Anne Miller, David Millard, Dana Wylder, and Shari Erickson. Al Cohen's Plaza, Raphune Hill, Rte. 38. © **340/777-3060.** www. mangotango-art.com.

Native Arts & Crafts Cooperative ★   This is the largest arts and crafts emporium in the U.S.V.I., combining the output of 90 different artisans into one sprawling shop. Contained within the former headquarters of the U.S. District Court, a 19th-century brick building adjacent to Charlotte Amalie's tourist information office, it specializes in items small enough to be packed into a suitcase or trunk. Examples include spice racks, paper towel racks, lamps crafted from conch shells, salad utensils and bowls, crocheted goods, and straw goods. Tarbor Gade 1. © **340/777-1153.**

Tillett Gardens Center for the Arts ★★   Since 1959, Tillett Gardens, once an old Danish farm, has been the island's arts-and-crafts center. This tropical compound is a series of buildings housing studios, galleries, and an outdoor garden restaurant and bar. Prints in the galleries start as low as $20. The best work of local artists is displayed here—originals in oils, watercolors, and acrylics. The Tillett prints on fine canvas are all one-of-a-kind. The famous Tillett maps on fine canvas are priced from $45. Tillett Gardens, 4126 Anna's Retreat, Tutu. © **340/775-1929.** www.tillettgardens.com. Take Rte. 38 east from Charlotte Amalie.

Cameras & Electronics

Boolchand's   This is the place to go when you're in the market for a camera. Famous throughout the Caribbean, this is the major retailer of not only cameras, but also electronics and digital products throughout the West Indies. Now into its eighth decade, it sells all the big names, from Kodak to Leica, and from Nikon to Fuji. In the electronics division are the latest in DVDs, minidiscs, and other items. There is also a jewelry department and a wide selection of watches. 31 Main St. © **340/776-0794.** www.boolchand.com.

Royal Caribbean ★ (**Value**)   This is the largest camera and electronics store in the Caribbean. It carries Nikon, Minolta, Pentax, Canon, and Panasonic products. It's a good source for watches, too, featuring such brand names as Seiko, Movado, Corum, Fendi, and Zodiac. There's also a complete collection of Philippe Charriol watches, jewelry, and leather bags, and a wide selection of Mikimoto pearls, 14- and 18-karat jewelry, and Lladró figurines. Another branch is located at Havensight Mall (© **340/776-8890**). 33 and 35 Main St. © **340/776-4110.** www.royalcaribbean.vi.

Clothing

Local Color   Located at the Waterfront, this retail outlet has a wide selection of affordable clothing for men, women, and children, as well as island furnishings and accessories such as handbags, hats, and jewelry. Royal Dane Mall at the Waterfront. © **340/774-2280.** www.usviweb.com/localcolor.

Tommy Hilfiger Boutique   The world knows this merchandise, of course, but prices here might be cheaper than stateside. There is a good selection of men's and women's sportswear, as well as shoes, jeans, children's clothing, home furnishings, and fragrances. Waterfront Hwy. at Trompeter Gade 30. © **340/777-1189.**

Crystal & China

The Crystal Shoppe ★ (**Finds**)   This family-run store offers a dazzling array of crystal from around the world. All the big names in glass—Hummel, Waterford, Swarovski, and Mats Jonasson—are on parade, along with some particularly good pieces from the Swedish firm of Kosta Boda. The porcelain Lladró figurines from Spain are also fast-moving items. 14 Main St. © **340/777-9835.** www.crystalshoppe.net.

Little Switzerland ★★   For half a century, this duty-free retailer has been familiar to visitors to various islands in the Caribbean. On St.

Thomas, its fine jewelry, watches, china, crystal, and accessories are showcased at three different locations, and the company also does a lively mail-order business. At any outlet, you can pick up a catalog. The finest crystal sold on the island is featured here, including Orrefors from Sweden as well as Waterford and Baccarat. 5 Dronnigens Gade (© 340/776-2010); Havensight Mall (© 340/776-2198); and 48 AB Norre Gade (© 340/776-4595).

Fragrances

Tropicana Perfume Shoppe ★ (Value This outlet is billed as the largest perfumery in the world. It offers all the famous names in perfumes, skin care, and cosmetics, including Lancôme. Men will find Europe's best colognes and after-shave lotions here. A very friendly and attentive staff will enhance your shopping experience. 2 Main St. © 800/233-7948. www.usvi.net/tropicana.

Gifts & Liquors

A. H. Riise Gift & Liquor Stores This is St. Thomas's oldest outlet for luxury items, such as jewelry, crystal, china, and perfumes. It also offers the widest sampling of liquors on the island. Everything is displayed in a 19th-century Danish warehouse that extends from Main Street to the Waterfront. The store boasts a collection of fine jewelry and watches from Europe's leading craftspeople, including Vacheron Constantin, Bulgari, Omega, and Gucci, as well as a wide selection of Greek gold, platinum, and precious gemstone jewelry. Imported cigars are stored in a climate-controlled walk-in humidor. There's also a vast selection of fragrances for both men and women, along with the world's best-known names in cosmetics and treatment products. Waterford, Lalique, Baccarat, and Rosenthal, among others, are featured in the china and crystal department. Specialty shops in the complex sell Caribbean gifts, books, clothing, food, art prints, note-cards, and designer sunglasses. Delivery to cruise ships and the airport is free. 37 Main St. at A. H. Riise Gift & Liquor Mall (perfume and liquor branch stores at the Havensight Mall). © 800/524-2037 or 340/776-2303.

Caribbean Marketplace The best selection of Caribbean spices is found here, including Sunny Caribbee products, a vast array of condiments (ranging from spicy peppercorns to nutmeg mustard), and botanical products. Do not expect very attentive service. Havensight Mall (Building III). © 340/776-5400.

Down Island Traders ★ (Finds The aroma of spices will lead you to this market, which has Charlotte Amalie's most attractive array of spices, teas, seasoning, candies, jellies, jams, and condiments, most of which are packaged from natural Caribbean products. The owner also carries a line of local cookbooks, as well as silk-screened T-shirts and

Diamonds Are Forever

Jewelry is the most common item for sale in St. Thomas. Look carefully over the selections of gold and gemstones (emeralds are traditionally considered the finest savings). Gold that is marked 24-karat in the United States and Canada is marked 999 (or 99.9% pure gold) on European items. Gold marked 18-karat in the United States and Canada has a European marking of 750 (or 75% pure), and 14-karat gold is marked 585 (or 58.5% pure).

bags, Haitian metal sculptures, handmade jewelry, Caribbean folk art, and children's gifts. Veterans Dr. (C) **340/776-4641.**

Jewelry

Azura Jewels   Replacing the Colombian Emeralds shop, here is another fine jewelry store carrying just about the same products, including emeralds, sapphires, tanzanite, and fine watches. Havensight Mall. (C) **340/774-2442.**

Cardow Jewelers   Often called the Tiffany's of the Caribbean, Cardow Jewelers boasts the largest selection of fine jewelry in the world. This fabulous shop, where more than 20,000 rings are displayed, offers savings because of its worldwide direct buying, large turnover, and duty-free prices. Unusual and traditional designs are offered in diamonds, emeralds, rubies, sapphires, and Brazilian stones, as well as pearls. Cardow also has a whole wall of Italian gold chains, and features antique-coin jewelry as well. 39 Main St. (C) **340/776-1140.** www.cardow.com.

Diamonds International ★★   If you believe that diamonds are a girl's best friend, you've come to the right place. These outlets have the largest selection of diamonds on the island. You can purchase tanzanite gems and emeralds as well. Patrons select the stone of their dreams and can have it mounted within an hour in the ring of their choice. With certain large purchases, women (or men) are rewarded with free diamond earrings. There are several on-island locations. 3 Drakes Passage in Charlotte Amalie ((C) **340-775-2010**); Havensight Mall, Route 30 ((C) **340/776-0040**); 31 Main St. in Charlotte Amalie ((C) **340/774-3707**); and Wyndham Sugar Bay Beach Club & Resort, Route 38, Estate Smith Bay ((C) **340/714-3248**). www.shopdi.com.

H. Stern Jewelers   This international jeweler is one of the most respected in the world, with some 175 outlets. It's Cardow's leading competitor (see above). Besides this branch, there are two more on

60-day exchange privilege. Havensight Mall. ✆ **800/524-2024** or 340/776-1223. www.hstern.net.

Leather

Longchamp Boutique ★   This store sells the best leather items around, each a French handcrafted product including handbags, wallets, briefcases, belts, and luggage. Their line of canvas and leather travel bags moves quickly. There is also the well-known nylon-and-leather "Pliage Shopping Bag" sold here as well as exquisite accessories, including a full line of signature scarves. 25 Main St., Charlotte Amalie. ✆ **800/233-7948.**

Linens

Mr. Tablecloth   This shop constantly receives new shipments of top-quality linens from China, including Hong Kong. It has the best selection of tablecloths and accessories, plus doilies, in Charlotte Amalie. Also check out the display of place mats, aprons, and runners. 6 Main St. ✆ **340/774-4343.** www.mrtablecloth-vi.com.

Music

Modern Music   This store features nearly every genre of music, from rock to jazz to classical, and especially Caribbean. You'll find new releases from big Caribbean stars such as Jamaica's Byron Lee and the Virgin Islands' The Violators, as well as U.S. artists. There's one other branch as well, at the Nisky Center (✆ **340/777-8787**). Across from Havensight Mall and cruise ship docks. ✆ **340/774-3100.**

---

9 ST. THOMAS AFTER DARK

St. Thomas has more nightlife than any other island in the U.S. or British Virgin Islands, but it's not as extensive as you might think. Charlotte Amalie is no longer the swinging town it used to be. Many of the streets are dangerous after dark, so visitors have stopped visiting the area for nightlife, with the exception of a few places, such as the Greenhouse. Much of the action has shifted to **Frenchtown** ★★, which has some great restaurants and bars. However, just as in Charlotte Amalie, some of these little hot spots are along dark, badly lit roads. The primary problem here is mugging, although some of the criminal activity appears to be drug-related. Sexual assault is known to occur, but happens rather infrequently.

The big hotels, such as Frenchman's Reef & Morning Star Marriott Beach Resort, Bolongo Bay, or the Ritz, have the most lively after-dark scenes. After a day of sightseeing and shopping in the hot West

Indies sun, sometimes your best bet is just to stay at your hotel in the evening, perhaps listening to a local fungi band playing traditional music on homemade instruments.

THE PERFORMING ARTS

Pistarckle Theater   On the grounds of **Tillett Gardens Center for the Arts** (p. 75), this professional theater presents four full-length plays as part of its subscription season. Occupying a vacant print shop, the 100-seat theater is air-conditioned. There is also a summer drama camp for children. Tillett Gardens, 4126 Anna's Retreat, Tutu. ℂ 340/775-7877. www.pistarckletheater.vi. Tickets $19–$30.

Reichhold Center for the Arts ★   This artistic center, the premier performing arts venue in the Caribbean, lies west of Charlotte Amalie. Past performances have included the Alvin Ailey American Dance Theater and the likes of Al Jarreau. Call the theater or check with the tourist office to see what's on at the time of your visit. The lobby displays a frequently changing free exhibit of paintings and sculptures by Caribbean artists. A Japanese-inspired amphitheater, permeated by the scent of gardenias, is set into a natural valley, with seating space for 1,196. Performances usually begin at 8pm. University of the Virgin Islands, 2 John Brewers Bay. ℂ 340/693-1559. www.reichhold center.com. Tickets $18–$45.

BARS & CLUBS

Banana Bar   There's piano bar entertainment Thursday, Saturday, and Sunday at this scenic spot overlooking the yacht harbor. It's a popular gathering ground for both residents and visitors, who are mainly in their 30s and 40s. You can dance from 7 to 10pm on Thursday and Saturday. Entertainment varies from month to month, but many nights are devoted to jazz. Open daily from 5 to 10pm. Bluebeard's Castle. ℂ 340/774-1600.

The Bar at Paradise Point   Any savvy insider will tell you to head to this bar to watch the sunset. It's located 740 feet above sea level, across from the cruise ship dock, and provides excellent photo ops and panoramic sunset views. Cruise ship passengers, usually a middle-aged crowd, flock to this bar. A tram takes you up the hill. Get the bartender to serve you a "Bushwacker" (his specialty). You can also order inexpensive food here during the day, such as pizza, hot dogs, and hamburgers, beginning at $8. Happy hour, with discounted drinks, begins at 5pm. Don't take the tram up if you plan on staying until closing. The last tram down is at 5pm. Otherwise, drive yourself or call a cab. Open 7 days a week from 9am to 8pm, except Wednesday, when it's open from 9am to 9pm. Paradise Point. ℂ 340/777-4540.

Epernay This stylish watering hole, with a view of the ocean, adds a touch of Europe to the neighborhood. You can order glasses of at least six different brands of champagne, or vintage wines also come by the glass. Appetizers include sushi and caviar, but there are also main courses, plus tempting desserts such as chocolate-dipped strawberries. A mature, sophisticated crowd seeks out this spot. Open Monday to Thursday 11:30am to 11pm, Friday 11:30am to midnight, and Saturday 5pm to midnight. Rue de St. Barthélemy, Frenchtown. ✆ 340/774-5348.

The Greenhouse Set directly on the Waterfront, this bar and restaurant is one of the few nightspots we recommend in the heart of Charlotte Amalie. You can park nearby and walk to the entrance. If you want to start early, come for dinner (p. 53). Each night, a different type of entertainment is featured, ranging from reggae to disco; there's also a daily happy hour from 4:30 to 7pm. Tuesday nights are the biggest draw with two-for-one drinks; there's a live reggae band on Friday nights. Almost all of the 30-something patrons are visitors. Open daily 11am until the last customer leaves. Veterans Dr. ✆ 340/774-7998. www.thegreenhouserestaurant.com.

Happy Buzzard Attracting a wide range of ages, this bar is situated along the Waterfront in the center of Charlotte Amalie. The bartenders offer a wide variety of beer, highballs, and shooters, including the "Head Butt," which contains Jägermeister, Bailey's, and amaretto. Special events are often presented here, such as live music on Tuesday nights. Open daily from 10am to 8pm, later on Friday and Saturday. 26A Royal Dane Mall. ✆ 340/777-8676.

Hull Bay Hideaway A 25-year-plus mainstay on the island scene, this funky surfer bar has a laid-back, casual atmosphere, attracting, in the words of a bartender, "people from all walks of life, from boaters to condo renters." Many locals and regulars like to spend lazy Sunday afternoons here. It's a cheap place to eat—hot dogs and hamburgers are served until 3:30pm. After 4pm, you can order affordable main courses in the restaurant, costing $5 to $18, including the catch of the day and the chef's pork stew. There is live music on Saturday nights beginning at 7pm and on Sunday afternoon from 4pm. There are also some gambling machines and a volleyball court, if that's your thing. Open daily 10am to 10pm. 10 Hull Bay. ✆ 340/777-1898. www.hullbay.com.

Iggies Bolongo This place functions during the day as an informal, open-air restaurant serving hamburgers, sandwiches, and salads. After dark, it presents karaoke and occasional live entertainment. This establishment attracts the broadest spectrum of age groups and professions in all of Charlotte Amalie. Call to find out what's happening.

Bolongo Bay Beach Resort, 7150 Bolongo. ✆ **340/693-2600.** www.iggies beachbar.com.

Latitude 18 This is the hot spot of the east coast, located where the ferryboats depart for St. John. The casual restaurant and bar, featuring a ceiling adorned with boat sails, offers live entertainment regularly, especially on Thursday through Sunday nights. Open daily from 11:30am to 10:30pm. Red Hook Marina. ✆ **340/777-4552.** www. stthomasusvirginislands.com/latitudes.

Turtle Rock Bar This popular bar presents live music and karaoke to a young crowd. There's space to dance, but most patrons just sway and listen. The steel-pan bands that play from 2pm to closing on Sundays are excellent. Burgers, salads, steaks, and grilled fish are available at the Iguana Grill, a few steps away. In the Iguana Grill at the Wyndham Sugar Bay Resort & Spa, 6500 Estate Smith Bay (a few minutes' drive west of Red Hook). ✆ **340/777-7100.**

GAY & LESBIAN NIGHTLIFE

St. Thomas might be the most cosmopolitan of the Virgin Islands, but it is no longer the "gay paradise" it was in the 1960s and 1970s. The major gay scene in the U.S. Virgins is now on St. Croix (see chapter 4). That doesn't mean that gay men and lesbians aren't drawn to St. Thomas. They are, but many attend predominantly straight establishments, such as the **Greenhouse** (see above).

St. John

East of St. Thomas, across a glistening turquoise channel known as Pillsbury Sound, lies St. John, the smallest and least densely populated of the three main U.S. Virgin Islands.

St. John is a wonder of unspoiled beauty. Along its rocky coastline are beautiful crescent-shaped bays and white-sand beaches. The interior is no less impressive. The variety of wildlife on St. John is the envy of naturalists around the world. And there are miles of hiking trails, leading past the ruins of 18th-century Danish plantations to panoramic views. At scattered spots along the trails, you can find mysteriously geometric petroglyphs of unknown age and origin incised into boulders and cliffs.

Today, St. John (unlike the other U.S. islands) remains pristine, its preservation enforced by the National Park Service. Thanks to the efforts of Laurance Rockefeller, who purchased many acres of land and donated them to the United States in 1956, the island's shoreline waters, as well as more than half of its surface area, make up the Virgin Islands National Park. The hundreds of coral gardens that surround St. John are protected rigorously—any attempt to damage or remove coral is punishable with large and strictly enforced fines.

Despite the unspoiled beauty of much of St. John, the island manages to provide visitors with modern amenities and travel services, including a sampling of restaurants, car-rental kiosks, yacht-supply facilities, hotels, and campgrounds. Cinnamon Bay, founded by the National Park Service in 1964, is the most famous campsite in the Caribbean. In addition, the roads are well-maintained; there's even a small commercial center, Cruz Bay, on the island's western tip. Don't come here for nightlife: St. John is definitely sleepy, and that's why people love it.

Thanks to the simple development of St. John, life is much more laid-back than on the other U.S. Virgins. It lies only a short ferry ride from the more commercialized St. Thomas, so there isn't even an airport here. On St. John, the local people actually have time to talk to you and perhaps provide you with directions and advice. While you may never meet the managers of most East End properties on St. Thomas, you could end up talking with your St. John innkeeper late into the night. If you show up for a visit same time next year, you might even be welcomed as one of the family; you'll certainly be considered a "regular."

1 ORIENTATION

GETTING THERE
By Boat

The easiest and most common way to get to St. John is by **ferry** (© **340/776-6282**), which leaves from the Red Hook landing pier on St. Thomas's eastern tip; the trip takes about 20 minutes each way. Beginning at 6:30am, boats depart more or less every hour. The last ferry back to Red Hook departs from St. John's Cruz Bay at 11pm. The service is frequent and efficient enough that even cruise ship passengers temporarily anchored in Charlotte Amalie can visit St. John for a quick island tour. The one-way fare is $6.10 for adults, $2.10 for children 11 and under. Schedules change without notice, so call in advance.

To reach the ferry, take the **Vitran** bus from the ferry dock near Market Square (in Charlotte Amalie) directly to Red Hook. The cost is $1 per person each way. In addition, privately owned taxis will negotiate a price to carry you from virtually anywhere on the island to the docks at Red Hook.

If you've just landed on St. Thomas and want to go straight to your chosen ferry dock, your best bet is to take a cab from the airport (Vitran buses run from Charlotte Amalie but don't serve the airport area). Depending on the traffic, the cab ride on St. Thomas could take 30 to 45 minutes, at a fare between $20 and $22. After disembarking from the ferry on St. John, you'll have to get another cab to your hotel.

It's also possible to board a **boat** for St. John directly at the Charlotte Amalie waterfront, from Vendors Plaza at the corner of Veterans Drive and Tolbod Gade, for a cost of $10 each way for adults and $1 for children 11 and under. The ride takes 45 minutes. The boats depart from Charlotte Amalie at 7:15am and continue at intervals of 2 hours, until the last boat departs around 5:30pm. (The last boat to leave St. John's Cruz Bay for Charlotte Amalie departs at 3:45pm.) Call © **340/776-6282** or visit www.vinow.com for more information.

VISITOR INFORMATION

The **tourist office** (© **340/776-6450**) is located near the Battery, a 1735 fort that's a short walk from the St. Thomas ferry dock in Cruz Bay. It's open Monday to Friday from 8am to 5pm. A **National Park visitor center** (© **340/776-6201**) is also found at Cruz Bay, offering two floors of information and wall-mounted wildlife displays, plus a video presentation about the culture of the Virgin Islands. Open daily 8am to 4:30pm.

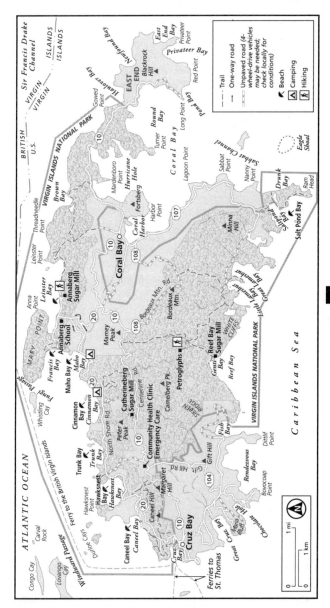

You can pick up a map of the island from the tourist office and also a copy of *St. John This Week,* which is distributed free.

ISLAND LAYOUT

Most visitors will arrive on St. John at **Cruz Bay,** on a ferry from St. Thomas. This tiny town, with its few restaurants and shops, is quite the departure from the bustle of Charlotte Amalie. Cruz Bay is also the first stop on any trip to **Virgin Islands National Park,** which sprawls through the interior and encompasses almost all the coastline. The park service runs an information center in town. Route 20 leads north out of Cruz Bay, and passes the beaches at Caneel, Hawksnest, Trunk, Cinnamon, and Maho bays. At the far north, Route 20 leads to the start of the **Annaberg Trail,** a historic hike through the ruins of 18th-century sugar plantations. Route 10 cuts through the center of the island. Dozens of foot trails lead off this road, making for easy exploration of the peaks and mountains. On the east end of the island is **Coral Bay,** a favorite among yachties and home to a smattering of small restaurants and bars. Crumbling ruins of forts and plantations also dot the coastline here. The far east end is undeveloped and pales in comparison to the lush greenery of the park. The south coast is a favorite hideaway for locals, but little-known by visitors. The coast here is sweeping and tranquil, yet rocky in parts and punctuated with a handful of small protected bays.

---

2 GETTING AROUND

The 20-minute ferry ride from St. Thomas will take you to **Cruz Bay,** the capital of St. John, which seems a century removed from the life you left behind. Cruz Bay is so small that its streets have no names, but it does have the **Mongoose Junction** shopping center (definitely worth a visit), a scattering of restaurants, and a small park. Cruise ships are nonexistent here, so you won't find hordes of milling shoppers. After a stroll around town, seek out the natural attractions of the island.

BY BUS

The most popular way to get around is by the local **Vitran** (© 340/774-0165) service, the same company that runs the buses on St. Thomas. Buses run between Cruz Bay and Coral Bay, costing $1 for adults and 75¢ for children.

BY TAXI

An open-air **surrey-style taxi** is more fun than taking a bus. Typical fares are $9 to Trunk Bay, $11 to Cinnamon Bay, or $14 to Maho

meet the ferries as they arrive in Cruz Bay, or you can hail one if you
see one. More than likely, you or your hotel will have to call one. Call
© 340/693-7530 for more information or **Paradise Taxi** at © 340/
714-7913.

BY CAR OR JEEP
One of the most exciting ways to see St. John is by a four-wheel-drive
vehicle, which you can rent in town (in winter it's best to reserve in
advance). The steep roadside panoramas are richly tinted with tones
of forest green and turquoise and liberally accented with flashes of
silver and gold from the strong Caribbean sun. Most visitors need a
car for only a day or two. *Remember:* Drive on the left and follow
posted speed limits, which are generally very low.

Unless you need to carry luggage, which should probably be locked
away in a trunk, you might consider one of the sturdy, open-sided,
jeeplike vehicles that offer the best view of the surroundings and are the
most fun way to tour St. John. Note that most of these vehicles have
manual transmission, which can be especially tricky in a car built to
drive on the left side of the road. They cost around $76 to $84 a day.

The largest car-rental agency on St. John is **Hertz** (© 800/654-
3001 in the U.S., or 340/776-6171; www.hertz.com). If you want a
local firm, try **St. John Car Rental,** across from the Catholic church
in Cruz Bay (© 340/776-6103; www.stjohncarrental.com).

ST. JOHN

3

FAST FACTS: ST. JOHN

ⓕ*Fast Facts*   St. John

Banks **First Bank Virgin Islands** is at 90C Cruz Bay (© 340/
776-6881).

Business Hours Stores are generally open Monday to Friday
9am to 5pm, Saturday 9am to 1pm.

Cameras & Film To purchase film or have it developed, go to
Sparky's, Cruz Bay Park (© 340/776-6284).

Currency Exchange Go to the branch of **First Bank Virgin
Islands** in Cruz Bay (© 340/776-6881).

Dentists The **Virgin Islands Dental Association** (© 340/775-
9110) is a member of the American Dental Association and
is also linked with various specialists. Call for information or
an appointment.

Doctors Call © **911** for a medical emergency. Otherwise, go
to **St. John Myrah Keating Smith Community Health Center,**
3B Sussanaberg (© 340/693-8900).

Drugstores Go to **Chelsea Drug Store,** Marketplace Shopping Center, Route 104, Cruz Bay (© **340/776-4888**). The staff here not only fills prescriptions but also sells film, cameras, magazines, and books. Hours are Monday to Saturday 9am to 6pm. The pharmacy is open Monday to Saturday 8:30am to 6pm and Sunday 10am to 4:30pm.

Emergencies For the police, an ambulance, or in case of fire, call © **911.**

Internet Access Go to **Connections,** Parcel Street, Suite 6D (© **340/776-6922;** www.connectionsstjohn.com). Expect to pay $5 for 30 minutes. You can also use the computers at the **Elaine Lone Sprauve Public Library,** Enighted Street (© **340/776-6359**), for a charge of $2 for 1 hour.

Laundry Try **Santo's Laundromat,** 1321 Cruz Bay Valley (© **340/693-7733**), or **Super Clean,** Enighted Street (© **340/693-7333**).

Maps See "Visitor Information," p. 84.

Newspapers & Magazines Copies of U.S. mainland newspapers, such as the *New York Times* and *The Miami Herald,* arrive daily and are for sale at **Mongoose Junction, Caneel Bay,** and the **Westin St. John Resort & Villas.** The latest copies of *Time* and *Newsweek* are also for sale. *What to Do: St. Thomas/ St. John,* the official guidebook of the St. Thomas and St. John Hotel Association, is available at the tourist office (see "Visitor Information," p. 84) and at hotels.

Post Office The **Cruz Bay Post Office** is at Cruz Bay (© **340/779-4227**). See "Fast Facts: St. Thomas" for current postal rates.

Safety There is some crime here, but it's relatively minor compared to St. Thomas. Most crime against tourists consists of muggings or petty theft, but rarely violent attacks. Precautions, of course, are always advised. You are most likely to be the victim of a crime if you leave valuables unguarded on Trunk Bay, as hundreds of people seem to do every year.

Taxes The only local tax is an 8% surcharge added to all hotel rates.

Telephone & Fax All island phone numbers have seven digits. It is not necessary to use the 340 area code when dialing within St. John. Make long-distance, international, and collect calls as you would on the U.S. mainland by dialing 0 or your long-distance provider.

3 WHERE TO STAY

The number of accommodations on St. John is limited, and that's how most die-hard fans would like to keep it. There are four basic types of choices here: luxury resorts, condominiums and villas, guesthouses, and campgrounds. Prices are often slashed in summer by 30% to 60%.

Chances are your location will be determined by your choice of resort. However, if you're dependent on public transportation and want to make one or two trips to St. Thomas by ferry, Cruz Bay is the most convenient place to stay. It also offers easy access to shopping, bars, and restaurants if you want to walk.

LUXURY RESORTS

Caneel Bay ★★★ (Kids)   Conceived by megamillionaire Laurance S. Rockefeller in 1956, this is the Caribbean's first eco-resort. Though it's long been one of the premier resorts of the Caribbean, Caneel Bay is definitely not one of the most luxurious. A devoted fan once told us, "It's like living at summer camp." That means no phones or TVs in the rooms. Nevertheless, the movers and shakers of the world continue to descend on this place, though younger people tend to head elsewhere.

The resort lies on a 170-acre portion of the national park, offering a choice of seven beaches. Surrounded by lush greenery, the main buildings are strung along the bays, with a Caribbean lounge and dining room at the core. Other buildings housing guest rooms stand along the beaches. Most rooms are set back on low cliffs or headlands. The decor within is understated, with Indonesian wicker furniture, hand-woven fabrics, sisal mats, and plantation fans.

The resort has consistently maintained a high level of cuisine, often quite formal for the laid-back Caribbean. In recent years the food has been considerably improved and modernized, with more variety and more healthy choices on the menu. In fact, **Equator** (p. 96) is one of our favorites on St. John.

Virgin Islands National Park, St. John, U.S.V.I. 00831. (℡) **888/767-3966** or 340/776-6111. Fax 340/693-8280. www.caneelbay.com. 166 units. Winter $450–$1,400 double; off season $375–$1,100 double. MAP (breakfast and dinner) $90 per person per day extra. 1 child 15 and under stays free in parent's room. AE, MC, V. **Amenities:** 5 restaurants; 2 bars; babysitting; children's center; concierge; health center & spa; pool (outdoor); room service; 11 tennis courts. *In room:* A/C, TV, hair dryer, minibar, Wi-Fi (free).

Westin St. John Resort & Villas ★★★ (Kids)   Come here if you like mega-resort flash and glitter as opposed to the "old-school ties" of Caneel Bay (see above). This is the most architecturally dramatic and visually appealing hotel on St. John. The complex is set on 34 acres of landscaped grounds on the southwest side of the island. It consists of 21 cedar-roofed postmodern buildings, each with ziggurat-shaped angles and soaring ceilings. Herringbone-patterned brick walkways connect the gardens (with 400 palms imported from Puerto Rico) to the 1,181-foot white-sand beach and one of the largest pools in the Virgin Islands. Some of the stylish accommodations contain fan-shaped windows and curved ceilings. Most units open onto private balconies, and some have their own whirlpools. Villas, of course, offer more space and come with a full kitchenette.

Cuisine options here are more varied than those at Caneel, featuring nouvelle cuisine, buffets, and even New York deli sandwiches. **Chloe & Bernard's** (p. 95) is an excellent choice for steak and seafood.

Great Cruz Bay, St. John, U.S.V.I. 00831. © **866/716-8108** in the U.S., or 340/693-8000. Fax 340/779-4985. www.westinresortstjohn.com. 321 units. Winter $649–$799 double, from $1,550 villa; off season $355–$495 double, from $1,150 villa. AE, DC, DISC, MC, V. Round-trip shuttle and private ferryboat transfers from St. Thomas airport $95 per adult, $80 ages 4–12. **Amenities:** 4 restaurants; 2 bars; airport transfers ($95 per adult, $80 ages 4–12); children's programs; concierge; golf nearby; pool (outdoor); room service; 6 lit tennis courts; extensive watersports equipment/rentals. In room: A/C, TV, hair dryer, Jacuzzi (in some), kitchenette (in some), minibar, Wi-Fi (free).

CONDOS & VILLAS

Villa vacations are on the rise in St. John for travelers who want a home away from home. There are actually more villa and condo beds available on St. John than there are hotel beds. These units offer spaciousness and comfort, as well as privacy and freedom, and they often come with fully equipped kitchens, dining areas, bedrooms, and such amenities as VCRs and patio grills. Rentals range from large multi-room resort homes to simply decorated one-bedroom condos.

Caribbean Villas & Resorts, P.O. Box 458, St. John, U.S.V.I. 00831 (© **800/338-0987** or 340/776-6152; fax 207/510-6308 in the U.S.; www.caribbeanvilla.com), the island's biggest real estate agency, is an excellent choice if you're seeking a villa, condo, or private home. Most condos go for between $125 and $295 per night, though private homes are more expensive.

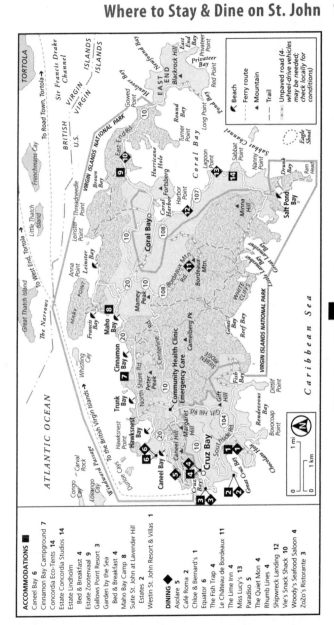

ST. JOHN

3

WHERE TO STAY

ACCOMMODATIONS ■

Caneel Bay 6
Cinnamon Bay Campground 7
Concordia Eco-Tents 14
Estate Concordia Studios 14
Estate Lindholm
Bed & Breakfast 4
Estate Zootenvaal 9
Gallows Point Resort 3
Garden by the Sea
Bed & Breakfast 4
Maho Bay Camp 8
Suite St. John at Lavender Hill
Estates 2
Westin St. John Resort & Villas 1

DINING ◆

Asolare 5
Café Roma 2
Chloe & Bernard's 1
Equator 6
The Fish Trap 4
Le Chateau de Bordeaux 11
The Lime Inn 4
Miss Lucy's 13
Paradiso 5
The Quiet Mon 4
Rhumb Lines 4
Shipwreck Landing 12
Vie's Snack Shack 10
Woody's Seafood Saloon 4
ZoZo's Ristorante 3

Expensive

Estate Zootenvaal ★ This property is located on 30 acres within the boundaries of the national park at the edge of a horseshoe-shaped bay. It's a good choice for escapees from urban life who want privacy. The accommodations have been renovated, now sporting designer fabrics in muted tones. Each has its own color scheme and comes with a fully equipped kitchen and a shower-only bathroom. Rooms have ceiling fans, but no telephones or televisions. Maid service can be arranged at an extra cost. Guests can use the private beach that's known for its great snorkeling.

Hurricane Hole, St. John, U.S.V.I. 00830. ✆ **340/776-6321** or 216/861-5337. www. estatezootenvaal.com. 4 units. Winter $275 1-bedroom, $360–$550 2-bedroom; off-season $180 1-bedroom, $240–$360 2-bedroom. Extra person $75–$175. No credit cards. *In room:* Ceiling fans, kitchen, no phone (in some).

Suite St. John at Lavender Hill Estates ★ (Kids) This outfit offers some of the best condo values on this tiny island. It's a short walk away from the shops, markets, restaurants, and safari buses of Cruz Bay. The two units overlook Cruz Bay Harbor, and both have a spacious central living/dining area opening onto a tiled deck, along with a fully equipped kitchen and one or two bedrooms.

P.O. Box 8306, Lavender Hill, Cruz Bay, St. John, U.S.V.I. 00831-8306. ✆ **800/348-8444** or 340/690-4692. Fax 301/977-4252. www.lavenderhillestates.com. 2 condo apts. Winter $350 1-bedroom apt; off season $195–$250 1-bedroom apt. Extra person $35 per night. MC, V. **Amenities:** Pool (outdoor). *In room:* A/C, TV, TV/DVD, CD player, kitchen, Wi-Fi (free).

Moderate

Estate Concordia Studios This environmentally sensitive 50-acre development has been widely praised for its integration with the local ecosystem. Its elevated structures were designed to coexist with the stunning southern edge of St. John. The secluded property is nestled on a low cliff above a salt pond, surrounded by hundreds of pristine National Park acres. It's best for those with rental vehicles. Each building was designed to protect mature trees and is connected to its neighbors with boardwalks. The nine studios are contained in five postmodern cottages. Each unit has a kitchen, a shower-only bathroom, a balcony, and a ceiling fan; some have an extra bedroom. For information on the on-site **Eco-Tents,** see "Campgrounds," below.

20–27 Estate Concordia, Coral Bay, St. John, U.S.V.I. 00830. ✆ **800/392-9004** in the U.S. and Canada, 212/472-9453 or 340/715-0501. Fax 340/776-6504. www. maho.org. 9 units. Winter $150–$225 double; off season $95–$160 double. MC, V. **Amenities:** Internet cafe ($10 per hour); pool (outdoor). *In room:* Ceiling fan, kitchen, no phone.

Estate Lindholm Bed & Breakfast ★ (Finds) The island's best B&B grew out of an estate originally settled by Dutch planters in the

1720s. Set among the Danish ruins, Estate Lindholm is a charming guesthouse on a hill overlooking Cruz Bay, each of its nonsmoking bedrooms opening onto a view. The spacious bedrooms are attractively and comfortably furnished, many resting under ceiling beams. Guests can enjoy private balconies as well. On the property is the **Asolare** restaurant, one of the island's best (p. 95). The staff is helpful in hooking you up with any number of outdoor activities, including everything from sea kayaking to windsurfing.

P.O. Box 1360, Cruz Bay, St. John, U.S.V.I. 00831. © **800/322-6335** in the U.S., or 340/776-6121. Fax 340/776-6141. www.estatelindholm.com. 10 units. Winter $340–$390 double; off season $190–$240 suite. Rates include continental breakfast. AE, DISC, MC, V. **Amenities:** Restaurant; exercise room; pool (outdoor). *In room:* A/C, TV, fridge.

Gallows Point Resort ★   The first complex of buildings you see as you arrive at Cruz Bay is this colony of condos just outside the town. Lying on a 5-acre peninsula, the complex blends into its setting, a tropical landscape with island-style architecture. You're within walking distance of the restaurants and shops of Cruz Bay. In all, there are 15 well-furnished buildings, each structure with four one-bedroom suites, coming with a full kitchen and spacious living area. The best views, of course, are in the apartments on the upper level. Harborside villas tend to get more noise. The beach nearby is small and rocky, so you may want to go farther afield for the sands. The garden suites are one story with sunken living rooms. The property also includes multilevel sunbathing decks. On-site is **ZoZo's Ristorante** (see recommendation below).

Gallows Point, St. John, U.S.V.I. 00831. © **800/323-7229** or 340/776-6434. Fax 340/776-6520. www.gallowspointresort.com. 60 units. Winter $465–$595 suite; off season $265–$495 suite. AE, MC, V. **Amenities:** Restaurant; bar; pool (outdoor). *In room:* A/C, TV, hair dryer, kitchen, Wi-Fi (free).

Garden by the Sea Bed & Breakfast ★ (Finds)   Overlooking the ocean, this B&B lies a 10-minute walk south of the little port of Cruz Bay. It has easy access to the north-shore beaches and lies between Frank and Turner bays. From the gardens of the house, a short path along Audubon Pond leads to Frank Bay Beach. Be sure to reserve a room ahead, as it offers only three bedrooms. Artifacts from around the world have been used to furnish the units. Each bedroom features elephant bamboo canopy beds, Japanese fountains, hardwood floors, and well-kept bathrooms. Don't expect phones or TVs, as this is a getaway, not a communications center. The 1970s house is designed in a Caribbean gingerbread style with cathedral beamed ceilings.

P.O. Box 37, Cruz Bay, St. John, U.S.V.I. 00831. ©/fax **340/779-4731.** www.garden bythesea.com. 3 units. Winter $250–$275 double; off season $160–$200 double. No credit cards. *In room:* A/C, ceiling fan, hair dryer, no phone.

Cinnamon Bay Campground ★★ (Kids)

This National Park Service campground is the most complete in the Caribbean. The site is directly on the beach, surrounded by thousands of acres of tropical vegetation. Life is simple here: You have a choice of a tent, a cottage, or a bare site. At the bare campsites, you get just the site, with no fancy extras. Each canvas tent is 10×14 feet and has a floor as well as a number of extras, including all cooking equipment; your linens are even changed weekly. Each cottage is 15×15 feet, consisting of a room with two concrete walls and two screen walls. Each cottage contains cooking facilities and four twin beds with thin mattresses; one cot can be added. Lavatories and cool-water showers are in separate buildings nearby. In winter, guests can camp for a maximum of 2 weeks; the rest of the year camping is limited to 30 days.

P.O. Box 720, Cruz Bay, St. John, U.S.V.I. 00831. (℃ **340/776-6330.** Fax 340/776-6458. www.cinnamonbay.com. 126 units, none with bathroom. Winter $120–$155 cottage for 2, $88 tent site, $30 bare site; off season $77–$100 cottage for 2, $64 tent site, $30 bare site. Extra person $19. AE, MC, V. Closed Sept. **Amenities:** Restaurant; extensive watersports equipment/rentals. *In room:* No phone.

Concordia Eco-Tents

On the southern tip of St. John, overlooking Salt Pond Bay and Ram Head Point, these solar- and wind-powered tent-cottages combine sustainable technology with some of the most spectacular views on the island. The light framing, fabric walls, and large screened-in windows lend a treehouse atmosphere to guests' experience. Set on the windward side of the island, the tent-cottages enjoy natural ventilation from the cooling trade winds. Inside, each has two twin beds with rather thin mattresses in each bedroom, one or two twin mattresses on a loft platform, and a queen-size futon in the living room area. (Each unit can sleep up to six people comfortably.) In addition, each Eco-Tent has a small solar-powered private shower, rather meager towels, and a composting toilet. The secluded hillside location, surrounded by hundreds of acres of pristine national park land, requires guests to arrange for a rental vehicle.

20–27 Estate Concordia, Coral Bay, St. John, U.S.V.I. 00830. (℃ **800/392-9004** in the U.S., or 212/472-9453. Fax 212/861-6210. www.maho.org. 18 units (4 are wheelchair accessible). Winter $155–$185 tent for 2; off season $95 tent for 2. Extra person $15. MC, V. **Amenities:** Pool (outdoor). *In room:* No phone.

Maho Bay Camps ★ (Kids)

Right on Maho Bay, this is an interesting concept in ecology vacationing, where you camp close to nature, but with considerable comfort. It's set on a hillside above the beach surrounded by the Virgin Islands National Park. To preserve the existing ground cover, all 114 tent-cottages are on platforms, above a thickly wooded slope. Utility lines and pipes are hidden under wooden boardwalks and stairs. Each tent-cottage, covered with canvas and screens, has two twin beds with thin mattresses, a couch, electric lamps and outlets, a dining table, chairs, a propane stove, an ice chest (cooler), linens, thin towels, and cooking and eating utensils. Guests share communal bathhouses. Maho Bay Camps is more intimate and slightly more luxurious than its nearest competitor, Cinnamon Bay.

P.O. Box 310, Cruz Bay, St. John, U.S.V.I. 00830. ✆ **800/392-9004** in the U.S., or 340/715-0501. Fax 340/776-6504 or 212/861-6210. www.maho.org. 114 units, none with bathroom. Winter $135 tent-cottage for 2 (minimum stay of 7 nights); off season $80 tent-cottage for 2. Extra person winter $15, off season $12. MC, V. **Amenities:** Restaurant; extensive watersports equipment/rentals.

4 WHERE TO DINE

St. John has some posh dining, particularly at the luxury resorts like Caneel Bay, but it also has West Indian restaurants with plenty of local color and flavor. Many of the restaurants command high prices, but you can lunch almost anywhere at reasonable rates. Dinner is often quite an event on St. John, since it's about the only form of nightlife the island has.

EXPENSIVE

Asolare ★ FRENCH/ASIAN This is the most beautiful and elegant restaurant on St. John, with the hippest and best-looking staff. Asolare is in the Estate Lindholm Bed & Breakfast and sits on top of a hill overlooking Cruz Bay and some of the British Virgin Islands. *Asolare* translates to "the leisurely passing of time without purpose" in Greek, and that's what many diners prefer to do here. The chef roams the world for inspiration and cooks with flavor and flair, using some of the best and freshest ingredients available on the island. To begin, you might try the grilled Asian barbecued shrimp or the squid and shrimp medley. For a main course, you will be tempted by the ginger lamb or the peppercorn-dusted filet of beef. Two truly excellent dishes are the chicken Kiev and the sashimi tuna with plum-passion fruit sake vinaigrette. For dessert, try the fresh berry dishes or the chocolate pyramid cake.

In the Estate Lindholm Bed & Breakfast (p. 92), Cruz Bay. ✆ **340/779-4747.** Reservations required. Main courses $30–$50. AE, MC, V. Daily 5:30–10:30pm.

Chloe & Bernard's ★★ AMERICAN At the Westin, this luxurious restaurant features one of the island's best dining experiences, especially if you like steak and seafood. Lying on the upper level of the open-air lobby, the restaurant is named after two fictional characters who spend their time traveling the world in search of delectable recipes to add to their mouthwatering menu. The inspiration is clear. The talented chefs turn out savory dishes redolent of Caribbean sunshine and full of flavor. Specialties of the chef include mahimahi and yellow-fin tuna as well as delectable crab cakes and a 2-pound lobster special.

In the Westin St. John Resort & Villas (p. 89), Great Cruz Bay. ⟲ 340/693-8000. Reservations recommended. Main courses $28–$38. AE, MC, V. Daily 6–9:30pm.

Equator ★ CARIBBEAN This restaurant lies behind the tower of an 18th-century sugar mill, where ponds with waterlilies fill former crystallization pits for hot molasses. A flight of stairs leads to a monumental circular dining room, with a wraparound veranda and sweeping views of the water and St. Thomas. In the center rises the stone column that horses and mules once circled to crush sugar cane stalks. A giant poinciana-like Asian tree of the *Albizia lebbeck* species—islanders call it "woman's tongue tree"—grows in the middle of the restaurant.

The cuisine is the most daring on the island, and for the most part, the chefs pull off their transcultural dishes. A spicy and tantalizing opener is lemon grass–and–ginger–cured salmon salad. Daily Caribbean selections are offered, such as a classic Caribbean callaloo soup, or you can opt for such fine dishes as seared Caribbean tuna, or penne pasta with shiitake mushrooms and roasted tomatoes in an herb-garlic cream sauce. There's always a dry, aged Angus steak or a grilled veal chop for the more traditional palate.

In the Caneel Bay hotel, Caneel Bay. ⟲ 340/776-6111. www.caneelbay.com/dine3.cfm. Reservations required. Main courses $22–$42. AE, MC, V. Days vary 6–9pm.

Le Château de Bordeaux ★ CONTINENTAL/CARIBBEAN This restaurant is 5 miles east of Cruz Bay, near the center of the island and close to one of its highest points. It's known for having some of the best views on St. John. A lunch grill on the patio serves burgers and drinks Monday through Saturday. In the evening, amid a Victorian decor with lace tablecloths, you can begin with a house-smoked chicken spring roll or a velvety carrot soup. After that, move on to one of the saffron-flavored pastas or a savory West Indian seafood chowder, the island's best. Smoked salmon and filet mignon are a bow to the international crowd, although the wild-game specials are more unusual. The well-flavored Dijon mustard and pecan-crusted roast rack of lamb with a shallot port reduction is also a good choice. For dessert, there's a changing array of cheesecakes, among other options. The specialty drink is a passion fruit daiquiri.

Junction 10, Bordeaux Mountain. ⟲ 340/776-6111. Reservations recommended. Main courses $28–$34. AE, MC, V. Sun–Fri 5:30–9:30pm.

Paradiso ★★ ITALIAN This is the most talked-about restaurant on St. John, other than Asolare (see above), and it's the only one that's air-conditioned. The interior has lots of brass, glowing hardwoods, and nautical antiques, not to mention the most beautiful bar on the island, crafted from mahogany, purpleheart, and angelique.

Try such appetizers as grilled chicken spring rolls with roasted sweet peppers. Roasted garlic Caesar salad with sun-dried tomatoes and Parmesan grissini is a new twist on this classic dish. But the main dishes truly shine, especially a pan-seared local yellowfin tuna with baby arugula, fennel, pear, and radicchio, and a grilled Kansas City sirloin marinated in garlic and fresh herbs. Another enticing choice is oven-roasted free-range chicken breast with roasted potatoes, carrots, and butternut squash.

Mongoose Junction. (C) **340/693-8899.** Reservations recommended. Main courses $28–$32. AE, MC, V. Daily 6–9pm; bar daily 6–10:30pm.

Rhumb Lines ★ (Kids) CARIBBEAN/PACIFIC RIM
In the heart of Cruz Bay, this restaurant with its West Indian courtyard has a South Seas ambience. The chefs take you on a culinary tour that travels from the Caribbean to the Pacific Ocean, seeking recipes to inspire them. Appetizers are among the island's best, ranging from hot and sour grilled duck breast glazed with rum punch to cracked pepper-crusted tuna over a seaweed salad. Ever had gazpacho made with mango? The main dishes are full of flavor and are delectable, especially the fresh mahimahi in banana leaf with a gingered banana beurre blanc or the tenderloin of Cuban pork marinated in garlic and citrus juices. For the adventurous palate, there is a special menu of Pupu, with everything from lemongrass and tofu cakes to spicy Szechuan noodles. There is also a kids' menu. The drink menu has some of the most imaginative drinks on the island.

Meada's Plaza, Cruz Bay. (C) **340/776-0303.** www.rhumblinesstjohn.com. Reservations recommended. $19–$27. MC, V. Daily 6–10pm.

ZoZo's Ristorante ITALIAN
An in-the-know crowd of locals and visitors flocks to this charming Italian trattoria, with an open-air terrace and a sweeping panoramic view over the sea. First-rate ingredients, style, and fresh seasonings contribute to such winning dishes as an eggplant tower (layers of eggplant, fontina, ricotta, and red peppers); littleneck clams in white wine, garlic, and plum tomatoes; and lump crab cakes with a roasted-pepper aïoli. The pastas are the island's best, especially the lobster ravioli with wild mushrooms and toasted pine nuts, and the basil-infused linguine. Tuck into such fish dishes as a grilled sea bass with an eggplant tapenade in a roasted garlic–shrimp sauce or pan-seared black grouper with a sauce flavored with orange and fresh basil. Their *osso buco* is slowly simmered in red wine, tomato, and veal stock and is a tasty main course.

Gallows Point. (C) **340/693-9200.** www.zozos.net. Reservations recommended. Main courses $33–$40. AE, MC, V. Nov–May daily 5:30–9pm; off season Mon–Sat 5:30–9pm.

MODERATE

Café Roma (Kids) ITALIAN   This restaurant in the center of Cruz Bay is not a place for great finesse in the kitchen, but it's a longtime favorite and has pleased a lot of families who just want a casual meal. To enter, you have to climb a flight of stairs. You might arrive early and have a strawberry colada, then enjoy a standard pasta, veal, seafood, or chicken dish. There are usually 30 to 40 vegetarian items on the menu. The owner claims, with justification, that his pizzas are the best on the island. Italian wines are sold by the glass or bottle, and you can end the evening with an espresso.

Cruz Bay. ✆ **340/776-6524.** www.stjohn-caferoma.com. Main courses $15–$30. MC, V. Daily 5–10pm.

The Fish Trap ★ SEAFOOD   This aptly named place serves St. John's best seafood. It's a casual, laid-back atmosphere with tables placed on a covered patio open to the trade winds, an easy walk up from the ferry dock. Chef Aaron Willis is the island's favorite, bringing his New York culinary training with him but showing a total familiarity with West Indian seasonings and flavors. Nobody on St. John does conch fritters better, and he's been praised by such national magazines as *Vogue* and *Gourmet*. Depending on the catch of the day, there will be a fresh fish special, most likely wahoo, shark, mahimahi, or snapper. The grilled tuna, for example, comes in a wasabi sauce and the swordfish is made more appetizing by the use of lemon grass. An array of steaks, tasty pastas, chicken cutlets, and burgers are always served.

Cruz Bay, next to Our Lady of Mount Carmel Church. ✆ **340/693-9994.** www. thefishtrap.com. Reservations required for groups of 6 or more. Main courses $13–$42. MC, V. Tues–Sun 4:30–10pm.

The Lime Inn SEAFOOD   This lively open-air restaurant is located at the Lemon Tree Mall in the heart of Cruz Bay. It's known for its fresh grilled Caribbean-style lobster. Other grilled seafood choices range from shrimp to the fresh catch of the day. The seared whole snapper, when served, is a delight. If you're not in the mood for seafood, try one of the daily chicken and pasta specials or one of the grilled steaks. There's also a tender grilled filet mignon stuffed with crabmeat. A beautifully prepared chicken Wellington is one of the chef's specialties. The most popular night of the week here is Wednesday with the all-you-can-eat, peel-and-eat shrimp feast for $19.

In the Lemon Tree Mall, Konges Gade, Cruz Bay. ✆ **340/776-6425.** www.limeinn. com. Reservations recommended. Main courses lunch $7.95–$13, dinner $19–$28. AE, MC, V. Mon–Fri 11:30am–3pm and 5:30–10pm; Sat 5:30–10pm. Closed Sept.

Miss Lucy's ★ (Kids) CARIBBEAN   For the broadest array of island cuisine, nobody does it better than Miss Lucy. Her food is the way it used to taste in the Caribbean long before anyone ever heard of upscale resorts. Before becoming the island's most famous female chef, Miss Lucy was a big hit with tourists as St. John's first female taxi driver. Her paella is scrumptious: a kettle brimming with hot Italian sausage, deep-fried chicken, shrimp, and mussels over perfectly cooked saffron rice. Traditional conch fritters appear with a picante sauce, and you can gobble them down with Miss Lucy's callaloo soup. She has a magic touch with this soup. Her fish is pulled from Caribbean waters, and does she ever know how to cook it! When a local fisherman catches a wahoo, he is often likely to bring it here for Miss Lucy to cook. Main dishes come with *fungi*, a cornmeal-and-okra side dish. At one of her "full moon parties," she'll cook a roast suckling pig. For dessert, try her banana pancakes.

Salt Pond Rd., near Estate Concordia, Coral Bay. ℂ **340/693-5244.** Reservations recommended. Main courses $18–$39. AE, MC, V. Tues–Sat 11am–3pm and 6–9pm; Sun 10am–2pm.

Shipwreck Landing SEAFOOD/CONTINENTAL   Eight miles east of Cruz Bay on the road to Salt Pond Beach, Shipwreck Landing has palms and tropical plants on a veranda overlooking the sea. The intimate bar specializes in tropical frozen drinks. Lunch features a lot more than just sandwiches, salads, and burgers—try pan-seared blackened snapper in Cajun spices, or the conch fritters. The chef shines at night, offering a pasta of the day along with such specialties as tantalizing Caribbean blackened shrimp. A lot of the fare is routine, including New York strip steak and fish and chips, but the grilled mahimahi in lime butter is worth the trip. Entertainment, mainly jazz, is featured Thursday and Sunday nights, with no cover.

34 Freeman's Ground, Rte. 107, Coral Bay. ℂ **340/693-5640.** Reservations requested. Lunch $6–$12; main courses $8–$25. AE, DISC, MC, V. Daily 11am–9pm (bar until 11pm).

INEXPENSIVE

The Quiet Mon (Finds AMERICAN   Many of us have heard the country singer Kenny Chesney sing of his life on Cinnamon Bay and his travels to Jost van Dyke in the B.V.I. He even sings of this pub, The Quiet Mon. The Knoxville-born Chesney has become even more famous for his brief marriage to Renee Zellweger. Chesney remains a frequent visitor, but count yourself lucky if he gets up late one night and sings such hits as "She Thinks My Tractor's Sexy."

The pub lies upstairs, close to the also-recommended Woody's Seafood Saloon (below). Tom Selleck and Alan Alda are just some of the celebrities who have visited here, ordering from a limited menu that consists mostly of hot dogs and French fries. You can also enjoy homemade chili and sloppy Joes. Look for lunch specials, including a homemade soup of the day. There are about six beers on tap.

Cruz Bay. ✆ **340/779-4799.** www.quietmon.com. Lunch plates $4–$7. No credit cards. Lunch specials Mon–Fri 12:30–6pm; bar daily 10am–4am.

Vie's Snack Shack ★ (Finds WEST INDIAN   Vie's looks like little more than a plywood-sided hut, but its charming and gregarious owner is known as one of the best local chefs on St. John. Her garlic chicken is famous. She also serves conch fritters, johnnycakes, island-style beans and rice with meat sauce, and coconut and pineapple tarts. Don't leave without a glass of homemade limeade. The place is open most days, but, as Vie says, "Some days, we might not be here at all"—so you'd better call before you head out.

East End Rd., Rte. 10 (13 miles east of Cruz Bay). ✆ **340/693-5033.** Main courses $5–$8. No credit cards. Tues–Sat 10am–5pm (but call first!).

Woody's Seafood Saloon SEAFOOD/AMERICAN   This local dive and hangout at Cruz Bay is more famous for its beers on tap than for its cuisine. A mix of local fishermen, taxi drivers, tour guides, aimless island drifters, and an occasional husband and wife show up here to sample the spicy conch fritters. Shrimp appears in various styles, and you can usually order fresh fish and other dishes, including burgers, blackened shark, drunken shellfish, and mussels and clams steamed in beer.

Cruz Bay (150 ft. from the ferry dock). ✆ **340/779-4625.** www.woodysseafood. com. Main courses $8–$17. AE, DISC, MC, V. Sun–Thurs 11am–1am; Fri–Sat 11am–2am.

5 BEACHES

The best beach, hands down, is **Trunk Bay ★★★**, the biggest attraction on St. John. To miss its picture-perfect shoreline of white sand would be like touring Paris and skipping the Eiffel Tower. One of the loveliest beaches in the Caribbean, it offers ideal conditions for diving, snorkeling, swimming, and sailing. There are even lifeguards on duty. The only drawback is the crowds (watch for pickpockets). Beginning snorkelers in particular are attracted to the underwater trail near the shore (see "Watersports," under "Fun in the Surf & Sun," below); you can rent snorkeling gear here. Admission is $4 per person for those over age 16. If you're coming from St. Thomas, both taxis and safari buses to Trunk Bay meet the ferries from St. Thomas when they dock at Cruz Bay.

　　Caneel Bay, the stomping ground of the rich and famous, has seven beautiful beaches on its 170 acres, and all are open to the public. **Caneel Bay Beach** is easy to reach from the main entrance of the Caneel Bay resort. A staff member at the gatehouse will provide directions. **Hawksnest Beach** is one of the most beautiful beaches near Caneel Bay, but since it's near Cruz Bay, where the ferry docks, it is the most crowded, especially when cruise ship passengers come over from St. Thomas. Safari buses and taxis from Cruz Bay will take you along Northshore Road.

The campgrounds of **Cinnamon Bay** have their own beach, where forest rangers sometimes have to remind visitors to put their swim trunks back on. This is our particular favorite, a beautiful strip of white sand with hiking trails, great windsurfing, ruins, and wild donkeys (don't feed or pet them!). Changing rooms and showers are available, and you can rent watersports equipment. Snorkeling is especially popular; you'll often see big schools of purple triggerfish. This beach is best in the morning and at midday, as afternoons are likely to be windy. A marked **nature trail,** with signs identifying the flora, loops through a tropical forest on even turf before leading up to Centerline Road.

Maho Bay Beach is immediately to the east of Cinnamon Bay, and it also borders campgrounds. As you lie on the sand, you can see a whole hillside of pitched tents. This is also a popular beach, often with the campers themselves.

Francis Bay Beach and **Watermelon Cay Beach** are just a few more of the beaches you'll encounter when traveling eastward along St. John's gently curving coastline. The beach at **Leinster Bay** is another haven for those seeking the solace of a private sunny retreat. You can swim in the bay's shallow water or snorkel over the spectacular and colorful coral reef, perhaps in the company of an occasional turtle or stingray.

The remote **Salt Pond Bay** is known to locals but often missed by visitors. It's on the beautiful coast in the southeast, adjacent to **Coral Bay.** The bay is tranquil, but the beach is somewhat rocky. It's a short walk down the hill from a parking lot. (*Beware:* A few cars have recently been broken into.) The snorkeling is good, and the bay has some fascinating tidal pools. The Ram Head Trail begins here and, winding for a mile, leads to a belvedere overlooking the bay. Facilities are meager but include an outhouse and a few tattered picnic tables.

If you want to escape the crowds, head for **Lameshur Bay Beach,** along the rugged south coast, west of Salt Pond Bay and accessible only via a bumpy dirt road. The sands are beautiful and the snorkeling is excellent. You can also take a 5-minute stroll down the road past the beach to explore the nearby ruins of an old plantation estate that was destroyed in a slave revolt.

Does St. John have a nude beach? Not officially, but lovely **Solomon Bay Beach** is a contender, although park rangers of late have sometimes asked people to give up their quest for the perfect tan.

Leave Cruz Bay on Route 20 and turn left at the park service sign, about ¼ mile past the visitor center. Park at the end of a cul-de-sac, then walk along the trail for about 15 minutes. Go early, and you'll practically have the beach to yourself. As we mentioned earlier, people also sometimes shed their swimwear at **Cinnamon Bay** (p. 94). Again, rangers frequently ask beachgoers to put their (only slightly more modest) bathing suits back on.

6 FUN IN THE SURF & SUN

St. John offers some of the best snorkeling, scuba diving, swimming, fishing, hiking, sailing, and underwater photography in the Caribbean. The island is known for Virgin Islands National Park, as well as for its coral-sand beaches, winding mountain roads, hidden coves, and trails that lead past old, bush-covered sugar cane plantations. Just don't visit St. John expecting to play golf.

WATERSPORTS

The most complete line of watersports equipment available, including rentals for windsurfing, snorkeling, kayaking, and sailing, is offered at the **Cinnamon Bay Watersports Center,** on Cinnamon Bay Beach (© 340/776-6330). One- and two-person sit-on-top kayaks rent for $15 to $30 per hour. You can also sail away in a 14-foot or 16-foot Hobie monohull **sailboat** for $30 to $50 per hour.

BOAT EXCURSIONS You can take half- and full-day boat trips, including a full-day excursion to the Baths at Virgin Gorda. **Cruz Bay Watersports** (© 340/776-6234) offers trips to the British Virgin Islands for $150, including food and beverages. *Note:* Be sure to bring your passport for any excursions to the British Virgin Islands.

Sail Safaris (© 866/820-6906; www.sailsafaris.net) offers guided tours with a captain, sailing lessons, and rentals of their fleet of Hobie catamarans. Right on the beach in Cruz Bay, just down from the ferry dock, this outfitter answers the often-asked question, "Where can we rent a small sailboat?" These catamarans, capable of sailing to the remote and wilder spots of the Virgin Islands, carry four passengers and feature a range of destinations not available by charter boat or kayak, including trips to uninhabited islands. On guided tours, passengers can go island-hopping in the B.V.I. Sail Safaris also has sailing lessons for those with an interest in sailing as a hobby. Half-day tours cost $70 per person; full-day jaunts, including lunch, go for $110; a 3-hour sailing lesson is $95.

FISHING Outfitters located on St. Thomas offer sport-fishing trips here—they'll come over and pick you up. Call the **Charter Boat**

$550 to $750 per party for a half-day of fishing. Fisherman can use hand-held rods to fish the waters in Virgin Islands National Park. Stop in at the tourist office at the St. Thomas ferry dock for a listing of fishing spots around the island.

SCUBA DIVING & SNORKELING ★★   Cruz Bay Watersports, P.O. Box 252, Cruz Bay, St. John (© **340/776-6234**; www.divestjohn. com), is a PADI and NAUI five-star diving center. Certifications can be arranged through a dive master, for $385. Beginner scuba lessons start at $110. Two-tank reef dives with all dive gear cost $95, and wreck dives, night dives, and dive packages are available. In addition, snorkel tours are offered daily for $65.

Divers can ask about scuba packages at **Low Key Watersports,** Wharfside Village (© **800/835-7718** in the U.S., or 340/693-8999; www.divelowkey.com). All wreck dives offered are two-tank/two-location dives and cost $90, with night dives also going for $90. Snorkel tours are also available at $50 per person. The center also rents watersports gear, including masks, fins, snorkels, and dive skins, and arranges day sailing trips, kayaking tours, and deep-sea fishing.

The best place for snorkeling is **Trunk Bay** (see "Beaches," above). Snorkeling gear can be rented from the Cinnamon Bay Watersports Center (see above) for $5, plus a $25 deposit. Two other choice **snorkeling spots** around St. John are **Leinster Bay** ★★ and **Haulover Bay** ★★. Usually uncrowded Leinster Bay offers some of the best snorkeling in the U.S. Virgins. The water is calm, clear, and filled with brilliantly hued tropical fish. Haulover Bay is a favorite among locals. It's often deserted, and the waters are often clearer than in other spots around St. John. The ledges, walls, and nooks here are set very close together, making the bay a lot of fun for anyone with a little bit of experience.

Beginning swimmers can experience a snorkel-like adventure with **Virgin Islands Snuba Excursions** (© **340/693-8063**; www.visnuba. com) at Trunk Bay. Divers use special equipment that allows them to breathe easily through a tube attached to an air tank above water. You'll see and experience everything as any other snorkeler would. Children ages 8 and up can participate; the fee is $65 per person.

SEA KAYAKING   **Arawak Expeditions,** based in Cruz Bay (© **800/238-8687** in the U.S., or 340/693-8312; www.arawakexp.com), provides kayaking gear, healthful meals, and experienced guides for full- and half-day outings. Trips cost $90 and $50, respectively. Multiday excursions with camping are also available; call their toll-free number if you'd like to arrange an entire vacation with them. These 5-day trips range in price from $1,100 to $2,500.

ST. JOHN

3

FUN IN THE SURF & SUN

> ## (Moments) A Water Wonderland
>
> At Trunk Bay, divers and snorkelers can follow the **National Park Underwater Trail** (© **340/776-6201**), which stretches for 650 feet and helps you identify what you see—everything from false coral to colonial anemones. You'll pass lavender sea fans and schools of silversides. Rangers are on hand to provide information. There is a $4 admission fee to access the beach.

WINDSURFING The windsurfing at Cinnamon Bay is some of the best anywhere, for either the beginner or the expert. The **Cinnamon Bay Watersports Center** (see above) rents high-quality equipment for all levels, even for kids. Boards cost $25 to $65 an hour; a 2-hour introductory lesson costs $80.

MORE OUTDOOR ADVENTURE

St. John has the most rewarding hiking in the Virgin Islands. The terrain ranges from arid and dry (in the east) to moist and semitropical (in the northwest). The island boasts more than 800 species of plants, 160 species of birds, and more than 20 trails maintained in fine form by the island's crew of park rangers. Much of the land on the island is designated as **Virgin Islands National Park.** Visitors must stop by the **Cruz Bay Visitor Center,** where you can pick up the park brochure, which includes a map of the park, and the *Virgin Islands National Park News,* which has the latest information on park activities. It's important to carry a lot of water and wear sunscreen and insect repellent when you hike.

St. John is laced with clearly marked walking paths. At least 20 of these originate from Northshore Road (Rte. 20) or from the island's main east-west artery, Centerline Road (Rte. 10). Each is marked at its starting point with a preplanned itinerary; the walks can last anywhere from 10 minutes to 2 hours. Maps are available from the national park headquarters at Cruz Bay.

One of our favorite hikes, the **Annaberg Historic Trail** (identified by the U.S. National Park Service as trail no. 10), requires only about a half-mile stroll. It departs from a clearly marked point along the island's north coast, near the junction of routes 10 and 20. This self-guided tour passes the partially restored ruins of a manor house built during the 1700s, and signs along the way give historical and botanical data. Visiting the ruins is free. If you want to prolong your hiking experience, take the **Leinster Bay Trail** (trail no. 11), which begins near the point where trail no. 10 ends. It leads past mangrove swamps and coral inlets rich with plant and marine life; markers identify some of the plants and animals. Scattered throughout the park, and sometimes hidden by plants, are mysterious petroglyphs incised into boulders and cliffs. Their age and origin are unknown.

Near the beach at **Cinnamon Bay,** there's a marked nature trail, with signs identifying the flora. It's a relatively flat walk through a tropical forest, eventually leading straight up to Centerline Road.

The **National Park Service** (© **340/776-6201;** www.nps.gov/viis) provides a number of ranger-led activities. One of the most popular is the guided 2.5-mile **Reef Bay Hike.** Included is a stop at the only known petroglyphs on the island and a tour of the sugar-mill ruins. A park ranger discusses the area's natural and cultural history along the way. The hike starts at 9:30am on Monday, Tuesday, Thursday, and Friday and costs $21 per person. Reservations are required and can be made by phone (at least 2–3 weeks in advance).

Another series of hikes traversing the more arid eastern section of St. John originates at clearly marked points along the island's **southeastern tip,** off Route 107. Many of the trails wind through the grounds of 18th-century plantations, past ruined schoolhouses, rum distilleries, molasses factories, and great houses, many of which are covered with lush, encroaching vines and trees.

---

7 EXPLORING ST. JOHN

The best way to see St. John quickly, especially if you're on a cruise ship layover, is to take a 2-hour **taxi tour.** The cost is $50 for one or two passengers, or $25 per person for three or more. If you want to go for 4 hours, expect to pay around $60. Almost any taxi at Cruz Bay will take you on these tours, or you can call the **St. John Taxi Association** (© **340/693-7530**).

Many visitors spend time at **Cruz Bay,** where the ferry docks. This village has interesting bars, restaurants, boutiques, and pastel-painted houses. It's a bit sleepy, but relaxing after the fast pace of St. Thomas.

Most cruise ship passengers dart through Cruz Bay and head for the island's biggest attraction, **Virgin Islands National Park ★★** (© **340/776-6201**). The park totals 12,624 acres, including submerged lands and water adjacent to St. John, and has more than 20 miles of hiking trails to explore. See "More Outdoor Adventure," above, for information on trails and organized park activities.

Other major sights on the island include **Trunk Bay** (see "Beaches," above), one of the world's most beautiful beaches, and **Fort Berg** (also called Fortsberg), at Coral Bay, which served as the base for the

> ## (Fun Facts St. John's Mascot
>
> The mongoose (plural *mongooses*) was brought to St. John to kill rats. It has practically been adopted as the island mascot—watch for mongooses darting across roads.

soldiers who brutally crushed the 1733 slave revolt. Finally, try to make time for the **Annaberg Ruins** on Leinster Bay Road, where the Danes maintained a thriving plantation and sugar mill after 1718. It's located off Northshore Road, east of Trunk Bay. Admission is free. On certain days of the week (dates vary), guided walks of the area are given by park rangers. For information on the **Annaberg Historic Trail,** see p. 104.

8 SHOPPING

Compared to St. Thomas, St. John's shopping isn't much, but what's here is interesting. The boutiques and shops of Cruz Bay are individualized and quite special. Most of the shops are clustered at **Mongoose Junction** (North Shore Rd., Cruz Bay), in a woodsy area beside the roadway, about a 5-minute walk from the ferry dock.

Before you leave the island, you'll want to visit the recently expanded **Wharfside Village** (© **340/693-8210;** www.wharfside village.com), just a few steps from the ferry departure point. This complex of courtyards, alleys, and shady patios is a mishmash of boutiques, along with some restaurants, fast-food joints, and bars.

Bajo El Sol, Mongoose Junction (© **340/693-7070;** www.bajo elsolgallery.com), is a cooperative and award-winning gallery displaying the work of many island artists. For sale are paintings, sculpture, ceramics, and jewelry.

Bamboula, Mongoose Junction (© **340/693-8699;** www. bamboulastjohn.com), has an exotic and very appealing collection of gifts from St. John, the Caribbean, India, Indonesia, and Central Africa. The store also has men and women's clothing under its own label—hand-batiked soft cottons and rayons made for comfort in a hot climate.

Here's your chance to pick up a unique item. A total of 100 artists, artisans, and designers have their work showcased at the **Best of Both Worlds** (© **340/639-8520;** www.thebestofstjohn.com), in Mongoose Junction. The shop is a great place for one-of-a-kind gifts and local art. Many award-winning designers display their work, ranging from jewelry to art glass, lamps, dishware, and clocks. You will find especially good buys in artistic glasswork.

If you're planning to hike the trails of lush St. John, and you've arrived unprepared, **Big Planet Adventure Outfitters,** Mongoose Junction (© **340/776-6638**), is the best place to go to stock up on outdoor clothing. Reef footwear and Naot sandals are sold, along with a selection of other durable items, including backpacks, luggage, sunglasses, and the like.

Sun Angels, Mongoose Junction (© **340/779-6274**), sells hand-painted clothing created in Costa Rica. This fine tropical clothing is designed for women only.

Coconut Coast Studios, Frank Bay (© **800/887-3798** or 340/776-6944; www.coconutcoaststudios.com), is the studio of Elaine Estern, best known for her Caribbean landscapes. It's 5 minutes from Cruz Bay; walk along the waterfront, bypassing Gallows Point. The outlet also sells calendars, gifts, limited edition prints, and lithographs. From December to May, the studio hosts a free sunset cocktail party Wednesday 5:30 to 7pm.

Donald Schnell Studio ★, next to the Texaco gas station, Cruz Bay (© **340/776-6420;** www.donaldschnell.com), is a working studio and gallery where Mr. Schnell and his assistants have created one of the finest collections of handmade pottery, sculpture, and blown glass in the Caribbean. The staff can be seen working daily. They're known for their rough-textured coral work. Water fountains are a specialty item, as are house signs and coral-pottery dinnerware. The studio will ship all over the world, so no need to worry about carrying it all back on the plane. Go in and discuss any particular design you may have in mind.

ⓘ Tips   The Best Shopping Day

The most fun shopping on the island takes place on **St. John Saturday** ★, a colorful, drum-beating, spicy feast for the senses, held on the last Saturday of every month. This daylong event begins early in the morning in the center of town and spills across the park. Vendors hawk handmade items, ranging from jewelry to handicrafts and clothing, and food made from local ingredients. One vendor concocts soothing salves from recipes passed on by her ancestors; another designs and makes porcelain earrings; another flavors chicken and burgers with her own wonderful secret hickory barbecue sauce; yet another hollows out and carves gourds from local calabash trees.

Every Ting, Bay Street, Cruz Bay (© **340/693-7730**), is the best of the all-purpose stores, and it's also a gathering point for locals and visitors alike. It's like a nerve center where you can drop in for a "cuppa" or to use the Internet. You can find reading material here for the beach along with music CDs, cotton resort wear, and of course campy picture frames decorated with pinkish shells gathered on the beach.

Fabric Mill, Mongoose Junction (© **340/776-6194**), features silk-screened and batik fabrics from around the world and around the corner. Vibrant rugs and bed, bathroom, and table linens can add a Caribbean flair to your home. Whimsical soft sculpture, sarongs, scarves, and handbags are also made here.

The Marketplace, Cruz Bay (© **800/626-3445** or 340/776-6455), with its dramatic architecture and native stone, is a cool place to shop on a hot day, thanks to its verandas and courtyards. It's ideal if you're renting a condo on St. John, as many visitors do, as the market here includes everything from a hardware shop to a video store, plus healthcare needs and a lot more.

R&I PATTON Goldsmithing, Mongoose Junction (© **340/776-6548;** http://pattongold.com), is one of the oldest businesses on the island. Three-quarters of the merchandise here is made on St. John, with a large selection of jewelry in sterling silver, gold, and precious stones. Also featured are the works of goldsmiths from outstanding American studios, as well as Spanish coins.

The location of the **Shop at Caneel Bay,** in the Caneel Bay resort (© **340/776-6111**), guarantees both an upscale clientele and an upscale assortment of merchandise. Scattered over two simple, elegant floors are drugstore items, books, sundries, and handicrafts, as well as some unusual artwork and pieces of expensive jewelry. There are also racks of resort wear and sportswear for men and women. The shop carries handbags and watches by top designers.

9 ST. JOHN AFTER DARK

Bring a good book. When it comes to nightlife, St. John is no St. Thomas, and everybody here seems to want to keep it that way. Most people are content to have a leisurely dinner and then head to bed.

The **Caneel Bay Bar,** at the Caneel Bay resort (© **340/776-6111**), has live music Tuesday to Sunday 8:30 to 10:30pm. The most popular drinks are the Cool Caneel (local rum with sugar, lime, and anisette) and the trademark Plantation Punch (lime and orange juice with three kinds of rum, bitters, and nutmeg).

If you'd like to drink and gossip with the locals, try **JJ's Texas Coast Café,** Cruz Bay (© 340/776-6908), a real dive, across the park from the ferry dock, open 8am to 9pm. The margaritas here are lethal. Also at Cruz Bay, check out the action at **Fred's** (© 340/776-6363), across from the Lime Inn. Fred's brings in bands and has dancing on Friday nights. It's just a little hole in the wall and can get crowded fast. It's open 8am to 7pm, but stays open until Saturday morning.

St. John's best sports bar is **Skinny Legs,** Emmaus, Coral Bay, beyond the fire station (© 340/779-4982). This shack made of tin and wood also happens to have the best burgers in St. John. (The chili dogs aren't bad, either.) The yachting crowd likes to hang out here, though you wouldn't know it at first glance—it often seems that the richer they are, the poorer they dress. The bar has a satellite dish, a dartboard, and horseshoe pits. There is live music on Friday and Saturday nights during high season when it stays open until midnight; regular hours are 11am to 9pm.

Morgan's Mango (© 340/693-8141), a restaurant, is also one of the hottest watering holes on the island. It's in Cruz Bay, across from the national park dock. Count yourself lucky if you get in on a crowded night in winter. The place became famous locally when it turned away Harrison Ford, who was vacationing at Caneel Bay. Thursday night is Margarita Night, and Tuesday night is Lobster Night.

Woody's Seafood Saloon, Cruz Bay (p. 100; © 340/779-4625), is the previously recommended local dive and hangout at Cruz Bay, 150 feet from the ferry dock. It draws both visitors and a cross section of island life from expats to villa owners. Michigan-born Woody Mann, the bartender, is often compared to the character of the same name on the sitcom *Cheers.* The place is particularly popular during happy hour from 3 to 6pm and it's about the only place on the island you can order food as late as 1am. The joint jumps Sunday to Thursday 11am to 1am, Friday and Saturday 11:50am to 2am.

Of course, there is also **The Quiet Mon** (p. 99), which is adjacent to Woody's. This is St. John's very own Irish pub and one of the hottest spots on the island.

4

St. Croix

At 84 square miles, St. Croix is the largest of the U.S. Virgin Islands. At the east end—which actually is the easternmost point of the United States—the terrain is rocky and arid. The west end is lusher and even includes a small "rain forest" of mango, mahogany, tree ferns, and dangling lianas. Between the two extremes are beautiful beaches, rolling hills, pastures, and, increasingly, miles of condos.

Christopher Columbus named the island Santa Cruz (Holy Cross) when he landed on November 14, 1493. He anchored his ship off the north shore but was quickly driven away by the spears, arrows, and axes of the Carib Indians. The French laid claim to the island in 1650; the Danes purchased it from them in 1733. Under their rule, the slave trade and sugar cane fields flourished until the latter half of the 19th century. Danish architecture and influence can still be seen on the island today.

You will find that St. Croix is more relaxed than St. Thomas, and the locals are friendlier, although there have been acts of violence and hostility against visitors in the past. While gambling has been introduced at one hotel, this has not changed the overall texture of the island. It has, however, attracted a more jaded Atlantic City– or Las Vegas–type visitor. St. Croix is being rapidly developed, but it has many years to go before approaching the mass tourism of St. Thomas.

1 ORIENTATION

GETTING THERE
By Plane
All flights to St. Croix land at the **Henry E. Rohlsen Airport,** Estate Mannings Bay (© **340/778-1012**), on the southern coast of the island. There are no ATMs at the airport, so come prepared with cash. Take a taxi to your hotel or rent a car. The major car-rental firms maintain kiosks here, but make reservations before you arrive.

American Airlines (© **800/433-7300;** www.aa.com) offers the most frequent and most reliable service to St. Croix. Passengers flying to the island connect through San Juan from either New York City's JFK airport or Newark, New Jersey. From San Juan, **American Eagle** (© **800/433-7300;** www.aa.com) offers several daily nonstop flights

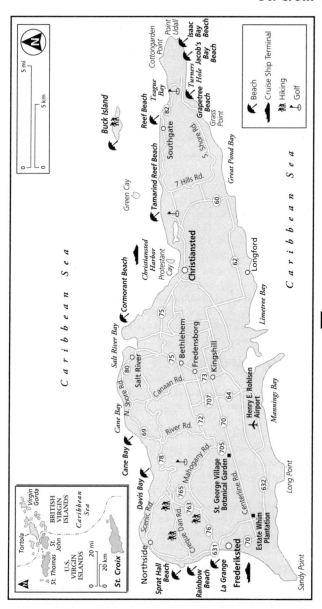

> ## Staying Safe on St. Croix
>
> Violent crime involving tourists on St. Croix is an uncommon
> occurrence. However, random acts of violence against visitors
> (even murder) have happened in the past. Even if St. Croix is
> your idea of paradise, you should still approach the island as
> you would any unknown territory. A few simple precautions
> can go a long way. Petty theft comprises the majority of com-
> plaints, so you'll be wise to keep valuables at your hotel (in
> the safe) and to lock your car. And remember, you should
> never walk to your hotel alone after a night out.

to St. Croix. There's also one flight daily from Miami, with one stop
(but no change of plane) in St. Thomas. The flight originates in
Dallas–Fort Worth, American's biggest hub.

Travel time to St. Croix from New York is 4 hours, from Chicago
5$1/2$ hours, from Miami 3$1/2$ hours, and from Puerto Rico 20 minutes.
There are no direct flights to St. Croix from Canada or the United
Kingdom; connections are made via Miami.

There are also easy air links between St. Thomas and St. Croix.
American Eagle (see American Airlines, above, for contact info) has
three daily flights; in addition, **Seaborne Airlines** (© **888/359-8687**
or 340/773-6442; www.seaborneairlines.com) offers 17 flights daily.
Flight time is only 25 minutes.

VISITOR INFORMATION

You can begin your explorations at the **St. Croix Visitor Bureau,** 53A
Company St., in Christiansted (© **340/773-0495**), a yellow building
across from the open-air market. It's open Monday to Friday 8am to
5pm.

The U.S. Virgin Islands Division of Tourism also has an office at
the Customs House Building, Strand Street (© **340/772-0357;** www.
stcroixtourism.com), in Frederiksted.

Tourist offices provide free maps to the island. *St. Croix This Week,*
distributed free to cruise ship and air passengers, has detailed maps of
Christiansted, Frederiksted, and the entire island, pinpointing individual attractions, hotels, shops, and restaurants. If you plan to do
extensive touring of the island, purchase *The Official Road Map of the
U.S. Virgin Islands,* available at island bookstores.

ISLAND LAYOUT

St. Croix has only two sizable towns: Christiansted on the north-
central shore and Frederiksted in the southwest. The Henry E.

Refinery, the major industry on the island. No roads circle St. Croix's coast.

To continue east from Christiansted, take Route 82 (also called the East End Rd.). Route 75 will take you west from Christiansted through the central heartland, then south to the Hess Oil Refinery. Melvin H. Evans Highway, Route 66, runs along the southern part of the island. You can connect with this route in Christiansted and head west all the way to Frederiksted.

Christiansted

This town's historic district is in the center bordering Veterans Drive, which runs along the waterfront. The district is split by Kronprinds-ens Gade (Rte. 308 or Main St.), which is connected to Veterans Drive by a number of shop-filled little streets, including Gutters Gade, Trompeter Gade, and Raadets Gade. The **visitor information center** is located at 53A Company St. The center of Christiansted can get very congested, and driving around is difficult because of the one-way streets. It's usually more practical to park your car and cover the small district on foot. You will find open-air parking on both sides of Fort Christiansvaern.

The North Shore

This coastal strip that stretches from Cottongarden Point, the eastern tip of the island, all the way west past Christiansted and up and around Salt River Bay, comes to an end as it reaches the settlement of Northside in the far west. It is the most touristy region of St. Croix, site of the best beaches, the most hotels, and the finest resorts and shopping. It is also the takeoff point (at Christiansted Harbor) for excursions to Buck Island, St. Croix's most popular attraction. Many visitors confine their stay in St. Croix entirely to the north coast. The northern coastline is not only long but also diverse, going from a lush tropical forest that envelops most of the northwest to the eastern sector, which is dry with palm-lined beaches.

The East End

The East End begins immediately east of Christiansted, the capital, taking in Tamarind Reef Beach and Reef Beach before it reaches Teague Bay, coming to an end at Cottongarden Point, the far eastern tip of St. Croix. This section of St. Croix is linked by Route 82 (also called East End Rd.). The Buccaneer, the major resort of St. Croix, is found here, along with the Tamarind Reef Hotel. The area is far less congested than the section immediately to the west of Christiansted, and many visitors prefer the relative isolation and tranquillity of the East End. This section of St. Croix is relatively dry, the landscape a bit arid, but its compensating factor is a number of palm-lined beaches. The best place for a beach picnic is Cramer Park at the far eastern tip, a U.S.V.I. territorial beach popular with islanders.

Frederiksted

It's hard to get lost in tiny Frederiksted. It is a port of call for cruises, so sometimes you can find yourself lost in a crowd. Most visitors head for the central historic district, where the Frederiksted Pier juts out into the sea. The two major streets, both of which run parallel to the water, are Strand Street and King Street.

---

2 GETTING AROUND

If you plan to do some serious sightseeing on the island, you'll need to rent a car, as getting around by public transportation is a slow, uneven process. There is bus service, but you might end up stranded somewhere and unable to reach your destination without a taxi.

BY CAR

Remember to **drive on the left.** In most rural areas, the speed limit is 35 mph; certain parts of the major artery, Route 66, are 55 mph. In towns and urban areas, the speed limit is 20 mph. Keep in mind that if you're going into the "bush country," the roads are very difficult. Sometimes the government smoothes the roads out before the rainy season begins (often in Oct or Nov), but they deteriorate rapidly.

St. Croix offers moderately priced car rentals, even on cars with automatic transmissions and air-conditioning. However, because of the island's higher-than-normal accident rate (which is partly the result of visitors who forget about driving on the left-hand side of the road), insurance costs are a bit higher than elsewhere. **Avis** (© 800/331-1212 or 340/778-9355; www.avis.com), **Budget** (© 800/472-3325 or 340/778-9636; www.budget.com), and **Hertz** (© 800/654-3131 or 340/778-1402; www.hertz.com) all maintain headquarters at the airport; look for their kiosks near the baggage-claim areas. Collision-damage insurance costs $14 per day, depending on the company and size of car, and we feel that it's a wise investment. Some credit card companies grant you collision-damage protection if you pay for the rental with their card. Verify coverage before you go.

BY TAXI

At Henry E. Rohlsen International Airport, official taxi rates are posted. From the airport, expect to pay about $16 to $32 to Christiansted and about $12 to $24 to Frederiksted. Cabs are unmetered, so agree on the rate before you get in. Taxis line up at the docks in

BY BUS

Air-conditioned **buses** run between Christiansted and Frederiksted about every 45 minutes daily between 5:30am and 8pm. They start at Tide Village, to the east of Christiansted, and go along Route 75 to the Golden Rock Shopping Center. They transfer along Route 70, with stopovers at the Sunny Isle Shopping Center, La Reine Shopping Center, St. George Village Botanical Garden, and Whim Plantation Museum before reaching Frederiksted. The fare is $1, or 55¢ for seniors. For more information, call *©* **340/773-1664.**

(*Fast Facts*) St. Croix

Banks Several major banks are represented in St. Croix. Most are open Monday to Thursday 9am to 3pm and Friday 9am to 4pm. Virgin Islands Community Bank has a branch at 6 King's St. (*©* **340/773-0504**) in Christiansted and another branch on Strand Street in Frederiksted.

Business Hours Typical business hours are Monday to Friday 9am to 5pm, Saturday 9am to 1pm.

Cameras & Film There is no specific outlet devoted to cameras and film. The best stock, however, is found at **Kmart** at the Sunny Isle Shopping Center, Space 1 (*©* **340/719-9190**).

Doctors For a referral, call **Sunny Isle Medical Center** (*©* **340/778-0069**).

Drugstores Try the **Golden Rock Pharmacy,** Golden Rock Shopping Center (*©* **340/773-7666**), open Monday to Saturday 8am to 7pm and Sunday 8am to 3pm.

Emergencies To reach the police, fire department, or an ambulance, call *©* **911.**

Hospitals The main facility is **Governor Juan F. Luis Hospital & Medical Center,** 4007 Estate Diamond Ruby (*©* **340/778-6311**).

Internet Access You can go to **A Better Copy,** 52 Company St., Christiansted (*©* **340/692-5303**), which charges $10 for every hour.

Laundry Try **Tropical Cleaners & Launderers,** 16–17 King Cross St. (*©* **340/773-3635**), in Christiansted. Hours are Monday to Saturday 7:30am to 5:30pm.

Maps See "Visitor Information," in "Orientation," above.

Newspapers & Magazines Newspapers such as *The Miami Herald* are flown into St. Croix daily. St. Croix also has its own newspaper, *St. Croix Avis*. *Time* and *Newsweek* are widely sold as well. Your best source of local information is *St. Croix This Week*, which is distributed free by the tourist offices.

Police Police headquarters is on Market Street in Christiansted. In case of emergency, dial (© **911;** for nonemergency assistance, call (© **340/778-2211.**

Post Office The post office is on Company Street ((© **340/773-3586**), in Christiansted. The hours of operation are Monday to Friday 8:30am to 4:30pm. See "Fast Facts: St. Thomas" for current postal rates.

Safety St. Croix is safer than St. Thomas. Although there have been random acts of violence against tourists in the past, even murder, most crime on the island is petty theft, usually of possessions left unguarded at the beach while vacationers go into the water for a swim, or muggings (rarely violent) of visitors wandering the dark streets and back alleys of Frederiksted and Christiansted at night. Exercise caution at night by sticking to the heart of Christiansted and not wandering around in Frederiksted. Avoid night strolls along beaches. Night driving in remote parts of the island can also be risky; you might be carjacked and robbed at knifepoint.

Taxes The only local tax is an 8% surcharge added to all hotel rates.

Taxis For an airport taxi, call (© **340/778-1088;** in Christiansted call (© **340/773-5020.**

Telephone & Fax You can dial direct to St. Croix from the mainland by using the 340 area code. Omit the 340 for local calls. A local call at a phone booth costs 25¢. Make long-distance, international, and collect calls as you would on the U.S. mainland by dialing 0 or your long-distance provider.

Toilets There are few public restrooms, except at the major beaches and the airport. In Christiansted, the National Park Service maintains some restrooms within the public park beside Fort Christiansvaern.

Tourist Offices See "Visitor Information," above.

3 WHERE TO STAY

St. Croix's deluxe resorts lie along the North Shore; its charming old waterfront inns are mostly in Christiansted. You may also choose to stay at a former plantation or in a condo complex, which offers privacy and the chance to save money by preparing your own meals. The choice is yours: a location in Christiansted or Frederiksted close to shops and nightlife, but away from the beach; or an isolated resort where, chances are, your accommodations will be either on the beach or a short walk from it. From such resorts, you'll have to drive into town for a shopping binge or for restaurants and clubs.

In general, rates are steep, but in summer, hotels slash prices by about 25% to 50%. All rooms are subject to an 8% hotel tax, not included in the rates given below.

Note: If you need a hair dryer, pack your own. Apparently, a lot of visitors have packed up hotel hair dryers upon departure, and some innkeepers are reluctant to provide them.

NORTH SHORE
Very Expensive
The Buccaneer ★★★ (Kids) This large, luxurious, family-owned resort has three of the island's best beaches, and the best sports program on St. Croix. The property was once a cattle ranch and a sugar plantation; its first estate house, which dates from the mid–17th century, stands near a freshwater pool. Accommodations are either in the main building or in one of the beachside properties. The baronially arched main building has a lobby opening onto landscaped terraces, with a sea vista on two sides and Christiansted to the west. The rooms are fresh and comfortable, though some of the standard units are a bit small. All have wicker or mahogany furnishings and full bathrooms. The best bathrooms are in the Beachside Doubloons, and come complete with whirlpool tubs. A free Kid's Camp is available year-round.

P.O. Box 25200, Gallows Bay (3km/2 miles east of Christiansted on Rte. 82), Christiansted, St. Croix, U.S.V.I. 00824. (C) **800/255-3881** in the U.S., or 340/712-2100. Fax 340/712-2105. www.thebuccaneer.com. 138 units. Winter $340–$695 double, $640–$990 suite; off season $295–$460 double, $440–$730 suite. Children 17 and under stay free in parent's room. Rates include American breakfast. AE, DISC, MC, V. **Amenities:** 4 restaurants; bar; babysitting; children's program; health club & spa; 2 pools (outdoor); room service; 8 tennis courts (2 lit); watersports equipment/rentals. *In room:* A/C, TV, fridge, hair dryer, Wi-Fi (free).

Expensive
Chenay Bay Beach Resort ★ (Kids) These West Indian–style cottages are nestled on a 30-acre beach. Home to one of the island's

finest beaches for swimming, snorkeling, and windsurfing, Chenay Bay is just 3 miles east of Christiansted and is a terrific choice for families thanks to the spacious cottages and the children's programs. With a quiet and barefoot-casual ambience, each cottage contains a fully equipped kitchenette and bathroom. The 20 original cottages are smaller and more weathered than the newer duplexes numbered 21 to 50. Accommodations are medium in size, with firm mattresses resting on comfortable beds. Most bathrooms are compact but with adequate shelf space and tubs.

Rte. 82, East End Rd. (P.O. Box 24600), St. Croix, U.S.V.I. 00824. ℂ **866/226-8677** in the U.S., or 340/773-2918. Fax 340/773-6665. www.chenaybay.com. 50 cottages. Winter $299–$683 cottage for 1 or 2; off season $211–$468 cottage for 1 or 2. Extra person $25. Children 17 and under stay free in parent's room. $50 per person for all meals. AE, DISC, MC, V. **Amenities:** Restaurant; bar; babysitting; children's program; pool (outdoor); 2 tennis courts (lit); watersports equipment/rentals; Wi-Fi (free in lobby). *In room:* A/C, TV, fridge, kitchenette.

Divi Carina Bay Resort and Casino ★   Opening onto 1,000 feet of sugar-white beach, this resort brought gambling to the U.S. Virgin Islands. That fact seems to obscure its success as a place of barefoot elegance and a top resort property. Accommodations feature oceanfront guest rooms and villa suites with views of the Caribbean. Rooms are good size and well equipped with computer/fax lines, VCRs, a small kitchen, full bathrooms, and balconies. We prefer the accommodations on the ground floor as they are closer to the water's edge. The 20 villas across the street are about a 3-minute walk from the sands. The most up-to-date building contains 50 oceanfront accommodations with balconies. You can simply go upstairs for a massage at the spa on the top floor.

5025 Estate Turner Hole, Christiansted, St. Croix, U.S.V.I. 00820. ℂ **800/823-9352** in the U.S., or 340/773-9700. Fax 340/773-6802. www.diviresorts.com. 180 units. Winter $216–$295 double, from $400 suite; off season $142–$195 double, from $265 suite. Children 15 and under stay free in parent's room. AE, MC, V. **Amenities:** 2 restaurants; 2 bars; babysitting; casino; health club & spa; 2 pools (outdoor); tennis court (lit); watersports equipment/rentals; Wi-Fi (free in lobby). *In room:* A/C, TV, hair dryer, kitchen (in some).

The Palms at Pelican Cove ★★   This family-oriented resort stands on 7 acres of beachfront property at a point 3 miles northwest of Christiansted. Its bedrooms are inviting in a Caribbean style with an upgraded decor. Designed in a boxy, modern-looking series of rectangles, it has outcroppings of exposed natural stone, striking a balance between seclusion and accessibility. Long Reef lies less than 100 feet offshore from the resort's sandy beachfront. The spacious guest rooms have a private balcony or patio with ocean views. Social life revolves around an open-air lounge, bar, and restaurant with sea views.

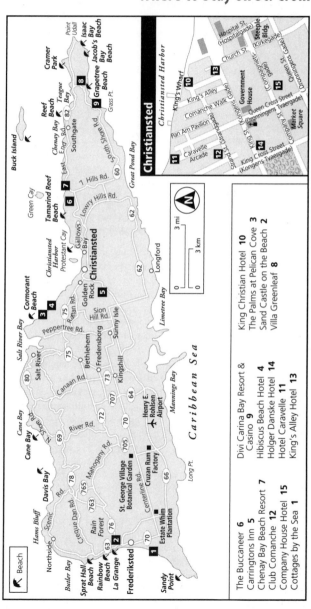

The Buccaneer **6**
Carringtons Inn **5**
Chenay Bay Beach Resort **7**
Club Comanche **12**
Company House Hotel **15**
Cottages by the Sea **1**

Divi Carina Bay Resort &
Casino **9**
Hibiscus Beach Hotel **4**
Holger Danske Hotel **14**
Hotel Caravelle **11**
King's Alley Hotel **13**

King Christian Hotel **10**
The Palms at Pelican Cove **3**
Sand Castle on the Beach **2**
Villa Greenleaf **8**

4126 La Grande Princesse, St. Croix, U.S.V.I. 00820. ℂ **800/548-4460** or 340/718-8920. Fax 340/718-0218. 35 units. $150–$269 double, $225–$309 suite. AE, MC, V. **Amenities:** Restaurant; bar; Internet (free); pool (outdoor); watersports (scuba).

CHRISTIANSTED
Moderate

Hibiscus Beach Hotel ★   This hotel, on one of the island's best beaches, attracts a lively clientele. The accommodations are in six two-story white-and-blue buildings. Each guest room is a retreat unto itself, with a private patio or balcony and a view of the Caribbean, plus tasteful Caribbean furnishings and floral prints. Shower-only bathrooms are small but well maintained. Guests who stay here are a bit isolated and will find a car useful.

4131 La Grande Princesse (about 3 miles northwest of Christiansted, beside Rte. 75, next to the Cormorant), St. Croix, U.S.V.I. 00820. ℂ **800/442-0121** in the U.S., or 340/718-4042. Fax 340/718-7668. www.1hibiscus.com. 38 units. Winter $190–$200 double; off season $140–$150 double. Honeymoon, dive, and golf packages available. AE, DISC, MC, V. **Amenities:** Restaurant; babysitting; pool (outdoor); watersports (snorkeling). *In room:* A/C, ceiling fan, hair dryer, Wi-Fi (free).

Hotel Caravelle ★ (Value)   The biggest hotel in the historic core of Christiansted, Hotel Caravelle often caters to international business travelers who prefer to be near the center of town. Many sports activities, such as sailing, deep-sea fishing, snorkeling, scuba, golf, and tennis, can be arranged at the reception desk. A swimming pool and sun deck face the water, and all the shopping and activities in town are close at hand. The Caribbean restaurant **RumRunners** (p. 128) sits right on the water.

   Accommodations, which are generally spacious and comfortably furnished, are priced according to their views. Bedrooms are a bit small but are still comfortable. We prefer the rooms on the third floor because they have high ceilings and the best views, although there are no elevators. The least expensive units open onto a parking lot. Be sure to ask when booking to avoid the view of your rental car.

44A Queen Cross St., Christiansted, St. Croix, U.S.V.I. 00820. ℂ **800/524-0410** or 340/773-0687. Fax 340/778-7004. www.hotelcaravelle.com. 44 units. Winter $150–$180 double, $299 suite; off season $128–$148 double, $209 suite. AE, DC, DISC, MC, V. **Amenities:** Restaurant; bar; pool (outdoor); Wi-Fi (free). *In room:* A/C, TV, fridge.

King Christian Hotel   This historic property is directly on the waterfront, right in the heart of everything. All of the front rooms have two double beds and a private balcony overlooking the harbor. The no-frills economy rooms have two single beds or one double and no view or balcony, although they have been recently redone with fresh mattresses and renewed fixtures in the tiny bathrooms. While it's not on a beach, there is a sun deck, pool, and shaded patio. The watersports center in the lobby offers daily trips to Buck Island's famous snorkeling trail. In this price category, however, we find King's Alley, a neighbor, far more appealing (see the review below).

59 King St., P.O. Box 24467, Christiansted, St. Croix, U.S.V.I. 00824. ✆ **800/524-2012** in the U.S., or 340/773-6330. Fax 340/773-9411. www.kingchristian.com. 38 units. Winter $120–$155 double; off season $115–$140 double. Children 11 and under stay free in parent's room. AE, DC, DISC, MC, V. **Amenities:** 2 restaurants; exercise room; pool (outdoor); extensive watersports. *In room:* A/C, ceiling fan, TV, Wi-Fi (free).

King's Alley Hotel ★ This inn, restored in 2007, stands at water's edge, near Christiansted Harbor's yacht basin. We like the atmosphere of the Alley much better than its neighbor, the King Christian Hotel (see above). Although short on amenities, this is one of our favorites in town. More charm. Better decor. More inviting ambience—a real St. Croix feeling. The King's Alley is furnished with a distinctly Mediterranean flair. Many of its rooms—which are small to medium-size—overlook its courtyard terrace surrounded by tropical plants. All rooms have twin or king-size beds with good mattresses, and the deluxe units have four-poster mahogany beds.

57 King St., Christiansted, St. Croix, U.S.V.I. 00820. ✆ **800/843-3574** or 340/773-0103. Fax 340/773-4431. 35 units. Winter $158 double; off season $89 double. AE, DC, DISC, MC, V. **Amenities:** 3 restaurants; pool (outdoor); watersports equipment/rentals; Wi-Fi (free in lobby). *In room:* A/C, TV.

Inexpensive

Club Comanche This famous old West Indian inn is right on the Christiansted waterfront. It's based around a 250-year-old Danish-inspired main house, once the home of Alexander Hamilton. Because accommodations come in such a wide range of styles and sizes, your opinion of this place is likely to be influenced almost entirely by your room assignment. Some of its small- to medium-size bedrooms have slanted ceilings (which can be either charming or cramping), old chests, and mahogany mirrors. A more modern addition is reached by a covered bridge that passes over a shopping street to the waterside. Most of the units face the pool instead of the ocean. Club Comanche also features **Comanche Club** (p. 128), the most popular restaurant in Christiansted.

1 Strand St., Christiansted, St. Croix, U.S.V.I. 00820. ✆ **800/524-2066** or 340/773-0210. Fax 340/713-9145. www.usvi.net/hotel/comanche. 42 units. Winter $100–$200 double; off season $65–$150 double. MC, V. **Amenities:** Restaurant; bar; pool (outdoor); watersports equipment/rentals. *In room:* A/C, TV, hair dryer, Internet (free).

Company House Hotel ★ For years this hotel in the heart of Christiansted was known as the Danish Manor, and, as such, it enjoyed a large fan base. Today it's been taken over and renamed; it's also been vastly restored and is better than ever. Lying 1¹/₂ blocks from the waterfront, the hotel has also been expanded and should have reached its potential of 33 rooms (see below) when you check in. This handsomely decorated hotel was once a warehouse for the Danish West Indies Company. All accommodations have a bright tropical decor. From some of the rooms there is no view of the sea; however, accommodations on the top (third) floor overlook the sands of Protestant Cay.

2 Company St., Christiansted, St. Croix, U.S.V.I. ✆ **340/773-1377.** Fax 340/719-5161. www.companyhousehotel.com. 33 units. Winter $125 double, $160 suite; off season $85 double, $150 suite. Rates include continental breakfast. AE, MC, V. **Amenities:** Piano bar; pool (outdoor). *In room:* A/C, TV, fridge, Wi-Fi (free).

Holger Danske Hotel (Value)   This hotel is one of the best bets in the heart of town for the budget traveler. It's located right on the boardwalk, with the harbor and docks for boating excursions only a breath away. The rooms are pleasantly furnished but small; each has a private furnished balcony. If you're looking to save even more money, book one of the units with an efficiency kitchen, where you can cook your own small meals. The property has a pool patio and a garden path walkway, but only the superior rooms open onto the harbor and the cay. On-site is the **Mix Lounge**, a fine addition to the food and nightlife scene in town, offering an eclectic choice of Asian and American cuisines, as well as a powerful Sunday brunch.

1200 King Cross St., Christiansted, St. Croix, U.S.V.I. 00820. ✆ **340/773-3600.** Fax 340/773-8828. www.holgerhotel.com. 39 units. Winter $125–$165 double; off season $115–$137 double. Children 17 and under stay free in parent's room. AE, DC, DISC, MC, V. **Amenities:** Restaurant; bar; room service; Wi-Fi (free in lobby). *In room:* A/C, TV, fridge, hair dryer.

FREDERIKSTED
Moderate
Cottages by the Sea (Value)   These isolated cottages are located on a wide and sandy beach right outside Frederiksted, about 6 miles from the airport, attracting honeymooners and families. Some cottages are made of cinder blocks, and others are wood. The paneled interiors are a bit worn and the whole look is a bit spartan, but reasonably comfortable. Most bedrooms have king-size or twin beds, with tight, compact bathrooms. All cottages have private patios. The hotel has kayaks and snorkel equipment free for guests to use at the beach. Due to the location, you'll have to depend on taxis or rent a car to get around the island. On the other hand, you can walk over to the center of Frederiksted for restaurants, bars, and shopping.

127A Smithfield, Frederiksted, St. Croix, U.S.V.I. 00840. ✆ **800/323-7252** or 340/772-0495. Fax 340/772-0495. www.caribbeancottages.com. 21 units. Winter

$155–$215 cottage for 2, $175–$215 villa for 4; off season $115–$165 cottage for 2, $145–$175 villa for 4. Extra person $15. Up to 2 children 17 and under stay free in parent's cottage. AE, DISC, MC, V. **Amenities:** Watersports equipment/rentals. *In room:* A/C, ceiling fan, TV, fridge, hair dryer, kitchen, Wi-Fi (free).

Sand Castle on the Beach   This small place is a well-known gay and lesbian hotel in Frederiksted. It lies just half a mile from the town's shopping and dining facilities. Rooms are comfortably furnished but small; all have good mattresses, tiny private bathrooms, and extras such as VCRs, kitchenettes, and coolers. There are two freshwater swimming pools (one is clothing-optional), a hot tub, and a beachfront patio, where you'll often encounter middle-aged men in G-strings. The resort's restaurant, Beach Side Café, has great atmosphere, right on the beach.

Frederiksted Beach, 127 Smith Field, Frederiksted, St. Croix, U.S.V.I. 00840. © **800/ 524-2018** or 340/772-1205. Fax 340/772-1757. www.sandcastleonthebeach.com. 21 units. Winter $149–$199 double, $259–$299 suite, $259–$449 villa for up to 4 people; off season $109–$159 double, $199–$249 suite, $239–$399 villa for up to 4 people. Rates include continental breakfast. AE, DISC, MC, V. **Amenities:** Restaurant; exercise room; Internet (free in lobby); 2 pools (outdoor); watersports equipment/rentals. *In room:* A/C, ceiling fan, TV, TV/VCR, fridge, hair dryer, kitchenette.

Bed & Breakfasts

Carringtons Inn ★ ⓕ**inds**   If you've read stories about celebrities such as screen legend Maureen O'Hara, who own villas on St. Croix, and you wonder what life is like in those villas, here's your chance to experience one firsthand. This grandly elegant B&B was once the home of a wealthy family who spent winters here. Much evidence of their former lifestyle remains. This is an intimate B&B with personalized attention and five spacious and beautifully furnished guest rooms with first-class private bathrooms. Some rooms have a king-size canopy bed, and wicker furnishings are in tasteful abundance. When guests gather around the pool, a house-party atmosphere prevails. Even your breakfast of such delights as rum-flavored French toast can be served poolside.

4001 Estate Hermon Hill (1 mile west of Christiansted), St. Croix, U.S.V.I. 00820. © **877/658-0508** in the U.S., or 340/713-0508. Fax 340/719-0841. www. carringtonsinn.com. 5 units. Winter $125–$165 double; off season $100–$125 double. Rates include breakfast. AE, MC, V. **Amenities:** Breakfast room; health club (nearby); outdoor pool; tennis courts (nearby). *In room:* A/C, ceiling fan, hair dryer, kitchenette (in some), Wi-Fi (free).

Villa Greenleaf ★★ ⓕ**inds**   This is one of the best B&Bs on the island, owned and operated by the same staff that made the Greenleaf Inn at Boothbay Harbor one of the leading inns of New England. This snug family retreat still adheres to its New England innkeeping tradition, offering personal service and the elegant ambience of a private home. It's very small, so make reservations well in advance. The building dates from the 1950s when it was a private home, but it's been completely renovated postmillennium. Four-poster beds are just some of the elegant details associated with the roomy bedrooms of this house. Each of the suites is individually decorated and imbued with muted Caribbean charm and grace. The location is to the west of Christiansted, so you'll need a car for excursions down from the hill.

Island Center Rd., Montpelier, St. Croix, U.S.V.I. 00821. © **888/282-1001** in the U.S., or 340/719-1958. Fax 340/772-5425. www.villagreenleaf.com. 5 units. Winter $320–$340 double, $365–$385 double with use of car; off season $220–$240 double, $265–$285 double with use of car. Rates include breakfast. AE, DC, MC, V. **Amenities:** Pool (outdoor). *In room:* A/C, ceiling fan, fridge, hair dryer, no phone, Wi-Fi (free).

4 WHERE TO DINE

Don't limit yourself to your hotel for dining. Most visitors sample diversity in their dining at lunch when, chances are, they are out indulging in beach life, shopping, or seeing the sights. Christiansted is filled with excellent restaurants offering lunch, but lunch in Frederiksted is a bit dicey if cruise ships have arrived. If so, the few restaurants here may be packed with your next-door neighbors (the ones you went to St. Croix to avoid).

At night, dining becomes more of a problem if you want to venture out. If you're not familiar with the badly lit roads and driving on the left, driving to the restaurant of your choice might present some difficulties. Of course, the easiest way to go is to have your hotel call a taxi and let the driver deliver you to a restaurant. Agree upon the hour you're to be picked up, and he'll even return for you, or the restaurant will summon a cab for you if you don't want to lock yourself into a time frame. Most of the resorts are along the north shore and dining at a different resort every night (unless you're on a meal plan) is easily arranged by taxi.

If you're staying at one of the small hotels or guesthouses in and around Christiansted, you can even walk to your restaurant of choice. If you're at a hotel in Frederiksted, the night is yours, as the cruise ship crowds have departed and there is a less expensive, earthier, and more laid-back feeling in the small dining rooms here.

NORTH SHORE
Expensive

The Terrace ★★ INTERNATIONAL   This is the island's finest dining room in a hotel. Menu items vary but are likely to include grilled local lobster cakes, served with lemon-caper beurre blanc and accented

Christiansted

The Terrace **7**
Tutto Bene **5**
Villa Morales **1**

The Avocado Pitt **11**
Blue Moon **3**
The Bombay Club **16**
Comanche Club **13**
Duggan's Reef **9**
Fort Christian Brew Pub **12**
The Galleon **8**
Harvey's **17**
Junie's Bar and Restaurant **4**

Kendrick's **6**
Le St. Tropez **2**
Los Angeles Café Bar & Restaurant **15**
Luncheria Mexican Food **19**
Paradise Café **18**
Pier 69 **2**
Restaurant Bacchus **14**
RumRunners **10**
Savant **20**

with fresh tarragon. You might also opt for the poached shrimp with a fresh lime cocktail sauce or a hand-cut New York strip steak in a tamarind dark-rum sauce. The delectable pecan-crusted roast pork tenderloin is served sliced over pesto mashed potatoes and red-eye gravy. The roast rack of lamb and the Thai barbecue salmon are classics.

At the Buccaneer (p. 117), Gallows Bay. ℂ **340/712-2100.** www.thebuccaneer. com/dine.htm. Reservations recommended. Main courses $25–$34. AE, DC, DISC, MC, V. Daily 7–10:30am and 6–9:30pm.

Moderate

Duggan's Reef CONTINENTAL/CARIBBEAN   This is one of the most popular restaurants on St. Croix. It's only 10 feet from the still waters of Reef Beach and makes an ideal perch for watching windsurfers and Hobie Cats. At lunch, an array of salads, crepes, and sandwiches are on offer. The more elaborate night menu features the popular house specialties: Duggan's Caribbean lobster pasta and Irish whiskey lobster. Begin with fried calamari or conch chowder. Other main dishes include New York strip steak, fish, and pastas. The local catch of the day can be baked, grilled, blackened Cajun-style, or served island-style (with tomato, pepper, and onion sauce).

East End Rd., Teague Bay. ℂ **340/773-9800.** Reservations required for dinner in winter. Main courses $20–$40; pastas $19–$27. MC, V. Daily noon–3pm and 6–9:30pm; Sun brunch 11am–2:30pm; bar daily noon–11:30pm. Closed for lunch off season.

The Galleon FRENCH/NORTHERN ITALIAN   This restaurant, which overlooks the ocean, is a local favorite, and deservedly so. It serves northern Italian and French cuisine, occasionally including *osso buco*, just as good as that dished up in Milan, although lunchtime offers include tacos and burgers. The dinner menu always offers at least one local fish, such as wahoo, tuna, swordfish, or mahimahi, or you might try the fresh Caribbean lobster. You can order a perfectly done rack of lamb, which will be carved right at your table. There's an extensive wine list, including many options sold by the glass. Music from a baby grand accompanies dinner several nights a week, and you can enjoy guitar music on Thursday and Saturday.

East End Rd., Green Cay Marina, 5000 Estate Southgate. ℂ **340/773-9949.** www. galleonrestaurant.com. Reservations recommended. Main courses $22–$70; lunch main courses $8–$17. MC, V. Daily 11am–4pm and 6–10pm; happy hour 4–6pm. Go east on Rte. 82 from Christiansted for 5 min.; after going 1 mile past the Buccaneer, turn left into Green Cay Marina.

CHRISTIANSTED
Expensive
Kendrick's ★★ FRENCH   Kendrick's, the island's toniest restaurant, lies in the historic Quin House complex at King Cross and

Company streets. Some of its recipes have been featured in *Bon Appétit,* and deservedly so. You'll immediately warm to such specialties as grilled filet mignon with a port-wine demi-glace and red-onion confit. The signature appetizer is king crab cakes with lemon-pepper aïoli. Another great choice is the pecan-crusted roast pork loin with ginger mayonnaise.

2132 Company St. ✆ 340/773-9199. Main courses $21–$33. AE, MC, V. Mon–Sat 6–9:30pm. Closed Mon Sept–Oct 31.

Restaurant Bacchus ★ STEAKHOUSE/CONTINENTAL In a restaurant dedicated to the god of wine, it's no surprise that the wine menu receives as much attention as the food. Both *Wine Spectator* and *Food & Wine* have praised the cellar here. The decor, the fine service, and the presentation of the dishes make for a fine evening out. The kitchen uses first-class ingredients, many imported, to craft a number of dishes that combine flavor and finesse. To finish, it doesn't get any better than the rum-infused sourdough bread pudding. Most dishes, except lobster, are at the lower end of the price scale.

Queen Cross St., off King St. ✆ 340/692-9922. www.restaurantbacchus.com. Reservations requested. Main courses $18–$42. AE, DC, DISC, MC, V. Tues–Sun 6–10pm.

Tutto Bene ITALIAN Lying directly east of Christiansted, this place seems more like a bistro-cantina than a full-fledged restaurant. The owners, Smokey Odom and Kelly Williams, believe in simple, hearty, and uncomplicated *paisano* dishes, the kind that mamma fed her sons back in the old country. You'll dine in a warehouse-like setting, amid warm colors and often lots of hubbub. The menu is written on a pair of oversize mirrors against one wall. The antipasti are some of the best on the island; an intriguing appetizer is the calamari stuffed with ground veal and served in a broth. Pizza lovers can start with pizza Sottile, with a thin crust and a choice of three toppings. A full range of delectable pastas and well-prepared seafood is offered nightly, along with steaks and chops. You can order a seafood pasta dish with mussels, clams, and shrimp in a white-wine pesto sauce over capellini. A fish of the day, based on the local catch, is served at market price (meaning the tab changes from day to day).

Boardwalk Building, Hospital St., Gallows Bay. ✆ 340/773-5229. www.tutto benerestaurant.com. Reservations recommended. Main courses $21–$42. AE, MC, V. Daily 6–10pm.

Moderate

The Bombay Club INTERNATIONAL This is one of the most enduring restaurants in Christiansted. It's concealed from the street by the brick foundations of an 18th-century planter's town house. You enter through a low stone tunnel and eventually end up near the bar and the courtyard that contains many of its tables. The food, though not overly fancy, is plentiful, full of flavor, and reasonably priced. The best items include the catch of the day and regional dishes such as conch, beef filet, and pasta. The island's best fresh lobster pasta is served here. On a recent visit, we enjoyed the grilled fish with sun-dried tomatoes and roasted garlic butter, and fettuccine with sliced prime rib.

5A King St. (©) **340/773-1838.** Reservations recommended. Main courses $14–$21. MC, V. Mon–Fri 11:30am–4pm and 5:30–10pm; Sat–Sun 6–10pm.

Comanche Club CARIBBEAN/CONTINENTAL   Relaxed yet elegant, Comanche is one of the island's most popular restaurants. It's not the best, but the specialties are eclectic—everything from fish and conch chowder to shark cakes. A different special and local dish is featured every night. Choices include salads and curries, and typical West Indian dishes such as conch Creole with *fungi* (a cornmeal and okra dish). There are also standard international dishes like a New York strip.

In Club Comanche (p. 121), 1 Strand St. (©) **340/773-0210.** Reservations recommended. Main courses $15–$26; lunch $7–$18. AE, MC, V. Mon–Sat 11:30am–2:30pm and 5:30–9:30pm.

RumRunners (Kids) CARIBBEAN   This open-air restaurant sits right on the boardwalk and offers some fabulous views to accompany the excellent dining. The ambience is purely Caribbean—the sound of waves in the background can put even the tensest of people at ease. Sunday brunch is even accompanied by a steel-pan band. Excellent choices here include the New York strip steak; the fresh, broiled whole lobster; the Caribbean pork tenderloin served with a grilled banana; and one of the house specials, baby back ribs slow-cooked in island spices and Guinness. The younger vacationers can pick from the children's menu.

In the Hotel Caravelle (p. 120), on the boardwalk at Queen Cross St. (©) **340/773-6585.** www.rumrunnersstcroix.com. Reservations recommended. Main courses $12–$28. AE, MC, V. Mon–Sat 7–10:30am, 11:30am–3pm, and 5:30–9:30pm; Sun 8am–2pm and 5:30–9:30pm.

Savant ★ (Finds) CARIBBEAN/THAI/MEXICAN   The spicy cuisines of one region and two nations are combined into a marvelous fusion to wake up your palate. The stylish bistro atmosphere is a delightful place to dine, but know that the chefs take the food seriously. We gravitate to the tantalizing Thai curries; most of them are mildly spiced for the average diner, but you can request the chef "to go nuclear" if that is your desire. The red coconut curry sauce is one of the best we've ever had on the island. Enchilada lovers will find much happiness here too, especially in the seafood enchiladas. The maple teriyaki pork tenderloin is one of the chef's specialties and deserves the praise heaped upon it. There are only 20 candlelit tables, so call for a reservation as far in advance as you can.

4C Hospital St. (℃) **340/713-8666.** Reservations required. Main courses $16–$33. AE, MC, V. Mon–Sat 6–10pm.

Inexpensive

The Avocado Pitt AMERICAN/VEGETARIAN This is an all-around good choice for breakfast or lunch while you explore the shops and attractions of Christiansted. One of the town's best breakfasts is served here, as patronage by locals reveal. Their omelets and pancakes are rib-sticking fare and full of flavor. Lunch options include "Kahuna burgers" and tuna sandwiches, but you can also find more creative offerings, including tofu with sautéed vegetables or fresh yellowfin tuna. Vegetarians rejoice for the veggie or soy burgers along with freshly made salads and a variety of protein-enriched fruit smoothies. The staff will also pack you a boxed lunch for your tour of the island or all-day sailing adventure. The cafe also serves as something of a small art gallery, displaying paintings by Caribbean artists. Many of the works are for sale.

Kings Wharf. (℃) **340/773-9843.** Main courses breakfast $3–$13, lunch $7–$15. AE, MC, V. Daily 7am–5pm.

Fort Christian Brew Pub CAJUN This fish house and brewery boasts one of the best harbor views in Christiansted. It's the only licensed microbrewery in the U.S.V.I. Rotating beer choices can include a pale ale (Hammerhead), a red ale (Blackbeard's), and a dark stout (West Indies Porter), all of which have earned a formidable reputation on the island. Many patrons come just to drink, staying until closing around 1am. A roster of burgers and sandwiches is served at lunch and dinner. In the evening, the upstairs dining room offers a two-fisted menu that includes a 16-ounce rib-eye with caramelized onions. A favorite of ours is Bourbon Street Jambalaya. Maybe it's better in New Orleans, but this version tastes very much of Louisiana, as does the shrimp étouffée, slow-cooked in a blend of Creole spices and stock. The blackened or pan-seared catfish also takes you way down south. For something West Indian, order the red snapper with *fungi*. There is also a microbrewery storefront in Charlotte Amalie that gives out free samples (and sells beer).

King's Alley Walk. (℃) **340/713-9820.** www.fortchristianbrewpub.com. Platters in brew pub $8–$10; main courses in upstairs restaurant $17–$25. MC, V. Mon–Sat 11am–10pm; Sun 11am–8pm.

Harvey's CARIBBEAN Forget the plastic and the flowery tablecloths that give this place a 1950s feel and enjoy the thoroughly zesty cooking of island matriarch Sarah Harvey, who takes joy in her work and aims to fill your stomach with her basic but hearty fare. Try one of her homemade soups, especially the callaloo or chicken. She'll even serve you conch in butter sauce as an appetizer. For a main dish you might choose from barbecue chicken, barbecue spareribs, boiled filet of snapper, and sometimes even lobster. *Fungi* comes with just about everything. For dessert, try one of the delectable tarts made from guava, pineapple, or coconut.

11B Company St. © **340/773-3433.** Main courses $8–$12. No credit cards. Mon–Sat 11:30am–4pm.

Junie's Bar and Restaurant ★ Finds CARIBBEAN A local favorite, particularly among the corps of taxi drivers, this restaurant occupies a white-painted cement building about a half-mile south of Christiansted, adjacent to a church and a discount store. Inside, wooden tables, metal chairs, bowls of cut flowers, and a well-scrubbed kind of simplicity add to the appeal. Your hosts, Junie Allen and her daughter Denise, prepare a flavor-filled but basic medley of West Indian staples, including a roster of drinks that you might not have tasted before. Sea moss (a kind of eggnog flavored with pulverized seaweed), *mauby* (fermented from rainwater and tree bark), and ginger beer are only some of the options. The menu features boiled fish, conch, lobster in butter sauce, stewed goat, stewed Creole-style lobster, and pork chops with greens and yams. Desserts include carrot cake, cheesecake, and Key lime pie. Because the place has been here for 30 years, it's known by virtually everybody on the island.

132 Peter's Rest. © **340/773-2801.** Main courses lunch $10–$22, dinner $10–$23. AE, MC, V. Mon–Sat 10am–10pm; Sun 10am–7pm.

Luncheria Mexican Food Value MEXICAN/CUBAN/PUERTO RICAN This restaurant is a bargain. You get the usual tacos, tostadas, burritos, nachos, and enchiladas, as well as chicken fajitas, enchiladas verdes, and *arroz con pollo* (spiced chicken with brown rice). Daily specials feature both low-calorie and vegetarian choices (the chef's refried beans are lard free), and whole-wheat tortillas are offered. The complimentary salsa bar has mild to hot sauces, plus jalapeños. Some Cuban and Puerto Rican dishes appear on the menu; these include a zesty chicken curry, black-bean soup, and roast pork. The bartender makes the island's best margaritas.

In the historic Apothecary Hall Courtyard, 2111 Company St. © **340/773-4247.** Main courses $5–$12. MC, V. Mon–Sat 11am–9pm.

Paradise Café Value DELI/AMERICAN This neighborhood favorite draws locals seeking good food and great value. Its brick walls and beamed ceiling were originally part of an 18th-century great house. New York–style deli fare is served during the day. The homemade soups are savory, and you can add grilled chicken or fish to the freshly made salads. At breakfast, you can select from an assortment of omelets, or try the steak and eggs. Dinners are more elaborate. The 12-ounce New York strip steak and the freshly made pasta specialties are good choices. Appetizers include mango chicken quesadillas and crab cakes.

53B Company St. (at Queen Cross St., across from Government House). (℃) **340/ 773-2985.** Breakfast $5.50–$10; lunch $7–$10; dinner $18–$26. No credit cards. Mon–Sat 7:30am–9pm.

IN & AROUND FREDERIKSTED
Moderate
Blue Moon INTERNATIONAL/CAJUN   The best little bistro in Frederiksted becomes a hot, hip spot during Sunday brunch and on Friday nights when it offers live entertainment. The 200-year-old stone house on the waterfront is a favorite of visiting jazz musicians, and tourists have discovered (but not spoiled) the fun. It's decorated with funky, homemade art from the States, including a trash-can-lid restaurant sign. The atmosphere is casual and cafe-like, with a frequently changing menu. You might begin with the "lunar pie," with feta cheese, cream cheese, onions, mushrooms, and celery in phyllo pastry, or the artichoke-and-spinach dip. Main courses include the catch of the day and, on occasion, Maine lobster. The clams served in garlic sauce are also from Maine. There's also the usual array of steak and chicken dishes. Save room for the brownie ice cream.

17 Strand St. (℃) **340/772-2222.** www.bluemoonstcroix.com. Reservations recommended. Main courses $23–$29. AE, MC, V. Tues–Fri 11:30am–2pm; Tues–Sat 6– 9pm; Sun 11am–2pm.

Le St. Tropez FRENCH   This is the most popular bistro in Frederiksted. It's small, so call ahead for a table. If you're visiting for the day, make this bright little cafe your lunch stop, and enjoy crepes, quiches, soups, or salads in the sunlit courtyard. At night, the atmosphere glows with candlelight and becomes more festive. Try the Mediterranean options, beginning with mushroom aïoli and escargots Provençal, or one of the freshly made soups. Main dishes are likely to include medallions of beef with mushrooms, the fish of the day, or a magret of duck.

Limetree Court, 227 King St. (℃) **340/772-3000.** Reservations recommended. Main courses $17–$36. AE, MC, V. Mon–Fri 11:30am–2:30pm; Mon–Sat 6–10pm.

Los Angeles Café Bar & Restaurant (Kids) AMERICAN   Here's another great spot favored by locals. Jean Claude Michelle, known as Bert, was an executive chef in Los Angeles, where he grew up, until he left to start a career in St. Croix. Bert runs this cafe with a jovial attitude that is nothing short of contagious. The menu is widely varied;

including everything from mozzarella sticks to mahimahi. The lobster with crabmeat is grilled to perfection and the fresh fish is always an excellent choice. The basics and more can be found on the children's menu.

King St., Frederiksted, St. Croix 00840. (*C*) **340/772-0016.** Reservations recommended. Main courses $12–$29. AE, MC. Hours are irregular and can change from month to month—always call in advance to see if it's open.

Villa Morales PUERTO RICAN   This inland spot is the premier Puerto Rican restaurant on St. Croix. But then again, no one will mind if you come here just to drink; a cozy bar is lined with the memorabilia collected by several generations of the family who maintain the place. Look for a broad cross section of Hispanic tastes here, including many that Puerto Ricans remember from childhood. Savory examples include fried snapper with white rice and beans, stewed conch, roasted or stewed goat, and stewed beef. Most of the dishes are at the lower end of the price scale. On special occasions, the owners transform the place into a dance hall, bringing in live salsa and merengue bands at no extra charge to patrons.

Plot 82C, Estate Whim (off Rte. 70 about 2 miles from Frederiksted). (*C*) **340/772-0556.** Reservations recommended. Main courses lunch $8–$15, dinner $8–$35. MC, V. Thurs–Sat 10am–10pm.

Inexpensive

Pier 69 AMERICAN/CARIBBEAN   You can get a decent platter of food here, but this place is far more interesting for its funky, Greenwich Village–style atmosphere than for its cuisine. New York–born Unise Tranberg is the earth mother/matriarch of the place, which looks like a warm and somewhat battered combination of a 1950s living room and a nautical bar. Counterculture fans make this their preferred drinking hangout, sometimes opting for a mango colada or a lime lambada. Menu items include a predictable array of salads, and sandwiches. Expect the likes of fried shrimp and potatoes, broiled red snapper served with a butter sauce, and steak with baked potatoes.

69 King St. (*C*) **340/772-0069.** Sandwiches and platters $5.75–$12; main courses $12–$24. DISC, MC, V. Mon–Tues 8am–7pm; Wed–Sun 8am–1am.

5 BEACHES

Beaches are St. Croix's big attraction. The problem is that getting to them from Christiansted, home to most of the hotels, isn't always easy. It can also be expensive, especially if you want to go back and forth each day of your stay. From Christiansted a taxi will cost about $30 for two people to Davis Bay, $24 to Cane Bay, $20 to Rainbow

Beach. Of course, you can rent a condo or stay in a hotel right on the water.

The most celebrated beach is offshore **Buck Island,** part of the U.S. National Park Service network. Buck Island is actually a volcanic islet surrounded by some of the most stunning underwater coral gardens in the Caribbean. The white-sand beaches on the southwest and west coasts are beautiful, but the snorkeling is even better. The islet's interior is filled with cactus, wild frangipani, and pigeonwood. There are picnic areas for those who want to make a day of it. Boat departures are from Kings Wharf in Christiansted; the ride takes half an hour. For more information, see the section "A Side Trip to Buck Island," later in this chapter.

Your best choice for a beach in Christiansted is the one at the **Hotel on the Cay.** This white-sand strip is on a palm-shaded island. To get here, take the ferry from the fort at Christiansted; it runs daily from 7am to midnight. The 4-minute trip costs $3 round-trip, free for guests of the Hotel on the Cay. Five miles west of Christiansted is the **Palms at Pelican Cove,** where some 1,200 feet of white sand shaded by palm trees attracts a gay and mixed crowd. Since a reef lies just off the shore, snorkeling conditions are ideal.

We highly recommend **Davis Bay** and **Cane Bay,** with swaying palms, white sand, and good swimming. Because they're on the north shore, these beaches are often windy, and as a result their waters are not always calm. The snorkeling at Cane Bay is truly spectacular; you'll see elkhorn and brain corals, all some 750 feet off the "Cane Bay Wall." Cane Bay adjoins Route 80 on the north shore. Davis Beach doesn't have a reef; it's more popular among bodysurfers than snorkelers. There are no changing facilities.

On Route 63, a short ride north of Frederiksted, lies **Rainbow Beach,** which has white sand and ideal snorkeling conditions. Nearby, also on Route 63, about 5 minutes north of Frederiksted, is another good beach, called **La Grange.** Lounge chairs can be rented here, and there's a bar nearby.

Sandy Point, directly south of Frederiksted, is the largest beach in all the U.S. Virgin Islands, but it's open to the public only on weekends from 10am to 4pm. Its waters are shallow and calm, perfect for swimming. Try to concentrate on the sands and not the unattractive zigzagging fences that line the beach. This beach is protected as a nesting spot for endangered sea turtles. Continue west from the western terminus of the Melvin Evans Highway (Rte. 66). For more on visiting the refuge, see p. 141.

There's an array of beaches at the east end of the island; they're somewhat difficult to get to, but much less crowded. The best choice here is **Isaac Bay Beach,** ideal for snorkeling, swimming, or sunbathing. Windsurfers like **Reef Beach,** which opens onto Teague Bay along Route 82, East End Road, a half-hour ride from Christiansted. You can get food at Duggan's Reef (p. 126). **Cramer Park** is a special public park operated by the Department of Agriculture. It's lined with sea-grape trees and has a delightful picnic area, a restaurant, and a bar. **Grapetree Beach** is off Route 60 (the South Shore Rd.), wide and sandy, with calm water. The beach is flanked only by a few private homes, although the beach at the Divi Carina is a short walk away.

---

6 FUN IN THE SURF & SUN

WATERSPORTS

FISHING The fishing grounds at **Lang Bank** are about 10 miles from St. Croix. Here you'll find kingfish, dolphin fish, and wahoo. Using light-tackle boats to glide along the reef, you'll probably turn up jack or bonefish. At **Clover Crest,** in Frederiksted, local anglers fish right from the rocks. For more information on legal shore-fishing spots around the island, contact the tourist office in Christiansted or Fredericksted.

Serious sport fishermen, and those who don't have their own dinghy, can board the *Island Girl II,* a 38-foot Bertram special. It's anchored at King's Alley Hotel at 59 Kings Wharf in Christiansted. Reservations can be made by calling © **340/773-2628** during the day. The cost for up to six passengers is $500 for 4 hours, $700 for 6 hours, and $900 for 8 hours with bait and tackle and drinks included.

KAYAKING The beauty of St. Croix is best seen from a kayak. Try the tour offered by **Caribbean Adventure Tours** (© **800/532-3483** or 340/778-1522; www.stcroixkayak.com). You use stable, sit-on-top ocean kayaks, enabling you to traverse the tranquil waters of Salt River, of Columbus landfall fame, and enjoy the park's ecology and wildlife. You also explore secluded mangrove estuaries. The highlight of the excursion is a dip for snorkeling on a pristine beach and paddling to where Christopher Columbus and his crew came ashore some 500 years ago. The tour, lasting 3 hours, costs $45 per person and includes water and a light snack.

SNORKELING & SCUBA DIVING ★★ Sponge life, black coral (the finest in the West Indies), and steep drop-offs near the shoreline make St. Croix a snorkeling and diving paradise. The island is home to the largest living reef in the Caribbean, including the fabled north-shore wall that begins in 25 to 30 feet of water and drops to 13,200 on good snorkeling beaches. The **St. Croix Water Sports Center** (© **340/773-7060;** www.caribbeandays.com) rents snorkeling equipment for $20 a day if your hotel doesn't supply it.

Buck Island ★★ is a major scuba diving site, with a visibility of some 100 feet. It also has an underwater snorkeling trail. Practically all outfitters on St. Croix offer scuba and snorkeling tours to Buck Island. For more information on the island, see the section "A Side Trip to Buck Island," later in this chapter.

Other favorite dive sites include the historic **Salt River Canyon** (northwest of Christiansted at Salt River Bay), for advanced divers. Submerged canyon walls are covered with purple tube sponges, deep-water gorgonians, and black coral saplings. You'll see schools of yellowtail snapper, turtles, and spotted eagle rays. We also like the gorgeous coral gardens of **Scotch Banks** (north of Christiansted) and **Eagle Ray** (also north of Christiansted), the latter so named because of the rays that cruise along the wall there. **Cane Bay** ★★ is known for its coral canyons.

Frederiksted Pier, near the historic area of Frederiksted, is the jumping-off point (literally) for a scuba voyage into a world of sponges, banded shrimp, plume worms, sea horses, and other creatures.

Davis Bay is the site of the 12,000-foot-deep Puerto Rico Trench. **Northstar Reef,** at the east end of Davis Bay, is a spectacular wall dive, recommended for intermediate or experienced divers only. The wall here is covered with stunning brain corals and staghorn thickets. At some 50 feet down, a sandy shelf leads to a cave where giant green moray eels hang out.

At **Butler Bay,** to the north of Frederiksted on the west shore, there are the submerged ruins of three ships: the *Suffolk Maid,* the *Northwind,* and the *Rosaomaira,* the latter sitting in 100 feet of water. These wrecks form the major part of an artificial reef system that also contains abandoned trucks and cars. This site is recommended for intermediate or experienced divers.

Anchor Dive Center, Salt River National Park (© **800/523-3483** in the U.S., or 340/778-1522; www.anchordivestcroix.com), is located within the most popular dive destination in St. Croix: Salt River National Park. It operates three boats and dives mainly in and around the park. The staff offers complete instruction, from resort courses through full certification, as well as night dives. A resort course is $90, with a two-tank dive going for $90. Dive packages begin at $250 for six dives.

Another recommended outfitter is the **Cane Bay Dive Shop** (© **800/338-3843** or 340/773-9913; www.canebayscuba.com), with five locations all around the island. The numerous locations means there's a variety of dive sites to choose from, without having to take a long boat ride. A beginner's lesson goes for $60, and packages go all the way up the scale to a six-tank dive package for $199.

WINDSURFING Head for the **St. Croix Water Sports Center** (© 340/773-7060), on the small offshore island in Christiansted Harbor and part of the Hotel on the Cay. It's open daily from 9am to 5pm. Windsurfing rentals are $25 per hour. Lessons are available.

More Outdoor Adventure

GOLF St. Croix has the best golf in the Virgin Islands. Guests staying on St. John and St. Thomas often fly over for a round on one of the island's three courses.

Carambola Golf & Country Club, on the northeast side of St. Croix (© 340/778-5638; www.golfcarambola.com), was created by Robert Trent Jones, Sr., who called it "the loveliest course I ever designed." It's been likened to a botanical garden. The par-3 holes here are known to golfing authorities as the best in the Tropics. The greens fee of $95 in winter, or $65 in the off season, allows you to play as many holes as you like. Carts are included.

The Buccaneer, Gallows Bay (p. 117; © 340/712-2144), 3 miles east of Christiansted, has a challenging 5,685-yard, 18-hole course with panoramic vistas. Nonguests pay $100 in winter or $60 off season, including the use of a cart.

The **Reef,** on the east end of the island at Teague Bay (© 340/773-8844), is a 3,100-yard, 9-hole course, charging greens fees of $20 for 9 holes and $35 for 18 holes. Golf carts can also be rented at an additional $12 for 9 holes or $18 for 18 holes. The longest hole here is a 465-yard par 5.

HIKING Scrub-covered hills make up much of St. Croix's landscape. The island's western district, however, includes a dense, 15-acre forest known as the **"Rain Forest"** (though it's not a real one). The network of footpaths here offers some fantastic nature walks. For more details on hiking in this area, see the section "Exploring the 'Rain Forest,'" below. **Buck Island** (see the section "A Side Trip to Buck Island," later in this chapter), just off St. Croix, also has nature trails.

The **St. Croix Environmental Association,** Arawak Building, Suite 3, Gallows Bay (© 340/773-1989; www.stxenvironmental. org), has regularly scheduled informative hikes to more remote sections of the island costing $10 per person.

HORSEBACK RIDING **Paul and Jill's Equestrian Stables,** 2 Sprat Hall Estate, Route 58 (© 340/772-2880; www.paulandjills.com), the largest equestrian stable in the Virgin Islands, is known throughout the Caribbean for its horses. It's set on the sprawling grounds of trail rides through the forests, along the beach, and past ruins of abandoned 18th-century plantations and sugar mills, to the tops of the hills of St. Croix's western end. Beginners and experienced riders alike are welcome. A 1½-hour trail ride costs $90. Tours usually depart daily in winter at 10:30am and 3pm, and in the off season at 4pm, with slight variations according to demand. Reserve at least a day in advance.

SAFARI TOURS St. Croix Safari Tours (© 340/773-6700; www. gotostcroix.com/safaritours) offers a tour in a 25-passenger open-air bus run by a hip tour guide who knows all about the botany, cuisine, and history of the island. Tours crisscross the island with stops at plantation houses, historic Frederiksted, the Salt River landfall of Columbus, and a drive through the rainforest, with a stop for lunch. There are lots of photo ops. The cost of the tour is $45 per person, including admission fees to the botanical garden, rum factory, and museum.

TENNIS Some authorities rate the tennis at the **Buccaneer ★★**, Gallows Bay (© 340/773-3036), as the best in the Caribbean. This resort offers a choice of eight courts, two lit for night play, all open to the public. Nonguests pay $8 daytime, $10 nighttime per person per hour; you must call to reserve a court at least a day in advance. A tennis pro is available for lessons, and there's also a pro shop.

---

7 SEEING THE SIGHTS

CHRISTIANSTED

The town is best seen by foot. The best time for a stroll is between 10am and 4pm, practically any day. You can see the major sites at a leisurely pace in less than 2 hours.

A good place to start exploring Christiansted is at **The Visitors Bureau** (53A Company St.). Located near the harborfront, this yellow-sided building with a cedar-capped roof was originally built as the Old Scalehouse in 1856, to replace a similar structure that had burned down. In its heyday, all taxable goods leaving and entering Christiansted's harbor were weighed here. In front of the building lies one of the most charming squares in the Caribbean. Its old-fashioned asymmetrical allure is still evident despite the mass of cars. Through the parking lot is a park named after Alexander Hamilton. The yellow-brick building with the ornately carved brick staircase is the **Old Customs House,** currently the headquarters of the National Park Service. The gracefully proportioned 16-step staircase was added in

1829 as an embellishment to an older building. (There are public toilets on the ground floor.)

Up the hill is **Fort Christiansvaern,** the best-preserved colonial fortification in the Virgin Islands. It's maintained as a historic monument by the National Park Service. Its original four-sided, diamond-shaped design was in accordance with the most advanced military planning of its era. The fort is the site of the St. Croix military museum, which documents police work on the island from the late 1800s to the present. Photos, weapons, and artifacts help bring to life the police force's past here. The admission price of $3 also includes admission to the Steeple Building (see below). The fort is open daily from 8am to 4:45pm.

Outside the fort and straight down the tree-lined path is the most visible steeple in Christiansted, the **Steeple Building.** Completed in 1753, the Steeple Building was embellished with a steeple between 1794 and 1796. For a time it served as the headquarters of the Church of Lord God of Sabaoth. The original structure can still be visited (see below). Inside is a local history museum. Hours are daily from 8am to 4:45pm; admission is included in the $3 ticket for Fort Christiansvaern (see above).

Across Company Street from the Steeple Building is **The Danish West India and Guinea Warehouse,** which is now a U.S. post office. Built in 1749 as the warehouse for the Danish West India and Guinea Company, the structure was once three times larger than it is today and included storerooms and lodging for staff. Go to the building's side entrance, on Church Street, and enter the rear courtyard. For many years, this was the site of some of the largest slave auctions in the Caribbean.

Down Company Street is **Hendricks Square,** St. Croix's largest outdoor market. The square was rebuilt in a timbered, 19th-century style after the 1989 hurricane. Fruits and vegetables are sold here Monday through Saturday from 7am to 6pm.

At Queen Cross Street and King Street is the unmarked arched iron gateway to the charming **Government House** garden. The European-style garden here contains a scattering of trees, flower beds, and walkways. The antique building that surrounds the gardens was formed from the union of two much older town houses in the 1830s. The gardens are open Monday to Friday, 8am to 5pm. At the same intersection is the original **Lord God of Sabaoth Lutheran Church,** which was established in 1734. Take a moment to admire its neoclassical facade.

A few blocks further down King Street is the **Limprecht Gardens and Memorial.** For 20 years (1888–1908) Peter Carl Limprecht served as governor of the Danish West Indies. Today, an occasional

FREDERIKSTED ★

This former Danish settlement at the western end of the island, about 17 miles from Christiansted, is a sleepy port town that comes to life only when a cruise ship docks at its pier. Frederiksted was destroyed by a fire in 1879, and the citizens rebuilt it by putting wood frames and clapboards on top of the old Danish stone and yellow-brick foundations.

Most visitors begin their tour at russet-colored **Fort Frederik,** at the northern end of Frederiksted next to the cruise ship pier (© **340/ 772-2021**). This fort, completed in 1760, is said to have been the first fort in the Caribbean to salute the flag of the new United States. An American brigantine, anchored at port in Frederiksted, hoisted a crudely made Old Glory. To show its support for the emerging American colonies, the head of the fort fired a cannon in the air to honor the Americans and their new independence. Such an act violated the rules of Danish neutrality. It was at this same fort, in July 3, 1848, that Governor-General Peter von Scholten emancipated the slaves in the Danish West Indies, in response to a slave uprising led by a young man named Moses "Buddhoe" Gottlieb. In 1998, a bust of Buddhoe was unveiled here. The fort has been restored to its 1840 appearance and today is a national historic landmark. You can explore the courtyard and stables. A local history museum has been installed in what was once the Garrison Room. Admission is $3 or free for children 15 and under. Open Monday through Friday from 8:30am to 4pm.

The Customs House, just east of the fort, is an 18th-century building with a 19th-century two-story gallery. To the south of the fort is the **visitor bureau** at Strand Street (© **340/772-0357**), where you can pick up a free map of the town.

EXPLORING THE "RAIN FOREST" ★

The island's western district contains a dense, 15-acre forest, called the "Rain Forest" (though it's not technically a rainforest). The area is thick with mahogany trees, kapok (silk-cotton) trees, turpentine (red-birch) trees, *samaan* (rain) trees, and all kinds of ferns and vines. Sweet limes, mangoes, hog plums, and breadfruit trees, all of which have grown in the wild since the days of the plantations, are also interspersed among the larger trees. Crested hummingbirds, pearly eyed thrashers, green-throated caribs, yellow warblers, and perky but drably camouflaged banana quits nest here. The 150-foot-high Creque Dam is the major man-made sight in the area.

The St. Croix Heritage Trail

A trail that leads into the past, **St. Croix Heritage Trail** helps visitors relive the island's Danish colonial past. All you need are a brochure and map, available at the tourist office in Christiansted (p. 113). This 72-mile itinerary includes a combination of asphalt-covered roadway, suitable for driving, and narrow woodland trails which must be navigated on foot. Many aficionados opt to drive along the route whenever practical, descending onto the footpaths wherever indicated, then returning to their cars for the continuation of the tour. En route, you'll be exposed to one of the Caribbean's densest concentrations of historical and cultural sites.

The route connects Christiansted and Frederiksted, going past the sites of former sugar plantations, and traverses the entire 28-mile length of St. Croix. The route consists mainly of existing roadways. The brochure will identify everything you're seeing: You will pass cattle farms, suburban communities, even industrial complexes and resorts. It's not all manicured and pretty, but much is scenic and worth the drive. Allow at least a day for this trail, with stops along the way.

Nearly everyone gets out of the car at **Point Udall,** the easternmost point under the U.S. flag in the Caribbean. You'll pass an eclectic mix of churches and even a prison.

The highlight of the trail is the **Estate Mount Washington** (p. 143), a strikingly well-preserved sugar plantation. Another highlight is **Estate Whim Plantation** (p. 143), one of the best of the restored great houses with a museum and gift shop. Another stop is along **Salt River Bay,** which cuts into the northern shoreline. This is the site of Columbus's landfall in 1493.

Of course, you'll want to stop and get to know the locals. We recommend a refreshment break at **Smithens Market.** Lying off Queen Mary Highway, vendors here offer freshly squeezed sugar cane juice and sell locally grown fruits and homemade chutneys.

The "Rain Forest" is private property, but the owner lets visitors go inside to explore. To experience its charm, some people opt to drive along Route 76 (also known as Mahogany Rd.), stopping beside the footpaths that meander off on either side of the highway into dry

hike along some of the little-traveled four-wheel-drive roads in the
area. Three of the best for hiking are the **Creque Dam Road** (Rte.
58/78), the **Scenic Road** (Rte. 78), and the **Western Scenic Road**
(Rte. 63/78).

Our favorite trail in this area takes about 2^1/$_2$ hours one-way. From
Frederiksted, drive north on Route 63 until you reach Creque Dam
Road, where you turn right, park the car, and start walking. About a
mile past the Creque Dam, you'll be deep within the forest's magnifi-
cent flora and fauna. Continue along the trail until you come to the
Western Scenic Road. Eventually, you reach Mahogany Road (Rte.
76), near St. Croix LEAP Project. This trail is moderate in difficulty.

You could also begin near the junction of Creque Dam Road and
Scenic Road. From here, your trek will cover a broad triangular swath,
heading north and then west along Scenic Road. The road will first
rise, and then descend toward the coastal lighthouse of the island's
extreme northwestern tip, **Hams Bluff.** Most trekkers decide to
retrace their steps after about 45 minutes of northwesterly hiking.
Real die-hards, however, will continue all the way to the coastline,
then head south along the coastal road (Butler Bay Rd.), and finally
head east along Creque Dam Road to their starting point at the junction of Creque Dam Road and Scenic Road. Embark on this longer
expedition only if you're really prepared for a hike lasting about 5
hours.

SANDY POINT WILDLIFE REFUGE ★

St. Croix's rarely visited southwestern tip is composed of salt marshes,
tidal pools, and low vegetation inhabited by birds, turtles, and other
wildlife. More than 3 miles of ecologically protected coastline lie
between Sandy Point (the island's westernmost tip) and the shallow
waters of the West End Salt Pond. This national wildlife refuge is one
of only two nesting grounds of the leatherback turtle in the United
States—the other is on Culebra, an offshore island of Puerto Rico. It's
also home to colonies of green and hawksbill turtles, and thousands
of birds, including herons, brown pelicans, Caribbean martins, black-
necked stilts, and white-crowned pigeons. As for flora, Sandy Point
gave its name to a rare form of orchid, a brown/purple variety. The
area consists of 360 acres of subtropical vegetation, including the largest salt pond in the Virgin Islands.

Park rangers are determined to keep the area pristine, and in doing
so they have to face such problems as the poaching of sea turtles and
their eggs, drug smuggling, dumping of trash, and the arrival of illegal
aliens. Even the mongoose and feral dogs are a menace to the nesting
female turtles.

Visitors are fascinated to see the leatherback sea turtle, the largest of its species, which can measure some six feet in length and weigh more than 1,000 pounds. Every two, perhaps three years, the turtles come back to this refuge to nest from March to July. The average female will deposit anywhere from 60 to 100 eggs in her nest. The survival rate is only one in 1,000 hatchlings. The refuge is also home to the green sea turtle, which can grow to a maximum of four feet and weigh about 400 pounds. These turtles come here only from June to September, when the females come to lay from 75 to 100 eggs.

Birdies also flock to Sandy Point to see more than 100 species of birds, five of which are endangered. Endangered brown pelicans, royal terns, laughing gulls, Caribbean elaenias, bananaquits, and yellow warblers are just some of the birds that call Sandy Point home. Three species of geckos (yes, that annoying insurance salesman), along with several species of reptiles also live here. The reptiles usually stay out of your way.

The wildlife refuge is only open to the public on Saturday and Sunday from 10am to 4pm (admission is free). Activities include hiking, nature photography, and wildlife observation. To reach the refuge, drive to the end of Route 66 (Melvin Evans Hwy.) and continue down a gravel road. For guided weekend visits, call (C) **340/773-4554** to make arrangements.

AROUND THE ISLAND

North of Frederiksted, you can drop in at **Sprat Hall,** the island's oldest plantation, or continue along to the "Rain Forest" (see above). Most visitors come to the area to see the jagged estuary of the northern coastline's **Salt River.** The Salt River was where Columbus landed on November 14, 1493. Marking the 500th anniversary of Columbus's arrival, former President George H. W. Bush signed a bill creating the 912-acre **Salt River Bay National Historical Park and Ecological Preserve.** The park contains the site of the original Carib village explored by Columbus and his men, including the only ceremonial ball court ever discovered in the Lesser Antilles. Also within the park is the largest mangrove forest in the Virgin Islands, sheltering many endangered animals and plants, plus an underwater canyon attracting divers from around the world. If you visit on your own, a taxi from Christiansted will cost $22. See "Fun in the Surf & Sun," earlier in the chapter, for suggestions on kayak and scuba tours to this very special park.

Carl and Marie Lawaetz Museum   The home of one of the island's oldest and most prestigious families can be visited for a rare glimpse into plantation life. This 1750 farmstead has been owned by the Lawaetz family since 1899. Set in a valley at La Grange, you can tour the estate with a member of the family. Originally a sugar plantation, the estate was later turned into a cattle ranch. On the grounds are the reminders of a bygone era, including a decaying sugar mill on a nearby hill. The 19 acres of land are filled with beautiful flowers and tropical trees and bushes.

Inside you can inspect the family heirlooms, many brought over from Denmark. Marie decorated the home with her paintings, still hanging in almost every room. You're even shown the mahogany four-poster bed in which all seven of the Lawaetz family were born.

Mahogany Rd., Rte. 76, Estate Little La Grange. ✆ 340/772-0598. www.stcroix landmarks.com. Admission $10 adults, $5 students and seniors, $4 children 6–12, free for children 5 and under. May–Oct Tues, Thurs, and Sat 10am–3pm; Nov–Apr Wed–Sat 10am–4pm.

Cruzan Rum Factory   This factory distills the famous Virgin Islands rum, which some consider the finest in the world. Guided tours depart from the visitor's pavilion and include a visit to the factory's old windmill. The whole affair is topped off with a complimentary mixed drink, of course. Call ahead for reservations.

Estate Diamond 3, W. Airport Rd., Rte. 64. ✆ 340/692-2280. www.cruzanrum.com. Admission $4 adults, $1 children 18 and under. Tours given Mon–Fri 9–11:30am and 1–4:15pm.

Estate Mount Washington Plantation   This is the island's best-preserved sugar plantation and a highlight along the St. Croix Heritage Trail. It flourished from 1780 to 1820, when St. Croix was the second-largest producer of sugar in the West Indies. The on-site private residence is closed to the public, but you can go on a self-guided tour of the 13 acres at any time of the day you wish (there is no admission charge, although donations are accepted). You'll see what is the best antiques store on St. Croix, but you can visit the little shop that houses them only by calling ✆ 340/772-1026 and asking for an appointment (see "Shopping," below).

At the very southwestern tip of the island, off Rte. 63, a mile inland from the highway that runs along the Frederiksted coast. Free admission.

Estate Whim Plantation Museum   This restored great house is unique among those of the many ruined sugar plantations that dot the island. It's composed of only three rooms. With 3-foot-thick walls made of stone, coral, and molasses, the house resembles a luxurious European château. A division of Baker Furniture Company used the Whim Plantation's collection of models for one of its most successful reproductions, the "Whim Museum–West Indies Collection." Upscale reproductions of some of the furniture is on display within the Whim Plantation, and are for sale on-site. Slightly different inventories are available from an associated store in downtown Christiansted:

The St. Croix Landmarks Museum Store, 58 Queen St. (② **340/713-8102**).

The ruins of the plantation's sugar-processing plant, complete with a restored windmill, also remain. The estate is also site of many events held by the St. Croix Landmarks Society, such as evening concerts and wine tastings. Check their website (www.stcroixlandmarks.com) to see what's happening during your visit.

Centerlrne Rd. (2 miles east of Frederiksted). ② **340/772-0598.** Admission $8 adults, $4 children. Mon–Sat 10am–4pm.

St. George Village Botanical Garden   This is a 16-acre Eden of tropical trees, shrubs, vines, and flowers. The garden is a feast for the eye and the camera, from the entrance drive bordered by royal palms and bougainvillea to the towering kapok and tamarind trees. It was built around the ruins of a 19th-century sugar cane workers' village. Self-guided walking-tour maps are available at the entrance to the garden's great hall. Facilities include restrooms and a gift shop.

127 Estate St., 1 St. George (just north of Centerline Rd.), 4 miles east of Frederiksted. ② **340/692-2874.** www.sgvbg.org. Admission $8 adults, $6 seniors, $1 children 12 and under; donations welcome. Daily 9am–5pm.

ORGANIZED TOURS

BUS TOURS   Organized tours operate according to demand. Many are conducted at least three times a week during the winter, with fewer departures in summer. A typical 4-hour tour costs $28 per person. Tours usually go through Christiansted and include visits to the botanical gardens, Whim Estate House, the rum distillery, the rainforest, the St. Croix LEAP mahogany workshop (see "Shopping," below), and the site of Columbus's landing at Salt River. Check with your hotel desk, or call **Travellers' Tours,** Henry E. Rohlsen Airport (② **340/778-1636**), for more information.

TAXI TOURS   Many visitors explore St. Croix on a taxi tour (② **340/778-1088**), which for a party of two costs about $100 for 3 hours. The fare should be negotiated in advance. Extra fees are charged for the following sights: $10 for the botanical gardens, $10 for the Whim Estate House, and $8 for the rum distillery. Taxi tours are far more personalized than bus tours; you can get on and off where you want and stay as long or as little as you wish at a destination.

WALKING TOURS   For a guided walking tour of either Christiansted or Frederiksted, contact **St. Croix House Tours** (② **340/772-0598**). The tour of Christiansted is available upon request, leaves at 9:30am, and costs $30 per person. The Frederiksted tour leaves on Wednesday at 9:30am, and costs $30 per person. Call for details and to arrange meeting places. Tours are given only in February and March.

8 SHOPPING

Christiansted is the shopping hub of St. Croix. The emphasis here is on hole-in-the-wall boutiques selling handmade goods. Most of the shops are compressed into a half-mile or so. Along the boardwalk is the **King's Alley Complex,** a pink-sided compound filled with the densest concentration of shops on St. Croix.

In recent years, **Frederiksted** has also become a popular shopping destination. Its urban mall appeals to cruise ship passengers arriving at Frederiksted Pier.

SHOPPING A TO Z IN CHRISTIANSTED
Antiques
Estate Mount Washington Antiques ★★ The owners are always there and you'll be able to browse through the best treasure-trove of colonial West Indian furniture and "flotsam" in the Virgin Islands. But you'll have to call first for an appointment. Afterward, you can walk around the grounds of an 18th-century sugar plantation, **Estate Mount Washington** (p. 143). Call for an appointment. 4 Estate Mount Washington. ✆ 340/772-1026.

Arts & Crafts
Folk Art Traders ★ (Finds) The operators of this store travel throughout the Caribbean ("in the bush") to add to their unique collection of local art and folk-art treasures—carnival masks, pottery, ceramics, original paintings, and hand-wrought jewelry. The assortment also includes batiks from Barbados and high-quality iron sculptures from Haiti. There's nothing else like it in the Virgin Islands. 1B Queen Cross St. ✆ 340/773-1900.

Clothes
The Coconut Vine This is one of the most colorful and popular little boutiques on the island. Hand-painted batiks for both men and women are the specialty. Strand St. ✆ 340/773-1991.

From the Gecko At this hip and eclectic outlet, you can find anything from hand-painted local cottons and silks to the old West Indian staple, batiks. We found the Indonesian collection here among the most imaginative in the U.S. Virgin Islands—everything from glass jewelry to banana-leaf knapsacks. 1233 Queen Cross St. ✆ 340/778-9433.

Gone Tropical About 60% of the merchandise in this unique shop is made in Indonesia (usually Bali). Prices of new, semi-antique, or antique sofas, beds, chests, tables, mirrors, and decorative carvings are the same as (and sometimes less than) those of new furniture in conventional stores. Gone Tropical also sells art objects, jewelry, batiks, candles, and baskets. 5 Company St. ✆ **340/773-4696.** www.gone tropical.com.

Urban Threadz This is the most comprehensive clothing store in Christiansted's historic core, with a two-story, big-city scale and appeal. It's the store where island residents prefer to shop because of the hip, urban styles. Men's items are on the street level, women's upstairs. The inventory includes everything from Bermuda shorts to lightweight summer blazers and men's suits. The store carries Calvin Klein, Polo, and Oakley, among others. 52C Company St. ✆ **340/773-2883.**

Gifts
Many Hands The merchandise here includes pottery and hand-made jewelry. The collection of local paintings is also intriguing, as is the year-round "Christmas tree." 110 Strand St. ✆ **340/773-1990.**

Purple Papaya This is the best place to go for inexpensive island gifts. It has the biggest array of embroidered T-shirts and sweatshirts on the island. Although you're in the Caribbean and not Hawaii, there is a large selection of Hawaiian shirts and dresses, if you're into hibiscus flowers. There's also beachwear for the whole family, plus island souvenirs. 39 Strand St., Pan Am Pavilion. ✆ **340/713-9412.**

Royal Poinciana ★ This is the most interesting gift shop on St. Croix, looking like an antique apothecary. You'll find such local items as hot sauces, seasoning blends for gumbos, island herbal teas, Antillean coffees, and a scented array of soaps, toiletries, lotions, and shampoos. There's also a selection of museum-reproduction greeting cards and calendars. Also featured are educational but fun gifts for children. 1111 Strand St. ✆ **340/773-9892.**

Jewelry
Crucian Gold ★ (Finds) This small West Indian cottage holds the gold and silver creations of island-born Brian Bishop. His most popular item is the Crucian bracelet, which contains a "True Lovers' Knot" in its design. Unusual items are pendants framed in gold or silver. These encase shards of china dating from the 1600s or 1700s and found along the beaches of St. Croix. The shards were once collected by island kids who called them "China money" or "chiny." Bishop claims that each pendant is "a little piece of the island's romantic history." The chiny are also incorporated into bracelets. The outlet also sells hand-tied knots (bound in gold wire), rings, pendants, and earrings. Strand St. ✆ **877/773-5241.** www.cruciangold.com.

Sonya Ltd. Sonya Hough is the matriarch of a cult of local residents who wouldn't leave home without wearing one of her bracelets.

She's most famous for her sterling silver or gold (from 14- to 24-karat) versions of her original design, the C-clasp bracelet. Locals say that if the cup of the "C" is turned toward your heart, it means you're emotionally committed; if the cup is turned outward, it means you're available. Prices range from $30 to $2,000. She also sells rings, earrings, and necklaces. 1 Company St. (C) **877/766-9284** or 340/773-8924. www.sonyaltd.com.

Perfume

Violette Boutique   This is a small department store, with many boutique areas carrying famous lines. Here you can get famous and exclusive fragrances and hard-to-find toiletry items, as well as the latest in Cartier, Fendi, Pequignet, and Gucci. A selection of children's gifts, Montblanc pens, and other famous brand names are sold here and found nowhere else on St. Croix (but are certainly found elsewhere in the Caribbean). In the Caravelle Arcade, 38 Strand St. (C) **800/ 544-5912** or 340/773-2148.

---

9 ST. CROIX AFTER DARK

St. Croix doesn't have the nightlife of St. Thomas. To keep abreast of the newest nightspots, you might consult the publication *St. Croix This Week,* which is distributed free to cruise ship and air passengers and is available at the tourist office.

Try to catch a performance of the **Quadrille Dancers** ★★★, a real cultural treat. Their dances have changed little since plantation days. The women wear long dresses, white gloves, and turbans, and the men wear flamboyant shirts, sashes, and tight black trousers. When you've learned their steps, you're invited to join the dancers on the floor. Ask at your hotel if and where they're performing.

Note: Women entering bars alone at night in Christiansted or Frederiksted should expect some advances from men. It is generally assumed here that a woman alone at a bar is seeking companionship and not necessarily just looking to have a drink and survey the scene. Nonetheless, women are fairly safe in bars providing they know how to deal with some leering. It is not wise to leave the bar alone and walk the lonely streets to your hotel. Take a taxi back—it's worth the investment.

THE CLUB & MUSIC SCENE

Blue Moon ★   This hip little dive, best known as a local stop for visiting jazz musicians, is not only a good bistro but also the hottest spot in Frederiksted on Friday, when a five-piece ensemble entertains until midnight. On Sunday, a jazz trio performs. Dinner is served Tuesday to Saturday, 6 to 9pm. 7 Strand St. ☎ 340/772-2222.

The Terrace Lounge This lounge off the main dining room of one of St. Croix's most upscale hotels welcomes some of the Caribbean's finest entertainers every night, often including a full band. Daily 4 to 11pm. In the Buccaneer (p. 117). ☎ 340/773-2100. Cover $6.

2 Plus 2 Disco This is a real Caribbean disco. It features the regional sounds of the islands, not only calypso and reggae but also salsa and soca (a hybrid of calypso and reggae). Usually there's a DJ, except on weekends when there are local bands. The place isn't fancy or large; it has a black-tile dance floor with a simple lighting system. Hours are Thursday and Sunday 10am to 1am and Friday and Saturday 9pm to 4 or 5am. 17 La Grande Princesse. ☎ 340/773-3710. Cover $10 when there's a live band.

THE BAR SCENE

The Palms This romantic bar lies within a resort about 3 miles northwest of Christiansted (p. 113). It caters to resort guests or visitors, gay or straight. You can sit at tables overlooking the ocean or around an open-centered mahogany bar, adjacent to a gazebo. The perfect accompaniment to the night out is one of their classic tropical drinks. Open Monday to Saturday 9am to midnight, Sunday 9am to 11pm. 4126 La Grande Princesse. ☎ 340/718-8920.

THE CASINO

Divi Carina Bay Casino After much protest and controversy, this casino introduced gambling to St. Croix in 2000. Many visitors who heretofore went to such islands as Aruba for gambling now stay within the realm of U.S. possessions. The 10,000-square-foot casino boasts 20 gaming tables and 300 slot machines. No passport is needed to enter, but you do need some form of ID. In lieu of a nightclub, the casino offers nightly live music on an open stage on the casino floor. There are two bars, plus a smaller cafe-style bar where you can order light meals. Open Monday to Thursday noon to 4am and Friday to Sunday 24 hours a day. In the Divi Carina Bay Resort (p. 118). ☎ 340/773-7529. www.divicarina.com.

10 A SIDE TRIP TO BUCK ISLAND ★★★

The crystal-clear waters and white-coral sands of **Buck Island,** a satellite of St. Croix, are legendary. Some call it the single-most-important attraction of the Caribbean. Only about a half-mile wide and a mile long, Buck Island lies 1¹/₂ miles off the northeastern coast of St. Croix. A barrier reef here shelters many reef fish, including queen angelfish and smooth trunkfish. In years past the island was frequented by the swashbuckling likes of Morgan, Lafitte, Blackbeard, and even Captain Kidd.

Buck Island's greatest attraction is its underwater snorkeling trails, which ring part of the island and are maintained by the National Park Service. Equipped with a face mask, swim fins, and a snorkel, you'll be treated to some of the most beautiful underwater views in the Caribbean. Plan on spending at least two-thirds of a day at this extremely famous ecological site. Labyrinths and grottoes await scuba divers. The sandy beach has picnic tables and barbecue pits, as well as restrooms and a small changing room. There are no concessions on the island.

You can hike the trails that twist around and over the island. Circumnavigating the island will take only about 2 hours. Trails meander from several points along the coastline to the sun-flooded summit, affording views over nearby St. Croix. *Warning:* The island's western edge has groves of poisonous manchineel trees, whose leaves, bark, and fruit cause extreme irritation when they come into contact with human skin. Always bring protection from the sun's merciless rays—including a hat and sunblock.

Sometimes small-boat operators trying to make an extra buck run people to Buck Island for a negotiated fee from Christiansted Harbor. These services are unscheduled and likely to be available in winter only. It's best to stick to the charter companies we recommend, as they are more reliable. Nearly all charters provide snorkeling equipment and allow for 1¹/₂ hours of snorkeling and swimming. See "Fun in the Surf & Sun," earlier in this chapter, for companies in addition to the two below.

Mile Mark Watersports, in the King Christian Hotel, 59 King's Wharf, Christiansted (✆ 340/773-2628), conducts two types of tours. The first option is a half-day tour aboard a glass-bottom boat departing daily from the King Christian Hotel, from 9:30am to 1pm and 1:30 to 5pm; it costs $65 per person. The second is a daily full-day tour, from 10am to 4pm, on a 40-foot trimaran for $95. Included in this excursion is a box lunch.

Captain Heinz (✆ 340/773-3161; fax 340/773-4041) is an Austrian-born skipper with more than 25 years of sailing experience. His trimaran, *Teroro II,* leaves the Green Cay Marina "H" Dock at 9am and 2pm, never filled with more than 23 passengers. This snorkeling trip costs $65 for adults, $45 for children 11 and under. The captain is also a considerate host: He will even take you around the outer reef, which the other guides do not, for an unforgettable underwater experience.

The British Virgin Islands

The British Virgin Islands embrace 40-odd islands, some no more than just rocks or spits of land in the sea. Only three of the islands are of any significant size: Virgin Gorda (Fat Virgin), Tortola (Dove of Peace), and Jost Van Dyke. These craggy and remote volcanic islands are just 15 minutes by air or 45 minutes by ferry from St. Thomas.

With its small bays and hidden coves, once havens for pirates, the British Virgin Islands are among the world's loveliest cruising areas. The islands mainly attract those who like to sail, although landlubbers will delight in the beaches. Despite predictions that mass tourism will invade, the islands are still an escapist's paradise. The smaller islands have colorful names, such as Fallen Jerusalem and Ginger. Norman Island is said to have been the prototype for Robert Louis Stevenson's novel *Treasure Island*. On Deadman's Bay, Blackbeard reputedly marooned 15 pirates and a bottle of rum, giving rise to the well-known ditty.

Even though they are part of the same archipelago, the British Virgin Islands and the U.S. Virgin Islands are as different as Dame Judi Dench and Julia Roberts. U.S. islands like St. Thomas are deep into mega-resort tourism, but it's still a bit sleepy over in the B.V.I., where the pace is much slower and laid-back, and the people seem more welcoming. Even the capital, Tortola, seems to exist in a bit of a time capsule.

Most of the resorts on Virgin Gorda are so isolated from each other that you'll feel your hotel has the island to itself. For those who want to be truly remote, there is a scattering of minor hotels on a handful of the smaller islands. Peter Island has the poshest lodgings, and there are modest inns on Jost Van Dyke and Anegada. Some places are so small that you'll get to know all the locals after a week. With no casinos, no nightlife, no splashy entertainment, and often no TV, what does one do at night? Jost Van Dyke has only 150 souls but six bars. Question answered.

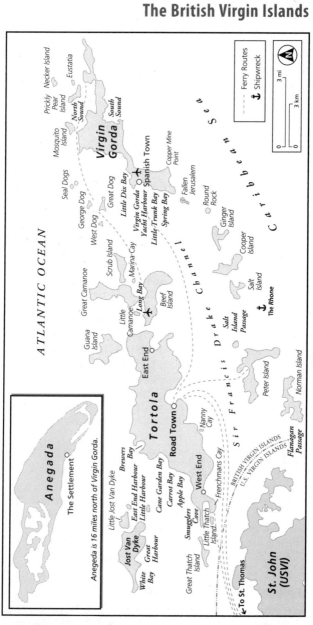

1 ESSENTIALS

GETTING THERE
By Plane

Your gateway to the B.V.I. will most likely be either Tortola or Virgin Gorda. **Beef Island,** the site of the major airport serving the British Virgins, the Terrence B. Lettsome Terminal, is connected to Tortola by the one-lane **Queen Elizabeth Bridge.** Supplies and services on the other islands are extremely limited.

There are no direct flights from North America or Europe to Tortola or any of the British Virgin Islands, but you can make easy connections from St. Thomas, St. Croix, or San Juan in Puerto Rico.

American Eagle (© 800/433-7300 in the U.S.; www.aa.com) has at least four daily flights from San Juan, Puerto Rico, to the airport at Beef Island. San Juan is serviced by dozens of daily nonstop flights from cities in North America, including Boston, Toronto, New York, Chicago, Miami, and Raleigh-Durham. You can also fly **American Airlines** (© 800/433-7300; www.aa.com) to St. Thomas, then hop on an American Eagle flight to Tortola. **Air Sunshine** (© 800/327-8900 or 284/495-8900; www.airsunshine.com) flies from San Juan or St. Thomas to Beef Island (connected to Tortola) and on to Virgin Gorda.

Another choice, if you're on one of Tortola's neighboring islands, is the much less reliable **LIAT** (© 888/844-5428 within the Caribbean, or 284/495-1187; www.liatairline.com). This Caribbean carrier makes short hops to Tortola from Antigua and St. Maarten in small planes not known for their careful scheduling.

Flying time to Tortola from San Juan is 30 minutes; from St. Thomas, 15 minutes; and from the most distant of the LIAT hubs (Antigua), 60 minutes.

By Boat

You can travel from Charlotte Amalie (St. Thomas) by public ferry to Road Town on Tortola, a 45-minute voyage. Boats making this run include **Native Son** (© 284/495-4617; www.nativesonferry.com), **Smith's Ferry Services** (© 284/495-4495; www.smithsferry.com), and **Inter-Island Boat Services** (© 284/495-4166). The latter specializes in a somewhat obscure routing—that is, from St. John to the West End on Tortola. One-way and round-trip fares range from $25 to $49.

VISITOR INFORMATION

Before you go, contact the **British Virgin Islands Tourist Board,** 1270 Broadway, Suite 705, New York, NY 10017 (© 800/835-8530

| (Tips) **Currency Note** |

The British Virgin Islands use the U.S. dollar as their form of currency. British pounds are not accepted.

---

or 212/696-0400). Other branches of the **British Virgin Islands Information Office** are located at 3450 Wilshire Blvd., Suite 1202, Los Angeles, CA 90010 (𝒞 **213/736-8931**), and at 1275 Shiloh Rd., Suite 2930, Kennesaw, GA 30144 (𝒞 **770/874-5951**). In the United Kingdom, contact the **B.V.I. Information Office,** 15 Upper Grosvenor St., London W1K 7PJ (𝒞 **207/355-9585**).

The tourist board's official website is **www.bvitourism.com**.

2 GETTING AROUND

BY BOAT
On Tortola, **Smith's Ferry** (𝒞 **284/495-4495;** www.smithsferry. com) and **Speedy's Fantasy** (𝒞 **284/495-5240**) operate ferry links to the Virgin Gorda Yacht Club (a 30-min. trip). The **North Sound Express** (𝒞 **284/495-2138**), near the airport on Beef Island, has daily connections to the Bitter End Yacht Club on Virgin Gorda. **Peter Island Boat** (𝒞 **284/495-2000**) also shuttles passengers between Road Town on Tortola and Peter Island at least seven times a day. The ferry cost for both round-trip and one-way is $15.

BY CAR, BUS, OR TAXI
There are car-rental agencies on Virgin Gorda and Tortola; flat-fare taxis also operate on these islands, as well as on some of the smaller ones. Bus service is available on Tortola and Virgin Gorda only. See the "Essentials" section for each island for further details.

3 TORTOLA ★★

Road Town, on Tortola's southern shore, is the capital of the British Virgin Islands and the site of the Government House and other administrative buildings. Wickham's Cay, a 28-hectare (69-acre) town center project, has brought in a large yacht-chartering business and has transformed the sleepy village capital into more of a bustling center.

The entire southern coast of this 62-sq.-km (24-sq.-mile) island, including Road Town, is characterized by rugged mountain peaks.

THE BRITISH VIRGIN ISLANDS

5

TORTOLA

On the northern coast are white-sand beaches, banana and mango trees, and clusters of palms. To the northeast lie Beef Island and the airport.

ESSENTIALS
Visitor Information

The **B.V.I. Tourist Board Office** (© 284/494-3134) is in the center of Road Town near the ferry dock, south of Wickham's Cay I. Here you'll find information about hotels, restaurants, tours, and more. Pick up a copy of *The Welcome Tourist Guide,* which has a useful map of the island.

Getting There

Close to Tortola's eastern end is **Beef Island,** the site of the main airport for all of the British Virgin Islands. This tiny island is connected to Tortola by the one-lane Queen Elizabeth Bridge. For more information on getting to Tortola by plane or by ferry, see "Getting There," in section 1, above.

Taxis meet every arriving flight. Government regulations prohibit anyone from renting a car at the airport—visitors must take a taxi to their hotels. The fare from the Beef Island airport to Road Town is $15 for one to three passengers.

Getting Around

BY TAXI The best driver we've found on Tortola is O'Dean "Mr. Quick" Chalwell. What he doesn't know about his island isn't worth knowing. Call **Quick's Taxi Service** at © 284/496-7127. For other taxi options in Road Town, dial © 284/494-2322; on Beef Island, © 284/495-1982. Your hotel can also call a taxi for you; there is a taxi stand in Road Town, near the ferry dock. A typical fare from Road Town to Cane Garden Bay is $25; from Road Town to Josiah's Bay on the north coast, $20.

BY BUS It's better to use taxis unless your budget is limited. If you wish to travel by bus, the **Scato's Bus Service** (© 284/494-2365) operates from the north end of the island to the west end, picking up passengers who hail it down. The bus runs Monday through Friday from 8am to dusk; it's most crowded in the morning when the school kids are picked up. Fares are $2 to $5.

BY CAR A handful of local companies and U.S.-based chains rent cars. **Itgo** (© 284/494-2639) is located at 1 Wickham's Cay, Road Town; **Avis** (© 800/331-1212 in the U.S., or 284/494-3322 on Tortola; www.avis.com) maintains offices opposite police headquarters in Road Town; and **Hertz** (© 800/654-3131 in the U.S., or 284/495-4405 on Tortola; www.hertz.com) has offices outside Road

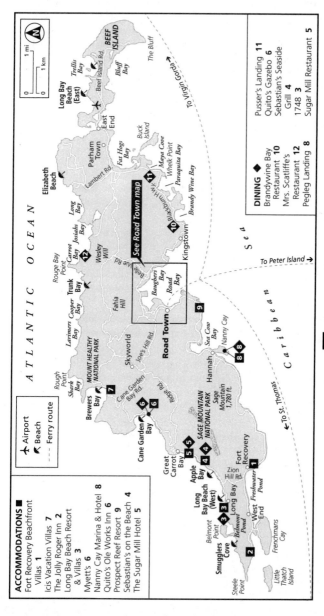

ACCOMMODATIONS ■
Fort Recovery Beachfront Villas **1**
Icis Vacation Villas **7**
The Jolly Roger Inn **2**
Long Bay Beach Resort & Villas **3**
Myett's **6**
Nanny Cay Marina & Hotel **8**
Quito's Ole Works Inn **6**
Prospect Reef Resort **9**
Sebastian's on the Beach **4**
The Sugar Mill Hotel **5**

DINING ◆
Brandywine Bay Restaurant **10**
Mrs. Scatliffe's Restaurant **12**
Pegleg Landing **8**
Pusser's Landing **11**
Quito's Gazebo **6**
Sebastian's Seaside Grill **4**
1748 **3**
Sugar Mill Restaurant **5**

✈ Airport
⚓ Beach
--- Ferry route

THE BRITISH VIRGIN ISLANDS

5

TORTOLA

BEEF ISLAND
The Bluff
Long Bay Beach Rd.
Trellis Bay
Bluff Bay
East End
To Virgin Gorda
Beef Island Rd.
Long Bay Beach (East)
Buck Island
Parham Town
Fat Hogs Bay
Maya Cove
Whelk Point
Paraquita Bay
Lambert Rd.
Elizabeth Beach
Blackburn Hwy.
Brandy Wine Bay
Long Bay
Josiahs Bay
Kingstown
Carrot Bay
Wesley Will
Rouge Point
Trunk Bay
See Road Town map
Cooper Bay
Larimers
Belle Vue Rd.
Fahia Hill
Baughers Bay
Road Bay
ATLANTIC OCEAN
Rough Point
Shark Bay
MOUNT HEALTHY NATIONAL PARK
Skyworld
Joe's Hill Rd.
Road Town
To Peter Island →
Sea
Brewers Bay
Cane Garden Bay Rd.
Ridge Rd.
Sea Cow Bay
Nanny Cay
Hannah
Cane Garden Bay
SAGE MOUNTAIN NATIONAL PARK
Sage Mountain 1,780 ft.
Caribbean
Great Carrot Bay
Apple Bay
Fort Recovery
Long Bay Beach (West)
Zion Hill Rd.
Long Bay
West End
Freshwater Pond
Belmont Point
Smugglers Cove
Belmont Pond
Frenchmans Cay
Steele Point
Little Thatch Island
To St. Thomas →

Town, on the island's West End, near the ferryboat landing dock. Rental companies will usually deliver your car to your hotel. All three companies require a valid driver's license and a temporary B.V.I. driver's license, which the car-rental agency can sell to you for $10; it's valid for 3 months. Because of the volume of tourism to Tortola, you should reserve a car in advance, especially in winter.

Remember: Drive on the left. Roads are pretty well paved; but they're often narrow, windy, and poorly lit, and they have few, if any, lines. Driving at night can be tricky. It's a good idea to take a taxi to that difficult-to-find beach, restaurant, or bar.

Fast Facts Tortola

American Express The local representative is **Travel Plan, Ltd.,** located at Waterfront Drive (📞 **284/494-4000**), in Road Town.

Banks Local bank branches include the **Bank of Nova Scotia** (Scotia Bank), Wickham's Cay I (📞 **284/494-2526**), and **First Caribbean National Bank,** Wickham's Cay I (📞 **284/494-2171**), both in Road Town. There's also a branch of **First Bank** on Wickham's Cay I in Road Town (📞 **284/494-2662**). Each has its own ATM.

Bookstores The best bookstore is the **National Educational Services Bookstore,** Wickham's Cay I, in Road Town (📞 **284/494-3921**).

Business Hours Most offices are open Monday to Friday 9am to 5pm. Government offices are open Monday to Friday 8:30am to 4:30pm. Shops are generally open Monday to Friday 9am to 5pm and Saturday 9am to 1pm.

Cameras & Film The best place for supplies and film developing is **Bolo's Brothers,** Wickham's Cay I, in Road Town (📞 **284/494-2867**).

Dentists For dental emergencies, contact **Dental Surgery** (📞 **284/494-3274**), which is in Road Town behind the police station, off Waterfront Drive.

Doctors Go to **Peebles Hospital,** Porter Road, Road Town (📞 **284/494-3497**).

Drugstores The best pharmacy is **Medicure Pharmacy,** Hodge Building, near Road Town Roundabout, Road Town (📞 **284/494-6189**).

Emergencies Call ℂ **999.** If you have a medical emergency, call **Peebles Hospital,** Porter Road, Road town, Tortola (ℂ **284/494-3497**), which has X-ray and laboratory facilities. Your hotel can also put you in touch with the local medical staff.

Hospitals In Road Town, you can go to **Peebles Hospital,** Porter Road (ℂ **284/494-3497**), which has X-ray and laboratory facilities.

Internet Access If there's no Web access at your hotel, try **Data Pro,** Road Town (ℂ **284/494-6633**), and **Copyright Systems,** Palmgrove House, behind First Caribbean International Bank (ℂ **284/494-5030**).

Laundry One of the best places is **Freeman's Laundry & Dry Cleaning,** Purcell Estate, Road Town (ℂ **284/494-2285**).

Police The main police headquarters is on Waterfront Drive near the ferry dock on Sir Olva Georges Plaza (ℂ **284/494-2945**).

WHERE TO STAY

Many of the island's hotels are small, informal, family-run guest-houses offering only the most basic amenities. Other lodgings are more elaborate, boasting a full range of resort-related facilities. None of them, however, is as big, splashy, and all-encompassing as the mega-resorts in the U.S. Virgin Islands, and many of the island's repeat visitors seem to like that just fine. Remember that all of Tortola's beaches are on the northern shore, so guests staying elsewhere (at Road Town, for example) will have to drive or take a taxi to reach them.

Note: All rates given within this chapter are subject to a 10% service charge and a 7% government tax. Rates are usually discounted significantly in summer. The term "MAP" stands for "Modified American Plan"; this means that the hotel provides breakfast and dinner (or lunch, if you prefer) for an extra charge.

In Road Town

If you want to be near the center of all the activity (such as there is), opt for a hotel in or around Road Town. Some visitors might want to combine a night or two in Road Town with a few other nights in a more secluded part of the island.

Maria's by the Sea   Right in the heart of Road Town, this hotel has a certain Caribbean charm, boasting little balconies that open right onto the harbor. At night, you can enjoy the harbor lights and the sound of the lapping waves from your balcony perch. During the day, you'll find it's a 10- to 15-minute drive to the nearest beach. The allure of the fairly minimalist bedrooms is the sea breeze that seems to blow here constantly. All units include a kitchenette, a balcony, and a small bathroom. The staff is friendly and helpful. Maria, the owner and manager, serves excellent local Caribbean cuisine at her on-site restaurant. From her famous conch chowder to her home-baked rolls fresh from the oven, dining here in the evening is a delight.

Road Town (P.O. Box 206), Tortola, B.V.I. 𝄴 **284/494-2595.** Fax 284/494-2420. www.mariasbythesea.com. 40 units. Winter $160–$200 double, $205 1-bedroom suite, $280 2-bedroom suite; off season $130–$170 double, $200 1-bedroom suite, $250 2-bedroom suite. AE, MC, V. **Amenities:** Restaurant; bar; pool (outdoor). *In room:* A/C, TV, fridge, Wi-Fi (free).

Treasure Isle Hotel ★   This landmark hotel has been completely restored and much improved. It was built at the eastern edge of Road Town, one mile from the center, on 6 hectares (15 acres) of steeply inclined hillside overlooking the coastal road and a marina (not the beach). Accommodations are rented with either water or garden views. All rooms have double or king-size beds. Rooms are designed with balconies or else private terraces on the hillside. The on-site Verandah Restaurant has been massively expanded to 250 seats and air-conditioned. The chefs serve Caribbean dishes but the menu has more of an international flair.

Pasea Estate (P.O. Box 68), Road Town, Tortola, B.V.I. 𝄴 **284/494-2501.** Fax 284/494-2507. www.pennhotels.com. 65 units. Winter $325–$425 double, $475 suite; off season $250–$350 double, $400 suite. AE, DISC, MC, V. **Amenities:** Restaurant; bar; pool (outdoor); room service. *In room:* A/C, TV, hair dryer, Internet (free).

Village Cay Hotel ★   Set in the heart of Road Town, this is the most centrally located full-service lodging. Yachties are often drawn here. The most expensive rooms (called "A" rooms) and the hotel restaurant directly overlook a marina filled with yachts from around the world; if you're seeking a beachfront location you'll have to look elsewhere. The "B" units are slightly smaller, and don't have balconies, but are a good value if you're on a budget. Anything you need is within a 5-minute walk of the premises, including ferry service to other islands, or taxi service to anywhere on Tortola. Sailing and motoring cruises can be booked directly through the hotel.

Wickham's Cay I, Road Town, Tortola, B.V.I. 𝄴 **284/494-2771.** Fax 284/494-2773. www.igy-villagecay.com. 21 units. Year-round $175–$220 double, $305–$405 1- or 2-bedroom waterfront suite. Children 11 and under stay free in parent's room.

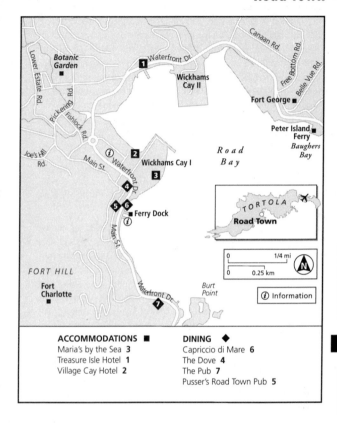

Map legend:

ACCOMMODATIONS ■
Maria's by the Sea **3**
Treasure Isle Hotel **1**
Village Cay Hotel **2**

DINING ◆
Capriccio di Mare **6**
The Dove **4**
The Pub **7**
Pusser's Road Town Pub **5**

Map labels: Canaan Rd., Waterfront Dr., Botanic Garden, Wickhams Cay II, Free Bottom Rd., Belle Vue Rd., Lower Estate Rd., Fort George, Pickering Rd., Fishlock Rd., Peter Island Ferry, Baughers Bay, Joe's Hill Rd., Main St., Waterfront Dr., Wickhams Cay I, *Road Bay*, Ferry Dock, TORTOLA, Road Town, FORT HILL, Fort Charlotte, Waterfront Dr., Burt Point, 0 1/4 mi, 0 0.25 km, ⓘ Information

THE BRITISH VIRGIN ISLANDS

5

TORTOLA

AE, MC, V. **Amenities:** Restaurant; bar; pool (outdoor); room service; watersports equipment/rentals. *In room:* A/C, TV, fridge, hair dryer, Internet ($12).

Around the Rest of the Island
Very Expensive

Long Bay Beach Resort & Villas ★   A favorite of travelers since the 1960s, this resort lies on a 2km-long (1¼-mile) sandy beach on the north shore, about 10 minutes from West End. It's the only full-service resort on the island, a low-rise complex set in a 21-hectare (52-acre) estate. Complaints about overbuilding and problems with maintenance have marred the once-stellar reputation of this resort, but there is still much to enjoy. Accommodations include hillside rooms and studios, plus two- and three-bedroom villas complete with a kitchen, a living area, and a large deck with a gas grill. The smallest and most basic units have simple furnishings, while the deluxe beach-front rooms and cabanas have either balconies or patios that overlook the ocean. Each unit does have an ocean view.

The two restaurants include **1748** (p. 166), built within the ruins of an old sugar mill, and the alfresco Palm Terrace, which serves a variety of local and international dishes in a more elegant and formal setting. The cuisine, especially the fresh fish, is among the finest at any hotel on the island, which is complemented by an extensive wine list.

Long Bay, Road Town, Tortola, B.V.I. (✆ **866/237-3491** in the U.S. and Canada, or 284/495-4252. Fax 284/495-4677. www.longbay.com. 152 units. Winter $250–$320 double, $395 junior suite, $610–$900 villa; off season $195–$265 double, $345 junior suite, $475–$730 villa. Extra person $35. Children 11 and under stay free in parent's room. MAP (breakfast and dinner) $48 per day. AE, DISC, MC, V. **Amenities:** 3 restaurants; 3 bars; babysitting; health club & spa; pool (outdoor); 2 tennis courts (lit); limited watersports; Wi-Fi (free in lobby). *In room:* A/C, TV, hair dryer, kitchen (in villas).

The Sugar Mill Hotel ★ Set in a lush tropical garden on the site of a 300-year-old sugar mill on the north side of Tortola, this secluded cottage colony sweeps down the hillside to its own little beach, with vibrant flowers and fruits brightening the grounds. The accommodations are contemporary and well-designed, ranging from suites and cottages to studios, all with kitchenettes. The latest addition, the Plantation House suites, relies on traditional Caribbean architectural tastes, complete with an airy porch and gingerbread detailing. Families might opt for a two-bedroom villa, or a pool suite, which has a sleeper couch.

Lunch is served down by the beach at Islands, which features standard Caribbean specialties such as jerk ribs and stuffed crab, plus burgers and salads. Dinner is offered at the acclaimed **Sugar Mill Restaurant** (p. 167).

Apple Bay (P.O. Box 425), Road Town, Tortola, B.V.I. (✆ **800/462-8834** in the U.S., or 284/495-4355. Fax 284/495-4696. www.sugarmillhotel.com. 23 units. Winter $340 double, $380 triple, $395 quad, $695 2-bedroom villa; off season $255–$275 double, $305 triple, $330–$350 quad, $275–$295 1-bedroom villa, $535–$585 2-bedroom villa. MAP (breakfast and dinner) $70 per person extra. Children 11 and under not accepted in winter, but stay free in parent's room Apr 15–Dec 20. AE, MC, V. Closed Aug–Sept. From Road Town, drive west 11km (6¾ miles), turn right (north) over Zion Hill, and turn right at the T-junction opposite Sebastian's; Sugar Mill is .8km (½ mile) down the road. **Amenities:** 2 restaurants; 2 bars; babysitting; concierge; pool (outdoor). *In room:* A/C, ceiling fan, TV (in some), hair dryer, Wi-Fi (free).

Expensive

Fort Recovery Beachfront Villas ★ Nestled in a small palm grove about 12km (7½ miles) from Road Town, this property faces the Sir Francis Drake Channel and fronts one of the best small beaches on this side of the island. A big plus at Fort Recovery is that the beach is perfect for swimming and snorkeling. The estate also contains the remnants of an old Dutch fort, including the stone lookout tower. Accommodations include villas and two houses, which are great for families. The large house has an art gallery hallway and a large wraparound porch. The resort has its own yoga instructor and classes are complimentary to guests, in case the sea breezes and the beach aren't relaxing enough.

If you book for 7 or more nights, dinner and a snorkeling trip are on the house.

The Towers, West End (P.O. Box 239), Road Town, Tortola, B.V.I. ✆ **800/367-8455** or 284/541-0955. Fax 284/495-4036. www.fortrecovery.com. 30 units. Winter $340–$360 villa for 2, $520 villa for 4, $750 villa for 6–8; off season $210–$250 villa for 2, $360 villa for 4, from $560 villa for 6–8. Extra person $50 per night; children 11 and under $35 per night. MAP (breakfast and dinner) $45 per day. AE, MC, V. **Amenities:** Restaurant; babysitting; bikes; exercise room; pool (outdoor); watersports equipment/rentals. *In room:* A/C, TV, hair dryer, kitchenette, Wi-Fi (free).

Myett's   Unlike some of the remote, tranquil inns we've recommended, Myett's stands in a beachfront garden right near the nightlife of Cane Garden Bay, the most happening place on the island when the sun goes down (not to mention one of the best places for swimming). The spacious bedrooms have air-conditioning, tropical decor, and a king-size bed. Extras include a small fridge and wet bar. There's no need to chance the hazardous roads of Tortola at night; you can stay right on the grounds, enjoying dinner or happy hour at Myett's Garden & Grille, offering a tasty Caribbean cuisine in a lush tropical-garden setting. Try the fresh lobster or the catch of the day along with more routine offerings such as shrimp, steak, and vegetarian dishes. Good music and live entertainment are presented on weekends. Ask the bartender to make you a "Sex in the Jungle," but don't bother to ask what's in it.

Cane Garden Bay, Tortola, B.V.I. ✆ **284/495-9649.** Fax 284/495-9579. www.myett ent.com. 6 units. Winter $200 double; off-season $130 double. AE, MC, V. **Amenities:** Restaurant; bar; Wi-Fi (free). *In room:* A/C, fridge.

Prospect Reef Resort ★   This is one of the largest resorts in the British Virgin Islands, rising above a private harbor in a compound of two-story concrete buildings scattered over 11 acres of sloping, landscaped terrain. The panoramic view of Sir Francis Drake Channel from the bedrooms is one of the best anywhere, though there's no beach to speak of.

All of the accommodations have private balconies or patios, and some of the larger units are suitable for families, complete with kitchenettes, living and dining areas, and separate sleeping areas.

The food at the hotel's restaurant is a combination of Continental specialties and island favorites.

Drake's Hwy. (P.O. Box 104), Road Town, Tortola, B.V.I. ☏ **800/356-8937** in the U.S., or 284/494-3311. Fax 284/494-7600. www.prospectreefbvi.com. 100 units. Winter $155–$195 double, $315–$480 suite; off season $120–$140 double, $255–$325 suite. AE, MC, V. **Amenities:** 4 restaurants; bar; babysitting; health club & spa; 2 pools (outdoor); 5 tennis courts (lit); watersports equipment/rentals; Wi-Fi (free in lobby). *In room:* A/C, ceiling fan, TV, Internet (in some; free).

Moderate

Nanny Cay Marina and Hotel   Few other resorts cater as aggressively to yacht owners as Nanny Cay, a sprawling, somewhat disorganized resort where great wealth (in the form of hyperexpensive yachts) lies cheek by jowl with more modest fishing craft. This place competes with Village Cay for the boat owner or sailor; we think Village Cay is superior. Accommodations are within a two-story motel-style building, where windows overlook open-air hallways. Each unit contains a refrigerator and comfortable (albeit bland) furniture. The heart and soul of the resort is the 180-slip marina, headquarters to at least three yacht-chartering companies and permanent home to many fishing and pleasure boats. The resort sprawls over 10 hectares (25 acres) of steamy flatlands, adjacent to a saltwater inlet that's favored because of the protection it offers boats during storms and hurricanes. Don't expect the spit and polish of a resort catering to conventional trade. This place is artfully and deliberately raffish, which seems to be the way folks here want to keep it. The restaurant, **Pegleg Landing** (p. 167), is a reasonable choice for standards like steak and grilled fish.

Road Town (P.O. Box 281), Tortola, B.V.I. ☏ **284/494-4895.** Fax 284/494-0555. www.nannycay.com. 40 studios. Winter $180–$220 double, $260 suite, $200–$240 triple; off season $120–$160 double, $210 suite, $140–$180 triple. Children 11 and under stay free in parent's room. MC, V. **Amenities:** Restaurant; bar; babysitting; exercise room; pool (outdoor); tennis court (lit); watersports equipment/rentals. *In room:* A/C, TV, hair dryer, kitchenette (in some), Wi-Fi (free).

Sebastian's on the Beach   This hotel is located at Little Apple Bay, about a 15-minute drive from Road Town, on a long beach that offers some of the best surfing in the British Virgin Islands. The rooms are housed in three buildings, with only one on the beach. All come with rattan furniture and balconies or porches. You should be careful here about room selection, as accommodations vary considerably. Most sought-after are the beachfront rooms, only steps from the surf; they have an airy tropical feeling, with tile floors, balconies, patios, and screened jalousies. The rear accommodations on the beach side are less desirable—not only do they lack views but they're also subject to traffic noise. Also, avoid the two noisy bedrooms above the commissary. The dozen less expensive, rather spartan rooms in the

Sebastian's Seaside Grill (p. 168) overlooks the bay and has live entertainment on Saturday and Sunday.

Little Apple Bay (P.O. Box 441), West End, Tortola, B.V.I. ✆ **800/336-4870** in the U.S., or 284/495-4212. Fax 284/495-4466. www.sebastiansbvi.com. 30 units. Winter $110–$325 double; off season $85–$145 double. MAP $45 per person extra; children 10 and under $23–$30. AE, DISC, MC, V. **Amenities:** Restaurant; bar, Wi-Fi (free in restaurant and courtyard). *In room:* A/C, TV, fridge, no phone (in some units).

Inexpensive

Icis Vacation Villas   These apartment units are located in a tranquil part of the island, just yards from Brewers Bay, which offers great swimming. Though the rooms are rather basic, they are spotlessly maintained. All the units, except the villa, have both air-conditioning and ceiling fans; each has a patio or porch. There are no room phones, but an on-site pay phone is available.

Brewers Beach (P.O. Box 383), Tortola, B.V.I. ✆ **284/494-6979.** Fax 284/494-6980. www.icisvillas.com. 15 units. Winter $145 efficiency, $180 1-bedroom apt, $290 3-bedroom apt, $185–$290 suite; off season $125 efficiency, $145 1-bedroom apt, $230 3-bedroom apt, $150–$230 suite. Extra person $25. Children 12 and under stay free in parent's unit. Rates include continental breakfast. AE, MC, V. **Amenities:** Restaurant; bar; babysitting; pool (outdoor); Wi-Fi (free). *In room:* A/C (in some), ceiling fans, TV, fridge, kitchenette.

The Jolly Roger Inn   This small harborfront hotel is located at Soper's Hole, a breath away from the ferry dock to St. Thomas and St. John. The accommodations are clean and very simple. The small rooms are comfortably and pleasantly decorated, but only two have a private bathroom. There's no air-conditioning in some units, but all the rooms do enjoy the sea breeze. The atmosphere is fun, casual, and definitely laid-back; the restaurant is a good place for dinner or a night out. The beach at Smuggler's Cove is a 20- to 30-minute walk over the hill.

West End, Tortola, B.V.I. ✆ **284/495-4559.** Fax 284/495-4184. www.jollyrogerbvi. com. 5 units. Winter $76–$82 double without bathroom, $95 double with bathroom, $86–$92 triple without bathroom, $105 triple with bathroom; off season $60–$70 double without bathroom, $80 double with bathroom, $70–$80 triple without bathroom, $90 triple with bathroom. AE, MC, V. Closed early Aug to Sept 30. **Amenities:** Restaurant; watersports equipment/rentals. *In room:* A/C (in some), no phone, Wi-Fi (free).

Quito's Ole Works Inn ★ (Finds)   This hotel occupies the historic premises of a 300-year-old sugar refinery. It is a far less expensive alternative to the Sugar Mill Hotel, although it doesn't have the cuisine or the facilities of that more famed property. Still, it puts you right on the beach. It's set inland from Cane Garden Bay, and has the best musical venue on Tortola—a rustic indoor/outdoor bar called **Quito's Gazebo** (p. 168). The rooms are cramped but cozy; many have water views, some with balconies. The bathrooms are all a bit too small. The most romantic unit is the large honeymoon suite in the tower. On the premises is a boutique-style art gallery showing watercolors by local artists and selling souvenirs.

The in-house bar is a magnet for fans of modern calypso music, largely because it's supervised by the hotel owner Quito (Enriquito) Rymer, who's the most famous recording star ever on Tortola. Quito himself performs Tuesday, Thursday, Saturday, and Sunday.

Cane Garden Bay (P.O. Box 560), Tortola, B.V.I. ℂ **284/495-4837.** Fax 284/495-9618. www.quitorymer.com. 17 units. Winter $120–$165 double; $180–$235 suite; off season $100–$135 double, $155–$185 suite. Extra person $35. Children 11 and under stay free in parent's room. AE, MC, V. **Amenities:** Restaurant; bar; pool (outdoor); Wi-Fi (free in bar). *In room:* A/C, ceiling fan, TV, fridge, kitchenette (in some).

WHERE TO DINE

Most guests dine at their hotels, but if you want to venture out, try one of the suggestions below. ***Note:*** Many of the less expensive restaurants on the island serve rotis, Indian-style turnovers stuffed with such treats as potatoes and peas or curried chicken.

In Road Town

Road Town offers the largest concentration of cheap and authentic Caribbean eateries in the B.V.I.

Expensive

The Dove ★★ FRENCH/ASIAN This is one of the best places for haute cuisine in town. You can begin by sipping a martini under the shade of the restaurant's mango tree or else drink in a luxurious bar while listening to jazz. The small menu changes every week, but offers inventive dishes prepared from both locally grown and imported ingredients. Seafood is flown in fresh daily, and sushi and soft-shell crab appetizers appear frequently on the menu. Main-course specialties include prawns seasoned with vanilla and jalapeño peppers or a five-peppercorn steak. The chef makes his own ice cream and sorbets, and a homemade chocolate soufflé is his specialty. A champagne happy hour is staged from 5 to 7pm Tuesday to Saturday featuring $3 champagne cocktails, and the restaurant boasts Tortola's largest wine *carte.*

67 Main St., Road Town. ℂ **284/494-0313.** Reservations recommended. Main courses $19–$35. MC, V. Tues–Sat 5–10pm.

Inexpensive

Capriccio di Mare ★ ITALIAN Created in a moment of whimsy by the owners of the more upscale **Brandywine Bay Restaurant**

(p. 166), this local favorite is small, casual, and laid-back. It's the most authentic-looking Italian cafe in the Virgin Islands. At breakfast time, many locals stop in for an Italian pastry along with a cappuccino, or even a full breakfast. If it's evening, you might try the mango Bellini, a variation of the famous champagne-based cocktail served at Harry's Bar in Venice. Begin with such appetizers as *piedini* (flour tortillas with various toppings), then move on to a selection of fresh pastas, the best pizzas on the island, or the well-stuffed sandwiches. We prefer the pizza topped with grilled eggplant. If you arrive on the right night, you might be treated to stuffed Cornish hen with scalloped potatoes.

Waterfront Dr., Road Town. ✆ **284/494-5369.** Main courses $8–$18. MC, V. Mon–Sat 8am–9pm.

The Pub INTERNATIONAL   This establishment attracts many of the island's yachties, as well as the local sports teams, who celebrate here after their games. More than 25 kinds of beer are available. You'll find the Pub housed in a low-slung timbered building on a narrow strip of land between the coastal road and the southern edge of Road Town's harbor. It has a barnlike interior and a rambling veranda built on piers over the water. If you're here for a meal, some of the best options include Bahamian fritters, Caesar or Greek salads, pastas, four kinds of steaks, and burgers. Locals and regulars are especially fond of the chef's jerk chicken and his combo platter of spareribs, chicken, and fried shrimp. The chef also prepares a catch of the day. Happy hour brings discounted drinks Saturday through Thursday from 5 to 7pm and on Friday, when hot wings and raw vegetable platters are offered.

In the Fort Burt Hotel, Harbour Rd. ✆ **284/494-2608.** Reservations recommended. Main courses $19–$35. AE, MC, V. Mon–Sat 6am–10pm; Sun 5pm–midnight.

Pusser's Road Town Pub CARIBBEAN/ENGLISH   Standing on the waterfront across from the ferry dock, the original Pusser's serves Caribbean fare, English pub grub, and good pizzas. This place is not as fancy as Pusser's Landing, in the West End (p. 167), nor is the food as good, but it's a lot more convenient and has faster service. The complete lunch and dinner menu includes savory English pies (*Gourmet* magazine once asked for the recipe for the chicken-and-asparagus pie) and deli-style sandwiches. John Courage ale is on draft, but the drink to order here is the famous Pusser's Rum, the same blend of five West Indian rums that the Royal Navy has served to its men for more than 300 years. Thursday is nickel-beer night.

Waterfront Dr. and Main St., Road Town. ✆ **284/494-3897.** www.pussers.com. Reservations recommended. Main courses $7.95–$20. AE, DISC, MC, V. Daily 10am–11pm.

Expensive

Brandywine Bay Restaurant ★★ ITALIAN   Set on a cobble-stone garden terrace along the south shore, overlooking Sir Francis Drake Channel, this is one of Tortola's most elegant and romantic restaurants. Davide Pugliese, the chef, and his wife, Cele, have earned a reputation for their outstanding Florentine fare. The skillful cooking produces dishes that range from classic to inspired. Davide changes his menu daily, based on the availability of fresh produce. The best dishes include beef carpaccio, roast duck, homemade pasta, his own special calf-liver dish (the recipe is a secret), and homemade mozzarella with fresh basil and tomatoes.

Brandywine Estate, Sir Francis Drake Hwy. ✆ **284/495-2301.** www.brandywine bay.com. Reservations and appropriate dress required. Main courses $25–$29. AE, MC, V. Mon–Sat 6:30–9:30pm. Closed Aug–Oct. Drive 5km (3 miles) east of Road Town (toward the airport) on South Shore Rd.

Mrs. Scatliffe's Restaurant ★ (Finds) WEST INDIAN   This Tortola mama offers home-cooked meals on the deck of her island home. Some of the vegetables come right from her garden, although others might be from a can. You'll enjoy excellent authentic West Indian dishes: perhaps spicy conch soup followed by curried goat, "old wife" fish (triggerfish, in this case filleted, boiled, and served with onion sauce), or chicken in a coconut shell. Service, usually from an inexperienced teenager, is not exactly efficient. Decide early in the evening you want to enjoy dinner here as there is only one seating and reservations must be made before 5pm.

You may be exposed to Mrs. Scatliffe's gentle preaching of her Christian faith. A Bible reading and a heartfelt rendition of a gospel song sometimes accompany a soft custard dessert.

Carrot Bay. ✆ **284/495-4556.** Fixed-price meal $35–$38. No credit cards. 1 seating daily begins 7–8pm.

1748 ★ CARIBBEAN/INTERNATIONAL   This is a good setting for a romantic dinner as it's set in a converted 18th-century sugar mill on Tortola's finest sandy beach. Its tables are arranged on two decks beneath sea-grape trees opening onto the white sands. The place is especially enticing on Tuesday and Thursday for pasta night, or on Wednesday and Sunday when an international buffet is served. The chefs do some of the finest grills on the island, especially in fresh fish, and they are also known for their beach barbecues and fresh-from-the-reef seafood. Sometimes visitors or hotel guests drop in for lunch just for a burger, drink, and dessert. At night the cuisine grows more elaborate, featuring mostly a Caribbean cuisine, though borrowing recipes from other cultures as well.

Sugar Mill Restaurant ★ CALIFORNIA/CARIBBEAN This transformed 3-century-old sugar mill is a romantic spot for dining. Colorful works by Haitian painters hang on the old stone walls, and big copper basins have been planted with tropical flowers. Before going to the dining room, once part of the old boiling house, visit the open-air bar on a deck that overlooks the sea.

Your hosts, the Morgans, know a lot about food and wine. Some of their recipes have even been printed in *Gourmet.* One of their most popular creations, published in *Bon Appétit,* is curried banana soup. You might also begin with the roasted pepper salad or the especially tasty wild mushroom soup. For a main course, we recommend such dishes as the pan-roasted duck breast served with Asian coleslaw and soba noodles, or the grilled fresh fish with a pineapple-pepper salsa.

In the Sugar Mill Hotel (p. 160), Apple Bay. ℰ **284/495-4355.** www.sugarmill hotel.com/restaurant. Reservations required. Main courses $26–$35. AE, MC, V. Daily 8–10am, noon–2pm, and 7–9pm. Closed Aug–Sept. From Road Town, drive west 11km (6¾ miles), turn right (north) over Zion Hill, and turn right at the T-junction opposite Sebastian's on the Beach; Sugar Mill is .8km (½ mile) down the road.

Moderate

Pegleg Landing INTERNATIONAL This restaurant lies 2.4km (1½ miles) southwest of Road Town, overlooking the yachts of the Nanny Cay Marina. You'll find accents of stained glass, mastheads from old clipper ships, lots of rustic paneling, and a nautical theme brought to life by the views and breezes from the sea. Food is competent, but hardly exciting. Specialties include charbroiled New York strip steak with mushrooms, and fresh filets of fish, such as dolphin (again, not Flipper), swordfish, tuna, and wahoo.

At the Nanny Cay Marina and Hotel (p. 162). ℰ **284/494-0028.** Reservations required. Main courses $18–$35. AE, MC, V. Daily 11:30am–midnight.

Pusser's Landing CARIBBEAN This Pusser's location, opening onto the water in West End, is more desirably situated than the original Pusser's Road Town Pub. In this nautical setting, you can enjoy fresh grilled fish of the day cooked to your requirements. Begin with a hearty soup, perhaps pumpkin or freshly made seafood chowder. Many of the main courses have real island flavor, the most justifiably popular being the grilled chicken breast with fresh pineapple salsa. A classic is the curried shrimp over rice. Mud pie remains the choice dessert here, but the Key lime pie and mango soufflé beckon as well. Happy hour is daily from 5 to 7pm.

Frenchman's Cay, West End. ℂ **284/495-4554.** www.pussers.com/outposts/
pussers_landing. Reservations required. Main courses $16–$35. AE, MC, V. Daily
11am–10pm.

Quito's Gazebo ★ (Finds) CARIBBEAN/INTERNATIONAL
This restaurant, owned by Quito Rymer, the island's most acclaimed
musician, is the most popular of those located along the shore of
Cane Bay. Quito himself performs after dinner several nights a week.
The restaurant, which is designed like an enlarged gazebo, is set
directly on the sand. Frothy rum-based drinks are the order of the day
here (ask for the piña colada or the Bushwacker, made with four kinds
of rum). Lunch includes sandwiches, salads, and platters. Evening
meals might feature conch or pumpkin fritters, mahimahi with a
wine-butter sauce, chicken roti, and steamed local mutton served
with a sauce of island tomatoes and pepper. On Wednesday, for only
$15, you can enjoy barbecue ribs, chicken roti, johnnycakes, and
more, from 3:30 to 5pm.

In Quito's Ole Works Inn (p. 163), Cane Garden Bay. ℂ **284/495-4837.** www.
quitorymer.com. Main courses $18–$32; lunch platters, sandwiches, and salads
$6–$14. AE, MC, V. Tues–Sun 11am–3pm and 6:30–9pm; bar Tues–Sun 11am–
midnight.

Inexpensive
Sebastian's Seaside Grill INTERNATIONAL   Sebastian's is a
good choice if you're in the West End area for lunch. The wooden
tables and rush-bottomed chairs here are scattered, Polynesian-style,
beneath a rustic yet comfortable pavilion a few feet from the waves.
Sun lovers sit within the open courtyard nearby. Choices include hot
sandwiches, West Indian fritters, a homemade soup of the day, and
burgers—nothing special, but it's all satisfying. At night, dishes have
more flair and flavor. Your best bet is the fresh fish of the day, which
can be pan-fried, grilled, or blackened, and is served with a choice of
sauces, including a local blend of seasonings and spices. You might
also try the Jamaican jerk chicken or vegetable casserole. Weekends
there is a live band at dinner.

In Sebastian's on the Beach (p. 162), West End. ℂ **284/495-4212.** www.
sebastiansbvi.com. Reservations required for dinner. Main courses lunch $5–$13,
dinner $18–$38. AE, DISC, MC, V. Daily 7am–10:30pm.

BEACHES
Beaches are rarely crowded on Tortola unless a cruise ship is in port.
If you take a taxi to the sands, don't forget to arrange a time to be
picked up.

Tortola's finest beach is **Cane Garden Bay** ★, on the aptly named
Cane Garden Bay Road, directly west of Road Town. You'll have to
navigate some roller coaster hills to get there, but these fine white

sands, with sheltering palm trees and gentle surf, are among the most popular in the B.V.I., and the lovely bay is many a yachtie's favorite. Outfitters here rent Hobie Cats, kayaks, and sailboards. Windsurfing is possible as well. There are seven places to eat along the beach, plus a handful of bars. Be prepared for crowds in the high season.

Surfers like **Apple Bay,** which is west of Cane Garden Bay along North Shore Road. The beach isn't very big, but that doesn't diminish activity when the surf's up. Conditions are best in January and February. After enjoying the white sands here, you can have a drink at the Bomba Surfside Shack, a classic dive of a beach bar at the water's edge (p. 173).

Smugglers Cove ★, known for its tranquillity and for the beauty of its sands, lies at the extreme western end of Tortola, opposite the offshore island of Great Thatch, and just north of St. John. It's a lovely crescent of white sand with calm turquoise waters. A favorite with locals, Smugglers Cove is also popular with snorkelers, who explore a world of sea fans, sponges, parrotfish, and elkhorn and brain corals. Beginning snorkelers in particular appreciate the fact that the reef is close to shore. The beach, sometimes called "Lower Belmont Bay," is located at the end of bumpy Belmont Road. Once you get here, even if you're a little worse for the wear, you'll find the crystal-clear water and the beautiful palm trees are worth the effort.

East of Cane Garden Bay, **Brewers Bay,** accessible via the long, steep Brewers Bay Road, is ideal for snorkelers and surfers. This clean, white-sand beach is a great place to enjoy walks in the early morning or at sunset. Or just sip a rum punch from the beach bar and watch the world go by. There is a campground here if you want to spend the night.

The 2km-long (1¼-mile) white-sand beach at **Long Bay West,** reached along Long Bay Road, is one of the most beautiful in the B.V.I. Joggers run along the water's edge, and spectacular sunsets make this spot perfect for romantic strolls. The Long Bay Beach Resort stands on the northeast side of the beach; many visitors like to book a table at the resort's restaurant overlooking the water.

If you'd like to escape from the crowds at Cane Garden Bay and Brewers Bay, head east along Ridge Road until you come to **Josiah's Bay Beach** on the north coast. This beach lies in the foreground of Buta Mountain. On most occasions we have found it either empty or with only a handful of bathers. If you visit in winter, beware: On many days there's a strong undertow, and there are no lifeguards.

At the very east end of the island, **Long Bay East,** reached along Beef Island Road across the Queen Elizabeth Bridge, is a great spot for swimming.

Travel Plan Tours, Romasco Place, Harbour House (P.O. Box 437), Road Town (℃ **284/494-4000;** www.aroundthebvi.com), offers a 3¹/₂-hour tour that touches on the natural highlights of Tortola (a minimum of four participants is required). The cost is $32 to $45 per person. The company also offers 3-hour **snorkeling tours** for $64 per person (with snacks included). A full-day **sailing tour** aboard a cata-maran that goes from Tortola to either Peter Island or Norman Island costs $165 per person; a full-day tour, which goes as far afield as the Baths at Virgin Gorda and includes lunch, costs $125 per person. And if **deep-sea fishing** appeals to you, book a half-day excursion, with equipment, for four fishermen and up to two "nonfishing observers" for $900, or a full-day excursion for $1,260.

A **taxi tour** of the island costs $65 for two passengers for 2 hours, or $85 for 3 hours. To call a taxi in Road Town, dial ℃ **284/494-2322;** on Beef Island, ℃ **284/495-1982.**

No visit to Tortola is complete without a trip to **Sage Mountain National Park ★,** rising to an elevation of 534m (1,752 ft.). Here, you'll find traces of a primeval rainforest, and you can enjoy a picnic while overlooking neighboring islets and cays. Covering 37 hectares (91 acres), the park protects the remnants of Tortola's original forests (those that were not burned or cleared during the island's plantation era). Go west from Road Town to reach the mountain. Before you head out, stop by the tourist office in Road Town and pick up the brochure *Sage Mountain National Park.* It has a location map, direc-tions to the forest and parking, and an outline of the main trails through the park. From the parking lot at the park, a trail leads to the park entrance. The two main trails are the Rainforest Trail and the Mahogany Forest Trail.

Shadow's Ranch, Todman's Estate (℃ **284/494-2262**), offers horseback rides through the national park or down to the shores of Cane Garden Bay. Call for details daily from 9am to 4pm. The cost is from $100 per hour.

OUTDOOR ACTIVITIES

SNORKELING A good beach for snorkeling is **Brewers Bay** (p. 169). Snorkelers should also consider heading to the islet of **Marina Cay,** or taking an excursion to or booking a room on **Cooper Island,** across the Sir Francis Drake Channel. Limited ferry service is run by the hotel. **Blue Water Divers** (see "The Wreck of the *Rhone* & Other Top Dive Sites," below) leads expeditions to both sites. Or consider a trip to **Norman Isle** (p. 173), the fabled setting of *Treasure Island,* for its caves and protected pools.

The Wreck of the *Rhone* & Other Top Dive Sites

The one site in the British Virgin Islands that lures divers over from St. Thomas is **the wreck of the HMS *Rhone* ★★**, which sank in 1867 near the western point of Salt Island. *Skin Diver* magazine called it "the world's most fantastic shipwreck dive." The wreck teems with marine life and coral formations, and was featured in the 1977 movie *The Deep*.

Although it's no *Rhone*, *Chikuzen* is another intriguing dive site off Tortola. It's an 81m (266-ft.) steel-hulled refrigerator ship, which sank off the island's eastern end in 1981. The hull, still intact under about 24m (79 ft.) of water, is now home to a vast array of tropical fish, including yellowtail, barracuda, black-tip sharks, octopus, and drum fish.

South of Ginger Island, **Alice in Wonderland** is a deepdive site with a wall that begins at around 3.6m (12 ft.) and slopes gently to 30m (98 ft.). It abounds with marine life such as lobsters, crabs, rainbow-hued fan coral, and mammoth mushroom-shaped coral. **Spyglass Wall** is another offshore dive site dropping to a sandy bottom and filled with sea fans and large coral heads. The drop is from 3 to 18m (10–59 ft.). Divers here should keep an eye out for tarpon, eagle rays, and stingrays.

Blue Water Divers, Road Town (✆ **284/494-2847;** www. bluewaterdiversbvi.com), is a PADI outfitter that offers various dive packages, including one to the wreck of the *Rhone*. A resort course costs $105; a PADI open-water certification is $410.

SHOPPING

Most of Tortola's shops are on Road Town's Main Street. Unfortunately, the British Virgins have no duty-free shopping. British goods are imported without duty, though, and you can find some good buys among these imported items, especially in English china. In general, store hours are Monday to Saturday from 9am to 4pm.

You might start your shopping expedition at **Crafts Alive,** an open-air market lying in the center of Road Town and impossible to miss. It consists of a series of old-fashioned West Indian–style buildings that are stocked with crafts, ranging from Caribbean dolls to straw hats, from crocheted doilies to the inevitable B.V.I. T-shirts.

Very few of these items, however, are made on the island; we noted that some, in fact, come from Panama.

In arts and crafts, you'll find higher-quality items at **Aragorn's Local Arts and Crafts Center ★**, Trellis Bay (© 284/495-1849; www.aragornsstudio.com), a showcase for the most talented artisans on the island. "A lot of Europeans used to look down on Caribbean art," Aragorn Dick-Read once told the press. But he has worked to create a greater appreciation of Caribbean culture among visitors. Here you will find an array of copper sculptures, island prints, local art, and jewelry, including the island's best selection of handcrafted pottery. The finest of woodcarving and metalwork is also displayed here in a newly expanded studio.

Sunny Caribbee Spice Co., 119 Main St., Road Town (© 284/494-2178; www.sunnycaribbee.com), in an old West Indian building, was the first hotel on Tortola. It's now a shop specializing in Caribbean spices, seasonings, teas, condiments, and handicrafts. With an aroma of spices permeating the air, this factory is an attraction in itself. You can buy two famous specialties here: the West Indian hangover cure and the Arawak love potion. A Caribbean cosmetics collection, Sunsations, includes herbal bath gels, island perfume, and sunscreens. There's a daily sampling of island products—perhaps tea, coffee, sauces, or dips.

Samarkand, Main Street, Road Town (© 284/494-6415), is an unusually good bet for jewelry and other items. Look for an intriguing selection of bracelets, pins, and pendants in both silver and gold, and pierced earrings. Caribbean motifs such as palms and seabirds often appear in the designs of the jewelry.

Pusser's Company Store, Main Street and Waterfront Road, Road Town (© 284/494-2467; www.pussers.com), has gourmet food items including meats, spices, fish, and a nice selection of wines. Pusser's Rum is one of the best-selling items here.

Arawak, on the dock at Nanny Cay (© 284/494-5240), is known for its household furnishings, such as place mats and candleholders, but also sells sporty clothing for adults and kids, along with a selection of gifts and souvenirs.

Flamboyance, Waterfront Drive (© 284/494-4099), is the best place to shop for perfume and upscale cosmetics.

If you've rented a villa or condo, or if your accommodations have a kitchenette, consider a visit to **Ample Hamper,** Villa Cay Marina, Wickham's Cay I, Road Town (© 284/494-2494; www.amplehamper.com). This outlet stocks some of the best packaged food and bottled wines on the island. It also offers fresh fruit and a tasty selection of cheeses.

Philatelists from all over the world flock to the **British Virgin Islands Post office,** Main Street, Road Town (© 284/494-3701, ext.

(Moments) Exploring Deserted "Treasure Island"

Across Drake Channel from Tortola lies **Norman Isle.** Although it used to be a pirate den with treasure ships at anchor in the 18th century, it is now deserted except by seabirds and small wild animals. Legend has it that Norman Isle was the inspiration for Robert Louis Stevenson's *Treasure Island,* first published in 1883. You can row a dinghy into the southernmost cave of the island—with bats overhead and phosphorescent patches—where Stevenson's Mr. Fleming supposedly stowed his precious treasure. Norman Isle has a series of other caves that are some of the best-known snorkeling spots in the B.V.I., teeming with spectacular fish, small octopuses, squid, and garden eels, and featuring colorful coral. Intrepid hikers climb through scrubland to the island's central ridge, Spy Glass Hill.

A private boat rental is the only way to reach Norman Isle. To cut costs, ask three or four other people to go with you. Contact **Moorings Limited,** P.O. Box 139, Road Town, Tortola (© **888/952-8420** or 284/494-2331; www.moorings. com). They rent 9.9 to 14m (32–46-ft.) catamarans that range from $1,090 to $1,400 per day for a 3-day minimum rental. A skipper onboard is optional for an extra $200 a day. Or contact **Travel Plan Tours** (p. 170) about their sailing tour.

4996), for its exquisite and unusual stamps in beautiful designs. Even though the stamps carry U.S. monetary designations, they can be used only in the B.V.I.

TORTOLA AFTER DARK

Ask around to find out which hotel might have entertainment on any given evening. Steel bands and fungi or scratch bands (African Caribbean musicians who improvise on locally available instruments) appear regularly, and nonresidents are usually welcome. Pick up a copy of *Limin' Times,* an entertainment magazine that lists what's happening locally; it's usually available at hotels.

Bomba Surfside Shack, Cappoon's Bay (© **284/495-4148;** www. bombasurfsideshack.com), is the oldest and most memorable hangout on the island, sitting on the beach near the West End and attracting an uninhibited crowd. It's covered with Day-Glo graffiti, and odds and ends of plywood, driftwood, and abandoned rubber tires. Despite its makeshift appearance, the shack has the sound system to create a real party. Every month (dates vary), Bomba stages a full-moon party, with free house tea spiked with hallucinogenic mushrooms. (The tea is free because it's illegal to sell it, although you have to buy the cup.) Note that the drug in this tea could be dangerous to your body. If one consumes it, as hundreds of tourists do every year, it should be done with caution. Or, better yet, not at all. This place is also wild on Wednesday and Sunday nights, when there's live music. It's open daily from 10am to midnight (or later, depending on business).

The bar at the **Moorings/Mariner Inn,** Wickham's Cay II (☏ 284/494-2333; www.bvimarinerinnhotel.com), is the preferred watering hole for upscale yacht owners. Interestingly, drink prices are low. Open to a view of its own marina, and bathed in a dim and flattering light, this place has a relaxed atmosphere.

Adjacent to the previously recommended Spaghetti Junction, and run by the same people, **The Bat Cave Bar** (☏ 284/494-4880; www.spaghettijunction.net/batcave.htm) is located at Baughers Bay and has a 93-sq.-m. (1,000-sq.-ft.) disco.

Other places worth a stop on a barhopping jaunt include the **Jolly Roger,** West End (☏ 284/495-4559; www.jollyrogerbvi.com), where you can hear local or sometimes American bands playing everything from reggae to blues. In the same area, visit **Stanley's Welcome Bar,** Cane Garden Bay (☏ 284/495-9424), where a rowdy frat-boy crowd gathers to drink, talk, and drink some more. Finally, check out **Sebastian's,** Apple Bay (p. 163; ☏ 284/495-4212), especially on Sunday, when you can dance to live music under the stars, at least in winter.

Rhymer's, on the popular stretch of beach at Cane Garden Bay (☏ 284/495-4639), serves up cold beer or tropical rum concoctions, along with a casual menu of ribs, conch chowder, and more. The beach bar and restaurant is open daily 8am to 9pm.

4 VIRGIN GORDA ★★★

The second-largest island in the British cluster, Virgin Gorda is 16km (10 miles) long and 3.2km (2 miles) wide, with a population of some 1,400 people. It's located 19km (12 miles) east of Tortola and 41km (25 miles) east of St. Thomas.

In 1493, on his second voyage to the New World, Christopher Columbus named the island Virgin Gorda, or "Fat Virgin," because the mountain on the island looked (in his opinion) like a protruding stomach.

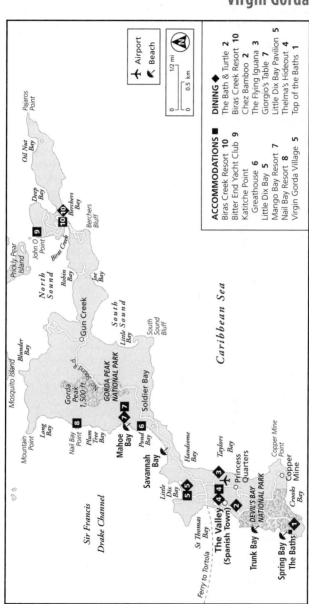

THE BRITISH VIRGIN ISLANDS

5

VIRGIN GORDA

ACCOMMODATIONS ■
Biras Creek Resort **10**
Bitter End Yacht Club **9**
Katitche Point
Greathouse **6**
Little Dix Bay **5**
Mango Bay Resort **7**
Nail Bay Resort **8**
Virgin Gorda Village **5**

DINING ◆
The Bath & Turtle **2**
Biras Creek Resort **10**
Chez Bamboo **2**
The Flying Iguana **3**
Giorgio's Table **7**
Little Dix Bay Pavilion **5**
Thelma's Hideout **4**
Top of the Baths **1**

Virgin Gorda was a fairly desolate agricultural community until Laurance Rockefeller established the resort of Little Dix here in the early 1960s, following his success with Caneel Bay on St. John in the 1950s. He envisioned a "wilderness beach," where privacy and solitude reigned. Other major hotels followed in the wake of Little Dix, but seclusion is still highly guarded and respected.

ESSENTIALS
Getting There

BY BOAT   Speedy's Fantasy (© 284/495-5240) operates a ferry service between Road Town, on Tortola, and Virgin Gorda. Monday to Saturday, at least four ferries a day leave from Road Town; three ferries make the trip on Sunday. The cost is $20 one-way or $30 round-trip. There is also service from St. Thomas to Virgin Gorda three times a week (on Tues, Thurs, and Sat), costing $40 one-way or $70 round-trip.

You'll also find that the more luxurious resorts have their own boats to take you from the airport on Beef Island to Virgin Gorda.

Getting Around

BY BUS   Independently operated open-sided **safari buses** run along the main road. Holding up to 22 passengers, these buses charge upward of $3 to $5 per person to transport a passenger, say, from the Valley to the Baths.

BY CAR   If you'd like to rent a car, try one of the local firms, including **Mahogany Rentals,** the Valley, Spanish Town (© 284/495-5469), across from the yacht harbor. This company has the least expensive rentals on the island, beginning at around $55 daily for a Suzuki Sidekick. Road conditions on Virgin Gorda range from good to extremely poor. *Remember:* Drive on the left.

An aerial view of the island shows what looks like three bulky masses connected by two very narrow isthmuses. The most northeasterly of these three masses (which contains two of the most interesting hotels) is not even accessible by road at all, requiring ferryboat transit from the more accessible parts of the island.

One possibility for exploring Virgin Gorda by car is to drive from the southwest to the northeast along the island's rocky and meandering spine. This route will take you to the **Baths** (in the extreme southeast), to **Spanish Harbour** (near the middle), and eventually, after skirting the mountainous edges of **Gorda Peak,** to the most northwesterly tip of the island's road system, near **North Sound.** Here, a miniarmada of infrequently scheduled ferryboats depart and arrive from Biras Creek and the Bitter End Yacht Club.

(Fast Facts) Virgin Gorda

American Express The local American Express representative is **Travel Plan,** Virgin Gorda Yacht Harbour (✆ **284/494-6239**).

Banks First Caribbean Bank (✆ **284/495-5217**) is located in Spanish Town at the Virgin Gorda Shopping Centre. It has the only ATM on the island.

Cameras & Film Try **Kysk Tropix,** Virgin Gorda Yacht Harbour (✆ **284/495-5636**), open daily 9:30am to 6pm.

Dentists & Doctors Contact **Medicure Health Center** at Spanish Town (✆ **284/495-5479**).

Drugstore Go to **Island Drug Centre** at Spanish Town (✆ **284/495-5449**).

Emergencies Call ✆ **999** or **911.**

Internet Access Go to the **Chandlery,** Yacht Harbour Marina (✆ **284/495-5628**), where the cost is $5 for the first 10 minutes, 50¢ per minute thereafter. You can also pay a flat fee of $20 per hour.

Laundry **Stevens Laundry & Dry Cleaning,** near the Virgin Gorda Yacht Harbour (✆ **284/495-5525**), is open daily 8am to noon and 1 to 9pm.

Police There is a station in the Valley at Spanish Town (✆ **284/495-7584**).

Tourist Information The island's tourist office is in Virgin Gorda Yacht Harbour, Spanish Town (✆ **284/495-5181**).

WHERE TO STAY

The best agency for a villa rental is **Virgin Gorda Villa Rentals Ltd.,** P.O. Box 63, Leverick Bay, Virgin Gorda, B.V.I. (✆ **800/848-7081** or 284/495-7421; www.virgingordabvi.com). This company manages villas throughout the island, most of which are quite expensive. A 5-night minimum stay is required in the off season, and a 7-night minimum stay is requested in winter. The cheapest weekly rentals in winter are $850 weekly, dropping to $725 per week in summer. Most accommodations have access to an outdoor pool, dining facilities, a spa, tennis courts, and extensive watersports. Wi-Fi is free in most rentals, but not available in all locations.

Biras Creek Resort ★★★ Stay at this sophisticated, relaxing hideaway if you want to retreat from the world. You can reach the resort only by boat. This private, romantic property is the classiest place on the island. Biras Creek stands at the northern end of Virgin Gorda on a 60-hectare (148-acre) estate with its own marina, and occupies a narrow neck of land flanked by the sea on three sides. All the attractive, tropically decorated units, all suites, have well-furnished bedrooms, private patios, and garden showers. There are no TVs in the rooms, but who needs TV when you have the luxury of an oceanview veranda? Guests get their own bikes for their stay, and there are lots of hiking trails near the property. The fitness center and restaurant have also received upgrades, as well as the available watersports equipment. The resort now has several Boston Whalers boats free for guests to take for 2-hour snorkeling trips to remote coves and beaches nearby.

The hotel restaurant is a longtime favorite, and the open-air bar is quietly elegant. There's always a table with a view. The food has won high praise, and the wine list is excellent. A barbecued lunch is served on the beach.

North Sound (P.O. Box 54), Virgin Gorda, B.V.I. © **877/883-0756** or 284/494-3555. Fax 284/494-3557. www.biras.com. 33 units. Winter $850–$2,500 suite; off season $700–$1,950 suite. Rates include all meals (no drinks). Ask about packages. AE, MC, V. Take the private motor launch from the Beef Island airport, $160 per person round-trip. No children under age 8. **Amenities:** Restaurant; bar; babysitting; exercise room; pool (outdoor); spa; 2 tennis courts (lit); watersports equipment/ rentals. *In room:* A/C, ceiling fan, TV, TV/DVD, fridge, hair dryer, MP3 docking station, Wi-Fi (free).

Bitter End Yacht Club ★★★ Kids This place is the liveliest of the B.V.I. resorts, and is even better equipped than the more exclusive Biras Creek. It's the best sailing and diving complex in the British chain, opening onto an unspoiled, secluded deep-water harbor, accessible only by boat. Guests have unlimited use of the resort's million-dollar fleet and a complimentary introductory course at the Nick Trotter Sailing and Windsurfing School. The Bitter End has informal yet elegant accommodations in either a hillside chalet or a well-appointed beachfront or hillside villa overlooking the sound. All villas have two twins, two queen-size, or a king-size bed, plus a shower with sea views and a patio or veranda.

For something novel, stay aboard a 9m (30-ft.) yacht, yours to sail, complete with dockage and daily maid service, meals in the Yacht Club dining room, and overnight provisions. Each yacht has a shower and can comfortably accommodate four.

First-rate meals are available in the Clubhouse Steak and Seafood Grille, the English Carvery, and the Pub, and entertainment is provided by a steel-drum or reggae band.

units, 5 yachts. Winter (double occupancy) $860–$1,840 beachfront villa, suite, yacht, or hillside villa; off season (double occupancy) $630–$1,560 all units. Rates include all meals. AE, MC, V. Take the private ferry from the Beef Island airport, $30 per person one-way. **Amenities:** 3 restaurants; pub; babysitting; exercise room; pool (outdoor); watersports equipment/rentals. *In room:* A/C (in some), ceiling fan (in some), TV, TV/VCR, fridge, Wi-Fi (free).

Katitche Point Greathouse ★★★ **Finds**   Designed by British architect Michael Helm, this luxurious and spacious "greathouse" serves the needs of the most discerning travelers. Affording total privacy, it can be rented as a complete villa for up to 13 people, with more than 185 sq. m (1,991 sq. ft.) of living space. Sometimes six couples or one or even two families share the villa like a first-class commune. It is also possible to rent just one of the suites or the master bedroom. The villa lies just above a panoramic sweep of Mahoe Bay and its beach. This luxury vacation spot has an infinity pool, four suites, and one master bedroom, which is secluded and set apart from the rest of the villa. The main structure of the villa is shaped like a pyramid, rising three floors. All the beds are made of handcrafted teak, and are furnished with a king-size, anti-allergic mattress. A steel ladder leads to the tallest point of the villa, a "Crow's Nest" at the top of the pyramid on the third level.

Plum Bay Rd., the Valley, Virgin Gorda, B.V.I. © **284/495-6274.** Fax 284/495-6275. www.katitchepoint.com. 5 units. Year-round $5,100 double; $7,500 quad. Rates are for 3 nights. MC, V. **Amenities:** Bar; pool (outdoor); watersports equipment/rentals. *In room:* A/C, TV, hair dryer, Internet (free).

Little Dix Bay ★★ **Kids**   This palace of low-key luxury is scattered along a .8km (¹/₂-mile) crescent-shaped, white-sand beach and private bay, on a 200-hectare (494-acre) preserve. Many guests find this resort too pricey and stuffy; we ourselves prefer the more casual elegance of Biras Creek Resort and the Bitter End Yacht Club, though Little Dix Bay does have an undeniably lovely setting, fine service, and an unmistakable elegance.

All rooms are surrounded by forest, and boast private terraces with views of the sea or gardens. Trade winds come through louvers and screens, and units also have ceiling fans and air-conditioning. Some units are two-story rondavels (think Tiki huts) raised on stilts to form their own breezeways. The furnishings and fabrics evoke Southeast Asia—beautiful wicker or reed furniture, bamboo beds, Balinese boxes and baskets, and ceramic objets d'art. The hotel has added two villas on an isolated stretch of white beach, each with dazzling white interiors, private pools, and alfresco dining pavilions.

The **Little Dix Bay Pavilion** (p. 182) is a romantic dinner spot on Virgin Gorda.

1km (²/₃ mile) north of Spanish Town (P.O. Box 70), Virgin Gorda, B.V.I. ⓒ **888/767-3966** in the U.S., or 284/495-5555. Fax 284/495-5661. www.littledixbay.com. 100 units. Winter $595–$950 double, from $1,200 suite; off season $395–$775 double, from $875 suite. Extra person $75. AE, DISC, MC, V. Take the private ferry from the Beef Island airport, $85 per person round-trip. **Amenities:** 3 restaurants; 2 bars; babysitting; children's programs; exercise room; room service; 7 tennis courts (lit); watersports equipment/rentals. *In room:* A/C, ceiling fan, TV, TV/DVD, movie library, hair dryer, Wi-Fi ($20).

Expensive

Nail Bay Resort ★   Near Gorda Peak National Park, and a short walk from a trio of usually deserted beaches, this resort enjoys an idyllic position. You can enjoy some of the best sunset views of Sir Francis Drake Channel and the Dog Islands from this 59-hectare (146-acre) site. Room options are wide-ranging, from deluxe bedrooms to suites, apartments, or villas. The villa community has a core of a dozen units in two structures on a hillside, with sitting areas amid old sugar mill ruins. Almost all the villas have their own pools. The most modest units are hotel-style bedrooms in the main building.

At night, Nail Bay evokes a luxury property in Asia, its landscaping highlighted by meandering stone walkways. One devotee told us that when she found the resort, it had the "terra-ultima exclusivity of Mustique, without that island's elitism."

Nail Bay (P.O. Box 69), Virgin Gorda, B.V.I. ⓒ **800/871-3551** in the U.S., 800/487-1839 in Canada, or 284/494-8000. Fax 284/495-5875. www.nailbay.com. 45 units. Winter $260–$495 double; off season $180–$395 double. AE, DISC, MC, V. **Amenities:** Restaurant; swim-up bar; babysitting; Jacuzzi; pool (outdoor); watersports equipment/rentals; Wi-Fi (free in restaurant). *In room:* A/C, TV, TV/DVD, TV/VCR, CD player, hair dryer, kitchen or kitchenette, MP3 docking station.

Virgin Gorda Village ★★   This place has some of the most up-to-date accommodations on the island—a choice of luxury studios; one-, two-, and three-bedroom apartments; and two-bedroom townhouses ranging from small to spacious. Surrounded by lush foliage, the complex faces the ocean, but the top floor has the most expansive views. Wide, breezy porches on each unit are another allure. The nearest and best beach lies at Savannah Bay, a 1.6km (1-mile) drive away. On-site is the Village Cafe, serving breakfast and lunch, and a commissary where you can purchase groceries.

The Valley, Virgin Gorda, B.V.I. ⓒ **284/495-5544.** Fax 284/495-5986. www.virgin gordavillage.com. 26 units. Winter (minimum 2 nights) $250 studio, $265–$295 1-bedroom, $310–$425 2-bedroom, $485 3-bedroom; off season (minimum 2 nights) $180 studio, $190–$210 1-bedroom, $225–$250 2-bedroom, $320 3-bedroom. MC, V. **Amenities:** Restaurant; bar; babysitting; children's playground;

health club & spa; watersports equipment/rentals; Wi-Fi (free at bar). *In room:* A/C, ceiling fans, TV, TV/DVD, hair dryer, kitchen.

Moderate

Mango Bay Resort ★ Ⓥⓐⓛⓤⓔ   This well-designed compound of eight villas is set on lushly landscaped grounds overlooking the scattered islets of Drake's Channel, on the island's western shore. You get good value for your money here. The accommodations are the most adaptable on the island—doors can be locked or unlocked to divide each villa into as many as four independent units. Costs vary with the proximity of your unit to the beach. Interiors are stylish yet simple, often dominated by the same turquoise as the seascape in front of you. There are also two large villas, with four or five bedrooms available only on a weekly basis. You can cook in, or dine at **Giorgio's Table** (p. 183), the island's best Italian restaurant, only a 5-minute walk away.

Mahoe Bay (P.O. Box 1062), Virgin Gorda, B.V.I. Ⓒ **284/495-5672.** Fax 284/495-5674. www.mangobayresort.com. 26 units. Winter $195–$355 studio, $275–$595 1-bedroom unit, $415–$995 2-bedroom unit, $645–$1,150 beachfront suite, $695 2-bedroom beachfront villa; off season $150–$220 studio, $205–$360 1-bedroom unit, $310–$580 2-bedroom unit, $440 beachfront suite, $580 2-bedroom beachfront villa. MC, V. **Amenities:** Restaurant; bar; pool (private villas only); limited watersports. *In room:* A/C, kitchen.

WHERE TO DINE

Many of the island's best restaurants are located in secluded resorts, accessible only by boat or resort ferry. Be sure to call ahead to find how to reach your desired table.

Expensive

Biras Creek Resort ★★ INTERNATIONAL   With even better cuisine than that of Little Dix Bay Pavilion (see below), this hilltop restaurant is our longtime island favorite, and for good reason. The resort hires the island's finest chefs, who turn out superb cuisine based on quality ingredients. The prix-fixe menu changes every night, but the panoramic view of North Sound doesn't. A recent sampling of the appetizers turned up such delights as five-spice duck salad, followed by a main course of pan-seared salmon wrapped in Parma ham in a lentil-cream sauce, and grilled grouper with an herby couscous. The chef's special, grilled lobster, is featured Sunday and Wednesday nights. Desserts are prepared fresh, and are likely to range from a chilled green-apple parfait to a choice of sorbets served with a chilled cantaloupe soup.

In Biras Creek Resort (p. 178), North Sound. Ⓒ **284/494-3555.** www.biras.com. Reservations required. Fixed-price dinner $85–$125. AE, MC, V. Seatings daily 7–8:45pm.

THE BRITISH VIRGIN ISLANDS

5

VIRGIN GORDA

Little Dix Bay Pavilion ★ INTERNATIONAL The most romantic of the dining spots on Virgin Gorda, this pavilion is our preferred choice at this deluxe resort, which also operates Sugar Mill Restaurant. Guests (most middle-aged and well-heeled) sit under a large thatched roof as trade winds breeze in through open doors. The chefs change the menu daily. Although many of the ingredients are shipped in frozen, especially meats, there is much that is fresh and good. The seafood keeps us returning again and again. Specialties include grilled halibut, seared snapper, and broiled lobster served with steamed broccoli in butter sauce with roasted almonds. Most dishes are at the lower end of the price range.

In Little Dix Bay hotel (p. 179), 1km (²/₃ mile) north of Spanish Town. (C) **284/495-5555.** www.littledixbay.com/dine2.cfm. Reservations required. Main courses $36–$42. AE, MC, V. Daily 8–10:30am, noon–2:30pm, and 6–9:30pm.

Moderate

Chez Bamboo ★ (Finds CAJUN This is the closest approxima-tion to a New Orleans supper club in the B.V.I. Located within a 5-minute walk north of the yacht club, the building features a big veranda. Inside, there's a wraparound mural showing a jazz band play-ing within a forest of bamboo; bamboo artifacts continue the theme. Owner Rose Giacinto and chef Joyce Rodriguez concoct superb dishes, including conch gumbo, Nassau grouper en papillote, and New Orleans–style strip steak covered with a creamy Worcestershire sauce. Desserts such as apple *crostini* and crème brûlée are among the very best on the island. Live music, usually blues or jazz of course, is presented every Friday night on the terrace.

Next to the Virgin Gorda Yacht Harbour, Spanish Town. (C) **284/495-5752.** Reser-vations recommended. Main courses $20–$35. AE, MC, V. Daily 5:30–10pm.

The Flying Iguana WEST INDIAN The owner of this place, Puck (aka Orlington Baptiste), studied his craft in Kansas City, with the Hilton Group, before setting up this amiable restaurant overlook-ing the airport's landing strip and the sea. Potted hibiscus and lots of effigies of iguanas, stuffed and carved, ornament a room that's a cel-ebration of West Indian mystique. The house drink is the Iguana Sunset, a concoction whose secret ingredients change according to the whim of the bartender. Whatever the recipe, it usually produces a lightheaded effect that goes well with the carefully conceived cuisine. Examples are not limited to combinations of fresh fish and shellfish, including calamari, shrimp, scallops, and conch: You'll also find steak, chicken, and lamb, seasoned in a way that evokes both the Caribbean and the Mediterranean. Happy hour is from 4 to 6pm daily.

The Valley, at the airport. (C) **284/495-5277.** www.flyingiguanabvi.com. Reserva-tions recommended. Main courses breakfast $6.50–$14, lunch $8.50–$20, dinner $9.50–$36. MC, V. Daily 6:30am–9pm.

Giorgio's Table ★ (Finds) ITALIAN   This is the only authentic Italian restaurant on the island, with chefs flown in for the season from Venice, Milan, and Florence. Lying a 15-minute drive north of Spanish Town, the restaurant opens onto a big covered terrace. We like to sit out here at night, with the sounds of the surf nearby. The varnished interior of the restaurant evokes a yacht. The chef says he cooks Italian instead of "American Italian," and the food is good, despite its reliance on a lot of imported ingredients. Fresh locally caught fish is generally the best bet. You can also order an array of succulent pastas and such standard Italian staples as veal scaloppine. Pizzas and sandwiches will fill you at lunch. We decided that the restaurant's owner, Giorgio, has an appropriate last name—Paradisio. *Note:* Giorgio's Table will be closed in November and December in 2010.

At the Mango Bay Resort (p. 181), Mahoe Bay. ✆ **284/495-5684.** Reservations recommended. Main courses $17–$42. AE, MC, V. Daily 12:30–2:30pm and 6–9pm.

Inexpensive

The Bath & Turtle INTERNATIONAL   At the end of the waterfront shopping plaza in Spanish Town sits the most popular pub on Virgin Gorda, packed with locals during happy hour, from 4:30 to 6:30pm. There are indoor and courtyard tables. Even if you're not hungry, you might want to join the regulars over midmorning mango coladas or peach daiquiris. If you're hungry, you can order fried fish fingers, tamarind-ginger wings, very spicy chili, or daily seafood specials such as conch fritters. There's live music every Wednesday and Friday night.

Virgin Gorda Yacht Harbour, Spanish Town. ✆ **284/495-5239.** Reservations recommended. Breakfast $7–$12; main courses lunch $10–$19, dinner $11–$25. AE, MC, V. Daily 7am–11pm.

Thelma's Hideout ★ (Finds) CARIBBEAN   Mrs. Thelma King, one of the most outspoken grande dames of Virgin Gorda (who worked in Manhattan for many years before returning to her native B.V.I.), runs this convivial gathering place for the island community. It's located in a concrete house with angles softened by ascending tiers of verandas. Food choices include steamed and grilled fish, fish filets, and West Indian stews of pork, mutton, goat, or chicken. Limeade or mauby are available, but many stick to rum or beer. Live music is presented on Saturday nights in winter, and every other Saturday off season. You have to call ahead to see if they are doing dinner.

The Valley. ✆ **284/495-5646.** Reservations required prior to 3pm for dinner. Main courses lunch $8–$12, dinner $18–$25. No credit cards. Daily 8:30–10am, 11:30am–2:30pm, and 6:30–9pm; bar daily 8am–9pm.

Top of the Baths CARIBBEAN   This aptly named green-and-white restaurant overlooks the famous Baths, and has a patio with a swimming pool. Locals gather here to enjoy the food they grew up on. At lunch, you can order an array of appetizers, including conch fritters, sandwiches, and salad plates. At night, the kitchen turns out good home-style fresh fish, lobster, chicken, steaks, and West Indian dishes. Look for one of the daily specials. And save room for a piece of that rum cake. Live steel bands perform on Sunday, and you're invited to swim in the pool either before or after dining.

The Baths. ✆ 284/495-5497. Dinner $15–$28; sandwiches and salads $9–$16. AE, MC, V. Daily 8:30am–10pm.

EXPLORING THE ISLAND

The northern side of Virgin Gorda is mountainous, with Gorda Peak reaching 417m (1,368 ft.), the highest spot on the island. In contrast, the southern half of the island is flat, with large boulders appearing at every turn.

If you're over for a day trip, the best way to see the island is to call **Andy Flax** at the Fischer's Cove Beach Hotel. He runs the **Virgin Gorda Tours Association** (✆ 284/495-5252), which will give you a tour of the island for $45 per person. You can be picked up at the ferry dock if you give 24-hour notice.

Surf & Sand

HITTING THE BEACH The best beaches are at **the Baths ★★**, where giant boulders form a series of tranquil pools and grottoes flooded with seawater. Nearby snorkeling is excellent, and you can rent gear on the beach. Scientists think the boulders were brought to the surface eons ago by volcanic activity. The Baths and surrounding areas are part of a proposed system of parks and protected areas in the B.V.I. The protected area encompasses 273 hectares (675 acres) of land, including sites at Little Fort, Spring Bay, and Devil's Bay on the east coast.

Devil's Bay National Park can be reached by a trail from the Baths. A 15-minute walk through boulders and dry coastal vegetation ends on a secluded coral-sand beach.

Neighboring the Baths is **Spring Bay,** one of the best of the island's beaches, with white sand, clear water, and good snorkeling. **Trunk Bay** is a wide, sandy beach reachable by boat or along a rough path from Spring Bay.

Savannah Bay is a sandy beach north of the yacht harbor, and **Mahoe Bay,** at the Mango Bay Resort, has a gently curving beach with neon-blue water.

DIVING **Kilbrides Sunchaser Scuba** is located at the Bitter End Yacht Club at North Sound (✆ 800/932-4286 in the U.S., or 284/495-9638; www.sunchaserscuba.com). Kilbrides offers the best diving in the British Virgin Islands, at 15 to 20 dive sites including the wreck of the ill-fated HMS *Rhone*. Prices range from $95 to $105 for a two-tank dive on one of the coral reefs. A one-tank dive in the afternoon costs $75. Equipment, except wet suits, is supplied at no charge. Hours are 7:45am to 5:30pm daily.

HIKING Consider a trek up the stairs and hiking paths that criss-cross Virgin Gorda's largest stretch of undeveloped land, the **Gorda Peak National Park.** To reach the best departure point for your uphill trek, drive north of the Valley on the only road leading to North Sound for about 15 minutes of very hilly driving (using a four-wheel-drive vehicle is a very good idea). Stop at the base of the stairway leading steeply uphill. There's a sign pointing to the Gorda Peak National Park.

It will take between 25 and 40 minutes to reach the summit of Gorda Peak, the highest point on the island, where views out over the scattered islets of the Virgin Islands archipelago await you. There's a tower at the summit, which you can climb for even better views. Admire the flora and the fauna (birds, lizards, and nonvenomous snakes) en route. Because the vegetation you'll encounter is not particularly lush, wear protection against the sun. Bring a picnic—tables are scattered along the hiking trails.

SHOPPING

There isn't much here. Your best bet is the **Virgin Gorda Craft Shop** at Yacht Harbour (© **284/495-5137**), which has some good arts and crafts, especially straw items. Some of the more upscale hotels have boutiques, notably the Bitter End Yacht Club's **Reeftique** (© **284/494-2745**), with its selection of sports clothing, including sundresses and logo wear. You can also purchase a hat here for protection from the sun. You might also check out **Island Silhouette in Flax Plaza** (no phone), located in Flax Plaza near Fischer's Cove Beach Hotel, which has a good selection of resort-style clothing that's been hand-painted by local artists. **Pusser's Company Store,** Leverick Bay (© **284/495-7369**), sells rum products, sportswear, and gift and souvenir items. **Tropical Gift Collections,** the Baths (© **284/495-5380**), is a good place to shop for local crafts. Here you'll find island spices, bags, T-shirts, wraps, jewelry, maps, and pottery on sale at good prices.

VIRGIN GORDA AFTER DARK

There isn't a lot of action at night, unless you want to make some of your own. **The Bath & Turtle Pub,** at Yacht Harbour (© **284/495-5239**), brings in local bands for dancing in the summer on Wednesday and Friday at 8:30pm. The **Bitter End Yacht Club** (© **284/494-2745**) has live music on Fridays. Accessible only by boat, this is the best bar on the island. With its dark wood, it evokes an English pub and even serves British brews. Call to see what's happening at the time of your visit, and see p. 178 for more on the resort.

Andy's Chateau de Pirate, at the Fischer's Cove Beach Hotel, the Valley (© **284/495-5252**), is a sprawling, sparsely furnished local hangout. It has a simple stage, a very long bar, and huge oceanfront windows, which almost never close.

5 JOST VAN DYKE

This 10-sq.-km (4-sq.-mile) rugged island (pop. 150) on the seaward (west) side of Tortola was named after a Dutch settler. In the 1700s, a Quaker colony settled here to develop sugar cane plantations. (One of the colonists, William Thornton, won a worldwide competition to design the Capitol in Washington, D.C.) Smaller islands surround this one, including Little Jost Van Dyke, the birthplace of Dr. John Lettsom, founder of the London Medical Society.

On the south shore are some good beaches, especially at **White Bay** and **Great Harbour.** The island has a handful of places to stay, but offers several dining choices, since it's a popular stopover point, not only for the yachting set but also for many cruise ships. Jost Van Dyke is very tranquil, but only when cruise ships aren't in port.

ESSENTIALS

GETTING THERE   Take the ferry to White Bay on Jost Van Dyke from either St. Thomas or Tortola. (*Be warned:* Departure times can vary widely throughout the year, and often don't adhere very closely to the printed timetables.) Ferries from St. Thomas depart from Red Hook 3 days a week (Fri–Sun), usually twice daily. A round-trip is $40, while one-way is $30. More convenient (and more frequent) are the daily ferryboat shuttles from Tortola's isolated West End. The latter depart five times a day for the 25-minute trip, and cost $20 for adults round-trip, $10 for children 12 and under round-trip. Call the **New Horizon Ferry Service Paradise Express** (© **284/495-9278;** www.jostvandykeferry.com) for information about departures from any of the above-mentioned points. If all else fails, negotiate a transportation fee with one of the handful of privately operated water taxis on Tortola. Fees start around $100 one-way.

GETTING AROUND   To get around the island, call **Bun Taxi** at © **284/495-9281.** Only two places on Jost Van Dyke rent Jeeps— **Abe's by the Sea** (© **284/495-9329**) at $60 to $80 per day and **Paradise Jeep Rentals** (© **284/495-9477**) at $55 to $70 per day.

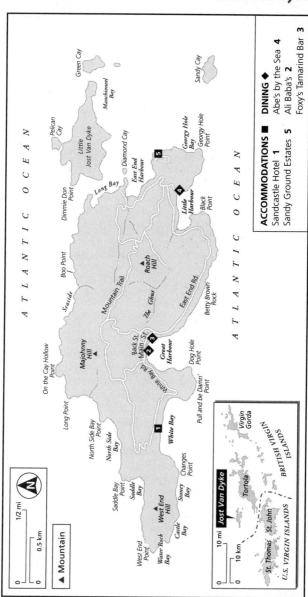

ACCOMMODATIONS ■
Sandcastle Hotel 1
Sandy Ground Estates 5

DINING ◆
Abe's by the Sea 4
Ali Baba's 2
Foxy's Tamarind Bar 3

THE BRITISH VIRGIN ISLANDS

5

JOST VAN DYKE

FAST FACTS In a medical emergency, call **VISAR** (Virgin Islands Search and Rescue) at ✆ 284/494-4357; you can be flown to Tortola. In the unlikely event that you need the police, call ✆ 284/495-9345. There are no banks, ATMs, or drugstores on the island. Stock up before you arrive here.

WHERE TO STAY

Sandcastle Hotel A retreat for escapists who want few neighbors and absolutely nothing to do, these six cottages are surrounded by flowering shrubbery and bougainvillea, and have panoramic views of a white-sand beach. Bedrooms are spacious, light, and airy, furnished in local art, rattan furnishings, daybeds, and king-size beds. Two units are air-conditioned, while the others have ceiling fans. You mix your own drinks at the beachside bar, the Soggy Dollar, and keep your own tab. Visiting boaters often drop in to enjoy the beachside informality and order a drink called the Painkiller. The restaurant is an old standard on the island and presents a candlelight, beachside dinner on Saturdays. A line in the guest book proclaims, "I thought places like this only existed in the movies."

White Bay Beach, Jost Van Dyke, B.V.I. ✆ **284/495-9888.** Fax 284/495-9999. www. soggydollar.com. 6 units. Winter $265–$295 double; off season $190–$230 double. Extra person $35–$45. 3-night minimum. Children 15 and under not permitted. MC, V. **Amenities:** Restaurant; bar; watersports equipment/rentals. *In room:* A/C (in some), ceiling fan, no phone, Wi-Fi (free).

Sandy Ground Estates These self-sufficient apartments are along the edge of a beach on a 7-hectare (17-acre) hill site on the eastern part of Jost Van Dyke. The complex rents two- and three-bedroom villas. One of our favorites is constructed on a cliff, and seems to hang about 25m (82 ft.) over the beach. The airy villas, each privately owned, are fully equipped with refrigerators and stoves. The interiors vary widely, from rather fashionable to bare-bones, but all have ceiling fans. The living space is generous, and extras include private balconies or terraces. The managers help guests with boat and watersports rentals. Diving, day sails, and other activities can be arranged. The rates quoted are for 1 week.

Sandy Ground Estate, Jost Van Dyke, B.V.I. ✆ **284/494-3391.** Fax 284/495-9379. www.sandyground.com. 7 units. Winter $1,950 villa for 2; off season $1,400 villa for 2. Extra person $500 per week in winter, $350 off season. MC, V. Take a private water taxi from Tortola or St. Thomas. **Amenities:** Watersports equipment/rentals. *In room:* Ceiling fan, kitchenette, no phone, Wi-Fi (free).

WHERE TO DINE

Abe's by the Sea WEST INDIAN Sailors are satisfied with a menu of fish, lobster, conch, ribs, and chicken at this local bar and restaurant. Prices are low, and it's money well spent. With each main course you also get peas, rice, and coleslaw.

Little Harbour. *©* **284/495-9329.** Reservations recommended for groups of 5 or more. Dinner $20–$45; nightly barbecue $24. MC, V. Daily 8am–10pm.

Ali Baba's ★ ⟨Finds⟩ CARIBBEAN Built of rustic-looking beams and unvarnished planks, this restaurant welcomes diners and drinkers to a breeze-flooded veranda near the edge of the harbor, immediately adjacent to the customs house. Inside, you're likely to meet Ali Baba himself (a member of the Baba family) and such friendly and charming staff members as Dominica-born Urinthia. Menu items focus on fresh grilled wahoo, kingfish (served with butter and braised onions), tuna, and snapper. Other dishes include lobster, West Indian conch, lime-garlic shrimp, and barbecued ribs or chicken. All main courses are accompanied by salad, vegetables, rice, and fried plantains. Drinks of choice include Painkillers and rum punches, but lots of the boat owners who come here seem to prefer beer—the colder, the better. If you're on the island in time for breakfast, drop in to join the locals for a tasty wake-up meal and what one visitor called "damn good coffee."

Great Harbour. *©* **284/495-9280.** Breakfast from $10; main courses lunch $9–$12, dinner $18–$22. AE, DISC, MC, V. Daily 9am–11pm.

Foxy's Tamarind Bar ★★ WEST INDIAN Arguably the most famous bar in the B.V.I., this mecca for yachties and other boat people is built entirely around sixth-generation Jost Van Dyke native Philicianno "Foxy" Callwood. He opened the place in the late 1960s, and guests have been coming back ever since. A songwriter and entertainer, Foxy is part of the draw. He creates impromptu calypso—almost in the Jamaican tradition—around his guests. If you're singled out, he'll embarrass you, but it's all in good fun. He also plays the guitar and takes a profound interest in preserving the environment of his native island.

Thursday through Saturday nights, a live band entertains. On other evenings, it's rock 'n' roll, reggae, or soca. The food and drink aren't neglected, either—try Foxy's Painkiller Punch. During the day, flying-fish sandwiches, rotis (West Indian burritos), and the usual burgers are served; evenings might bring freshly caught lobster, spicy steamed shrimp, or even grilled fish, depending on the catch of the day. They also have a big barbecue on the weekends.

Great Harbour. *©* **284/495-9258.** www.foxysbar.com. Reservations recommended. Lunch $10–$15; dinner $18–$45. AE, MC, V. Daily 11am–10pm.

DIVE SITES

Increasingly, Jost Van Dyke attracts divers. They are drawn in particular to the north coast of Little Jost Van Dyke, with its Twin towers, a pair of rock formations jutting up some 27m (90 ft.). The best dive operator is **JVD Scuba and BVI Eco-tours,** great Harbour (© 284/ 495-0271; www.bvi-ecotours.com). A one-tank dive goes for $70, a two-tank dive for $110. You can also arrange rentals here for snorkel gear, scuba equipment, kayaks, surfboards, windsurfers, small boats, or fishing equipment. You can also book boat excursions to nearby islands, costing $750 for 1 day for up to four passengers, including the services of a captain; half-day tours are $375.

6 PETER ISLAND ★

Half of this island, boasting a good marina and docking facilities, is devoted to the yacht club. The other part is deserted. A gorgeous beach is found at palm-fringed Deadman's Bay, which faces the Atlantic but is protected by a reef. All goods and services are at the one resort (see below).

The island is so sparsely populated that except for an occasional mason at work, about the only company you'll encounter will be an iguana or a feral cat whose ancestors were abandoned generations ago by shippers (the cats are said to have virtually eliminated the island's rodent population).

A complimentary, hotel-operated ferry, **Peter Island Ferry** (© 284/ 495-2000), departs Tortola from the pier at Trellis Bay, near the airport. Other boats depart six or seven times a day from Baugher's Bay in Road Town, on Tortola. Passengers must notify the hotel 2 weeks before their arrival so transportation can be arranged.

WHERE TO STAY & DINE

Peter Island Resort ★★★ This 720-hectare (1,779-acre) tropical island is solely dedicated to Peter Island Resort guests and to yacht owners who moor their crafts here. The island's tropical gardens and hillside are bordered by five gorgeous private beaches, including Deadman's Beach (in spite of its name, it's often voted one of the world's most romantic beaches).

The resort contains 32 rooms facing Sprat Bay and Sir Francis Drake Channel, and 20 larger rooms on Deadman's Bay Beach. There are also several (less desirable) gardenview rooms. Designed with a casual elegance, all the rooms have a balcony or terrace. The least desirable rooms are the smallest, housed in two-story, A-frame structures next to the harbor. Bathrooms range from standard motel-unit types to spectacularly luxurious offerings, depending on your room assignment. The Crow's Nest, a luxurious four-bedroom villa, overlooks the harbor and Deadman's Bay, and features a private swimming pool. The Hawk's Nest villas are three-bedroom villas situated on a tropical hillside.

The resort has two restaurants. For the day-tripper, the **Deadman's Beach Bar and Grill** is the more casual of the two, although reservations are recommended. Set right on the beach, it enjoys a secluded setting in the midst of sea-grape trees and towering palms. The restaurant has a wood-fired pizza oven and an expansive salad bar buffet, which also includes freshly made desserts. At lunch expect an array of sandwiches, even one made from a big portobello mushroom. Other selections include Jamaican jerk chicken, tuna tartare, and roti. Dinner includes the fresh catch of the day, succulent lamb kebabs, and more. On Sunday afternoons a live steel-drum band plays, and on Monday nights there's a West Indian buffet.

Peter Island (P.O. Box 211), Road Town, Tortola, B.V.I. 🕐 **800/346-4451** in the U.S., or 284/495-2000. Fax 284/495-2500. www.peterisland.com. 55 units. Winter $660–$1,335 double, $910–$1,585 3-bedroom villa, $1,495–$1,835 4-bedroom villa; off season $575–$875 double, $825–$1,245 3-bedroom villa, $1,375–$1,495 4-bedroom villa. Rates include all meals. AE, MC, V. **Amenities:** 2 restaurants; 2 bars; babysitting; health club & spa; pool (outdoor); 4 tennis courts (lit); watersports equipment/rentals; Wi-Fi (free in lobby and clubhouse). *In room:* A/C, hair dryer, minibar.

Fast Facts

1 FAST FACTS: THE VIRGIN ISLANDS

AREA CODES   The area code for the U.S.V.I. is **340;** in the B.V.I., it's **284.** You can dial direct from North America; from outside North America, dial 001, plus the number for the U.S.V.I., and 011-44 plus the number for the B.V.I.

AUTOMOBILE ORGANIZATIONS   Motor clubs will supply maps, suggested routes, guidebooks, accident and bail bond insurance, and emergency road service. The **American Automobile Association (AAA)** is the major auto club in the United States. If you belong to a motor club in your home country, inquire about AAA reciprocity before you leave. You may be able to join AAA even if you're not a member of a reciprocal club; to inquire, call AAA (© **800/222-4357;** www.aaa.com). AAA has a nationwide emergency road service telephone number (© 800/AAA-HELP [222-4357]).

BUSINESS HOURS   See "Fast Facts" in individual island chapters for information on business hours.

DRINKING LAWS   In the U.S. Virgins, the legal age for purchase and consumption of alcoholic beverages is 18; proof of age is required and often requested at bars, nightclubs, and restaurants, so it's always a good idea to bring ID when you go out.

Do not carry open containers of alcohol in your car or any public area that isn't zoned for alcohol consumption. The police can fine you on the spot. Don't even think about driving while intoxicated. Although 18-year-olds can purchase, drink, and order alcohol, they cannot transport bottles back to the United States with them. If an attempt is made, the alcohol will be confiscated at the Customs check point. The same holds true for the B.V.I.

In the B.V.I., the legal minimum age for purchasing liquor or drinking alcohol in bars or restaurants is 18. Alcoholic beverages can be sold any day of the week, including Sunday. You can have an open container on the beach, but be careful not to litter or you might be fined.

DRIVING RULES   In both the U.S.V.I. and the B.V.I., you must drive on the left. See "Getting Around," p. 13.

ELECTRICITY The electrical current in the Virgin Islands is the same as on the U.S. mainland and Canada: 110 to 120 volts AC (60 cycles), compared to 220 to 240 volts AC (50 cycles) in most of Europe, Australia, and New Zealand. Downward converters that change 220–240 volts to 110–120 volts are difficult to find in the United States, so bring one with you.

EMBASSIES & CONSULATES There are no embassies or consulates in the Virgin Islands. If you have a passport issue, go to the local police station, which in all islands is located at the center of government agencies. Relay your problem to whomever is at reception, and you'll be given advice about which agencies can help you.

EMERGENCIES Call ⓒ **911** in the U.S.V.I. or **999** in the B.V.I.

GASOLINE (PETROL) Taxes are already included in the printed price. One U.S. gallon equals 3.8 liters or .85 imperial gallons.

HOLIDAYS In addition to the standard legal holidays observed in the United States, **U.S. Virgin Islanders** also observe the following holidays: Three Kings' Day (Jan 6); Transfer Day, commemorating the transfer of the Danish Virgin Islands to the Americans (Mar 31); Organic Act Day, honoring the legislation that granted voting rights to the islanders (June 20); Emancipation Day, celebrating the freeing of the slaves by the Danish in 1848 (July 3); Hurricane Supplication Day (July 25); Hurricane Thanksgiving Day (Oct 17); Liberty Day (Nov 1); and Christmas Second Day (Dec 26). The islands also celebrate 2 carnival days on the last Friday and Saturday in April: Children's Carnival Parade and the Grand Carnival Parade.

In the **British Virgin Islands,** public holidays include the following: New Year's Day, Commonwealth Day (Mar 12), Good Friday, Easter Monday, Whitmonday (sometime in July), Territory Day Sunday (usually July 1), Festival Monday and Tuesday (during the first week of Aug), St. Ursula's Day (Oct 21), Birthday of the Heir to the Throne (Nov 14), Christmas Day, and Boxing Day (Dec 26).

INSURANCE For information on traveler's insurance, trip-cancellation insurance, and medical insurance while traveling, visit www.frommers.com/planning.

INTERNET ACCESS There is limited Internet access on the major islands in the Virgin Islands chain, including St. Thomas (which has the best), St. Croix, St. John, Tortola, and Virgin Gorda. On some of the more remote islands, you may be completely out of luck. Many visitors log on at their hotel. See "Fast Facts" for individual chapters.

LANGUAGE English is the official language of both the U.S. and British Virgin Islands.

LEGAL AID   If you are "pulled over" for a minor infraction (such as speeding), never attempt to pay the fine directly to a police officer; this could be construed as attempted bribery, a much more serious crime. Pay fines by mail, or directly into the hands of the clerk of the court. If accused of a more serious offense, say and do nothing before consulting a lawyer. Here the burden is on the state to prove a person's guilt beyond a reasonable doubt, and everyone has the right to remain silent, whether he or she is suspected of a crime or actually arrested. Once arrested, a person can make one telephone call to a party of his or her choice. International visitors should call their embassy or consulate.

MAIL   At press time, U.S. domestic postage rates were 28¢ for a postcard and 44¢ for a letter. For international mail, a first-class letter of up to 1 ounce costs 98¢ (75¢ to Canada and 79¢ to Mexico); a first-class postcard costs the same as a letter. For more information go to **www.usps.com**.

If you aren't sure what your address will be in the U.S. Virgin Islands, mail can be sent to you, in your name, c/o General Delivery at the main post office of the city or region where you expect to be. (Call ℂ **800/275-8777** for information on the nearest post office.) The addressee must pick up mail in person and must produce proof of identity (driver's license, passport, and so on). Most post offices will hold your mail for up to 1 month, and are open Monday to Friday 8am to 6pm, and Saturday 9am to 3pm.

Always include zip codes when mailing items in the U.S. If you don't know your zip code, visit **www.usps.com/zip4**.

Postal rates in the British Virgin Islands are 35¢ for a postcard (airmail) to the United States or Canada, 50¢ for a first-class airmail letter (¹/₂ oz.) to the United States or Canada. Mailing a postcard to the U.K. costs 50¢ and a first-class letter via airmail costs 75¢ (¹/₂ oz.).

NEWSPAPERS & MAGAZINES   Daily U.S. newspapers are flown into St. Thomas, St. Croix, Tortola, and Virgin Gorda. For local papers, see "Fast Facts" in individual island chapters. The B.V.I. have no daily newspaper, but the *Island Sun,* published Wednesday and Friday, is a good source of information on local entertainment, as is the *BVI Beacon,* published on Thursday. *Standpoint* is another helpful publication that comes out on Monday and Saturday. You can find these in most supermarkets and shops.

PASSPORTS   See www.frommers.com/planning for information on how to obtain a passport. See "Embassies & Consulates," above, for whom to contact if you lose your passport while traveling in the U.S. Virgin Islands. For other information, please contact the following agencies.

For Residents of Australia Contact the **Australian Passport Information Service** at ☏ **131-232,** or visit the government website at www.passports.gov.au.

For Residents of Canada Contact the central **Passport Office,** Department of Foreign Affairs and International Trade, Ottawa, ON K1A 0G3 (☏ **800/567-6868;** www.ppt.gc.ca).

For Residents of Ireland Contact the **Passport Office,** Setanta Centre, Molesworth Street, Dublin 2 (☏ **01/671-1633;** www.irlgov. ie/iveagh).

For Residents of New Zealand Contact the **Passports Office** at ☏ **0800/225-050** in New Zealand or 04/474-8100, or log on to www.passports.govt.nz.

For Residents of the United Kingdom Visit your nearest passport office, major post office, or travel agency or contact the **United Kingdom Passport Service** at ☏ **0870/521-0410** or search its website at www.ukpa.gov.uk.

For Residents of the United States To find your regional passport office, either check the U.S. State Department website or call the **National Passport Information Center** toll-free number (☏ **877/487-2778**) for automated information.

PETS To bring your pet to the U.S.V.I., you must have a health certificate from a mainland veterinarian and show proof of vaccination against rabies. Very few hotels allow animals, so check in advance. If you're strolling with your dog through the national park on St. John, you must keep it on a leash. Pets are not allowed at campgrounds, in picnic areas, or on public beaches. Both St. Croix and St. Thomas have veterinarians listed in the Yellow Pages.

Your dog or cat is permitted entry into the B.V.I. without quarantine if accompanied by an Animal Health Certificate issued by the Veterinary Authority in your country of origin. This certificate has a number of requirements, including a guarantee of vaccination against rabies.

POLICE Dial ☏ **911** for emergencies in the U.S.V.I. In the B.V.I., the main police headquarters is on Waterfront Drive near the ferry docks on Sir Olva Georges Plaza (☏ **284/494-3822**) in Tortola. There are also police stations on Virgin Gorda (☏ **284/495-9828**) and on Jost Van Dyke (☏ **284-495-9345**). See individual island chapters for more detailed information.

TAXES For the U.S. Virgin Islands, the United States has no value-added tax (VAT) or other indirect tax at the national level. The U.S.V.I. may levy their own local taxes on all purchases, including hotel and restaurant checks and airline tickets. These taxes will not appear on price tags.

In the British Virgin Islands, there is a departure tax of $5 per person for those leaving by boat or $20 if by airplane. Most hotels add a service charge in the $5 to $18 range; some restaurants will also tack on a 10% surcharge if you pay by credit card. There's also a 7% government tax on hotel rooms, but no sales tax.

TELEPHONES   See "Staying Connected," in chapter 1, p. 26.

TIME   The Virgin Islands are on Atlantic Standard Time, which is 1 hour ahead of Eastern Standard Time. However, the islands do not observe daylight saving time, so in the summer, the Virgin Islands and the East Coast of the U.S. are on the same time. In winter, when it's 6am in Charlotte Amalie, it's 5am in Miami; during daylight saving time it's 6am in both places.

TIPPING   In hotels, tip **bellhops** at least $1 per bag ($2–$3 if you have a lot of luggage) and tip the **chamber staff** $1 to $2 per day (more if you've left a disaster area for him or her to clean up). Tip the **doorman** or **concierge** only if he or she has provided you with some specific service (for example, calling a cab for you or obtaining difficult-to-get theater tickets). Tip the **valet-parking attendant** $1 every time you get your car.

In restaurants, bars, and nightclubs, tip **service staff** and **bartenders** 15% to 20% of the check, tip checkroom attendants $1 per garment, and tip **valet-parking attendants** $1 per vehicle.

As for other service personnel, tip cab drivers 15% of the fare; tip skycaps at airports at least $1 per bag ($2–$3 if you have a lot of luggage); and tip hairdressers and barbers 15% to 20%.

TOILETS   You won't find public toilets or "restrooms" on the streets but they can be found in hotel lobbies, bars, restaurants, museums, department stores, bus stations, and service stations. Large hotels and fast-food restaurants are often the best bet for clean facilities. Restaurants and bars in resorts or heavily visited areas may reserve their restrooms for patrons.

VISAS   Visitors to the U.S. Virgin Islands from other nations should have a U.S. visa; those visitors may also be asked to produce an onward ticket. In the British Virgin Islands, visitors who stay for less than 6 months don't need a visa if they possess a return or onward ticket.

For information about U.S. Visas go to **http://travel.state.gov** and click on "Visas." Or go to one of the following websites:

Australian citizens can obtain up-to-date visa information from the **U.S. Embassy Canberra,** Moonah Place, Yarralumla, ACT 2600 (② **02/6214-5600**), or by checking the U.S. Diplomatic Mission's website at **http://usembassy-australia.state.gov/consular**.

British subjects can obtain up-to-date visa information by calling the **U.S. Embassy Visa Information Line** (② **0891/200-290**) or by visiting the "Visas to the U.S." section of the American Embassy London's website at **www.usembassy.org.uk**.

Irish citizens can obtain up-to-date visa information through the **Embassy of the USA Dublin,** 42 Elgin Rd., Dublin 4, Ireland (② **353/1-668-8777;** or by checking the "Visas to the U.S." section of the website at **http://dublin.usembassy.gov**.

Citizens of **New Zealand** can obtain up-to-date visa information by contacting the **U.S. Embassy New Zealand,** 29 Fitzherbert Terrace, Thorndon, Wellington (② **644/472-2068**), or get the information directly from the website at **http://wellington.usembassy. gov**.

VISITOR INFORMATION You can surf the **U.S.V.I. Division of Tourism**'s website at www.usvitourism.vi. The **British Virgin Islands Tourist Board** can be found at www.bvitourism.com.

In the U.S.: Before you take off for the U.S. Virgin Islands, you can get information from the **U.S. Virgin Islands Division of Tourism,** 1 W. 34th St., Suite 302, New York, NY 10001 (② **800/372-USVI** [372-8784]). There are additional offices at the following locations: 1275 Shiloh Rd., Kennesaw, GA 30144 (② **770/874-5951**); 401 N. Michigan Ave., Suite 1200, Chicago, IL 60611 (② **312/836-3723**); 444 N. Capitol St. NW, Suite 305, Washington, DC 20001 (② **202/ 624-3590**); 2655 Le Jeune Rd., Suite 907, Coral Gables, FL 33134 (② **305/442-7200**); and 3450 Wilshire Blvd., Suite 1202, Los Angeles, CA 90010 (② **213/739-8931**).

For details on the British Virgin Islands, get in touch with the **British Virgin Islands Tourist Board** at 3450 Wilshire Blvd., Suite 1202, Los Angeles, CA 90010 (② **213/736-8931**).

In the U.K.: Information for the British Virgin Islands is available at the **B.V.I. Information Office,** 15 Upper Grosvenor St., London W1K 7PS (② **020/7355-9585**).

WATER Many visitors to both the U.S. and British Virgins drink the local tap water with no harmful effects. To be prudent, especially if you have a delicate stomach, stick to bottled water.

2 AIRLINE, HOTEL & CAR-RENTAL WEBSITES

AIRLINES THAT FLY TO THE U.S.V.I.

American Airlines
www.aa.com

Continental Airlines
www.continental.com

Delta Airlines
www.delta.com

United Airlines
www.united.com

US Airways
www.usairways.com

LOCAL CARRIERS THAT FLY TO THE B.V.I.

Air Sunshine
www.airsunshine.com

Bohlke Airlines
www.bohlke.com

Caribbean Wings
www.bvi-airlines.com

Fly BVI
www.fly-bvi.com

Island Birds
www.islandbirds.com

Island Helicopter Int.
www.helicoptersbvi.com

LIAT Airlines
www.liatairline.com

Seaborne Airlines
www.seaborneairlines.com

MAJOR HOTEL & MOTEL CHAINS

Best Western International
www.bestwestern.com

Divi Hotels
www.divicarina.com

Holiday Inn
www.holidayinn.com

Marriott
www.marriott.com

Westin Hotels & Resorts
www.starwoodhotels.com/
westin

Wyndham Hotels & Resorts
www.wyndham.com

CAR-RENTAL AGENCIES

Avis Car Rental
www.avis.com

Budget Car Rental
www.budget.com

Dollar Car Rental
www.dollar.com

Hertz
www.hertz.com

Local Car-Rental Agencies
On St. Thomas
Dependable Car Rental
www.dependablecar.com

Discount Car Rentals
www.discountcar.vi

On St. John
St. John Car Rental
www.stjohncarrental.com

On St. Croix
Centerline Car Rentals
www.centerlinecarrentals.com

Judy of Croix Car Rental
www.villadawn.com/st_croix/
info/judi_car_rental.htm

Olympic Rent-a-Car
www.olympicstcroix.com

Skyline Car Rentals
www.villadawn.com/st_croix/
info/skyline_car_rental.htm

In the British Virgin Islands
Abe's Car Rentals (Jost Van Dyke)
www.bvitourism.com/Getting
Around/Rentals

Andy's Taxi and Jeep Rental (Virgin Gorda)
www.bvitourism.com/Getting
Around/Rentals

Anegada Reef Hotel Jeep Rentals (Aneganda)
www.anegadareef.com

D&D Car Rental (Tortola)
www.bvitourism.com/Getting
Around/Rentals

Speedy's Car Rental (Virgin Gorda)
www.bvitourism.com/Getting
Around/Rentals

FAST FACTS

6

AIRLINE, HOTEL & CAR-RENTAL WEBSITES

INDEX

See also Accommodations and Restaurant indexes, below.

RESTAURANTS